M/10

CRIME, PROTEST AND POLICE IN MODERN BRITISH SOCIETY

David Jones

CRIME, PROTEST AND POLICE IN MODERN BRITISH SOCIETY

Essays in Memory of David J. V. Jones

Edited by

DAVID W. HOWELL and KENNETH O. MORGAN

UNIVERSITY OF WALES PRESS
CARDIFF
1999

© The Contributors, 1999

British Library Cataloguing-in-Publication Data
A catalogue record for this book is available from the British Library

ISBN 0-7083-1555-0

All rights reserved. No part of this book may be reproduced, stored in a retrieval system, or transmitted, in any form or by any means, electronic, mechanical, photocopying, recording or otherwise, without clearance from the University of Wales Press, 6 Gwennyth Street, Cardiff, CF2 4YD.

Typeset by Action Publishing Technology, Gloucester
Printed in Great Britain by Gwasg Dinefwr, Llandybïe

Contents

Foreword	vii
The Editors and Contributors	ix
Introduction DAVID W. HOWELL AND KENNETH O. MORGAN	1
David Jones: An Appreciation DOROTHY THOMPSON	9
Consensus and Conflict in Modern Welsh History KENNETH O. MORGAN	16
Riots and Public Disorder in Eighteenth-Century Wales DAVID W. HOWELL	42
Beccaria and Britain HUGH DUNTHORNE	73
PC Dixon and *Commissaire* Maigret: Some Myths and Realities in the Development of English and Continental Police CLIVE EMSLEY	97
W. E. Adams, Chartist and Republican in Victorian England OWEN R. ASHTON	120
'A Reckless Spirit of Enterprise': Game-Preserving and Poaching in Nineteenth-Century Lancashire JOHN E. ARCHER	149
'South Wales has been Roused as Never Before': Marching against the Means Test, 1934–1936 NEIL EVANS	176

'It's Not All about Nicking Folks': Dramatizing the Police   207
    PETER STEAD

David Jones: A Bibliography   238
    DWYRYD W. JONES

Index   241

List of Subscribers   246

Foreword

The tragically early death of Professor David Jones from cancer on 30 October 1994 at the age of only fifty-three was a deeply shocking event. His many friends and colleagues lost a charming and gentle personality, of immense academic and intellectual gifts. His pupils were deprived of a dedicated and stimulating teacher of modern social history. The historical world in general mourned the loss of an outstanding historian of crime and protest in modern Britain and modern Wales. Numerous obituaries in the national press emphasized his remarkable and highly original contribution to the historical understanding of movements of social protest, the texture of the lives of poor and oppressed peasantry and proletariat, the historical relationship of crime and the community, and the issues underlying the history of modern policing and the policed society. It was immediately felt, therefore, by his colleagues in Swansea that a memorial volume should be published to honour his work and to suggest the quality and depth of the rare achievement of a sadly brief life. The present volume is the result. It attempts to give an indication of his work on aspects of the dynamics of social history and popular protest, rural and industrial; key themes in modern Wales and modern Britain; his writings on the Chartist uprising; his work on the roots and significance of crime, and on the popular impact of the police on the public consciousness in Britain and elsewhere. We hope very much that the variety of this memorial volume will give an idea of the extraordinary range of David's historical research and writing. We trust that it will offer a flavour also of the integrity, intellectual honesty and warmth of personality of a man whose work will endure for as long the Welsh and the British are concerned with their history.

The publication of this book has been assisted by grants from the Scouloudi Foundation in association with the Institute of

Historical Research, the Marc Fitch Fund and the Lipman-Miliband Trust; we are immensely grateful for this valuable assistance. We are also, of course, greatly indebted to those colleagues who have contributed so willingly and enthusiastically to this book. Their promptness in so doing suggests the admiration and affection in which David Jones was so universally held. In addition to the authors, we must also mention the late Mrs Audrey Philpin, an M.Phil. student of David's, who was due to write a chapter on 'Women and Crime in Pembrokeshire' before, sadly, she too died. Among those whose advice has been especially valuable are Sir Glanmor Williams, Professor David Eastwood, Professor Ralph Griffiths, Susan Jenkins and Ceinwen Jones of the University of Wales Press. The jacket illustration was chosen with the help of D. Huw Owen of the National Library of Wales. We are also deeply grateful for the secretarial and administrative help of Mrs Jane Buse of the Swansea History Department. Finally, this volume could not have been written without the advice and moral support of Gwenda Jones, David's wife.

DAVID W. HOWELL
KENNETH O. MORGAN
Swansea, January 1999

The Editors and Contributors

Owen R. Ashton is Reader in Modern British Social History at Staffordshire University. He wrote *W. E. Adams, Chartist, Radical and Journalist (1832–1906)* in 1991. He co-produced *The Chartist Movement: A New and Annotated Bibliography* (1995) and co-edited and contributed to *The Duty of Discontent: Essays for Dorothy Thompson* (1995). He was David Jones's first postgraduate student at Swansea in 1972.

John Archer graduated from the University of Wales Swansea, and gained his doctorate from the University of East Anglia. He is currently a Senior Lecturer in History at Edgehill College of Higher Education. His research has until now concentrated on rural crime and protest, but the recent award of an ESRC grant will enable him to study violence in Liverpool and Manchester between 1850 and 1914.

Hugh Dunthorne is a Senior Lecturer in History at Swansea where he has taught since 1971. His publications include *The Maritime Powers* (1987) and other studies in Anglo-Dutch history. He is at present writing a book on the Enlightenment.

Clive Emsley is Professor of History at the Open University and currently president of the International Association for the History of Crime and Criminal Justice. He has taught at universities in Australia, Canada and France. His publications include *Crime and Society in England 1750–1900* and *The English Police: A Political and Social History*. His comparative study, *Gendarmes and the State in Nineteenth-Century Europe* is to appear in 1999.

Neil Evans graduated in History at Swansea University College in 1969 and completed an MA there in 1973. At present he is Tutor in History at Coleg Harlech and Honorary Lecturer in the School of History and Welsh History at University of Wales, Bangor. He has published extensively in the field of modern British social history and is joint editor of *Llafur, the Journal of Welsh Labour History*.

x The Editors and Contributors

David W. Howell studied at Aberystwyth University College and LSE before joining the History Department at Swansea in 1970, where he has remained throughout his career. A specialist in modern Welsh rural history, his two books are *Land and People in Nineteenth-Century Wales* (1978) and *Patriarchs and Parasites: The Gentry of South-West Wales in the Eighteenth Century* (1986). He is at present writing the centenary history of the Royal Welsh Agricultural Society.

Dwyryd Wynn Jones is a graduate of Aberystwyth and Oxford, and a member of the History Department at the University of York, since 1965. He is a historian of the London cloth markets in the sixteenth and seventeenth centuries, and author of *War and Economy in the Age of William III and Marlborough* (1988).

Kenneth O. Morgan is Research Professor at Aberystwyth, Honorary Professor and Honorary Fellow at Swansea and Honorary Fellow of The Queen's College, Oxford. He was formerly Lecturer at Swansea, 1958–66; Fellow and Praelector of The Queen's College, Oxford, 1966–89, and Vice-Chancellor of the University of Wales, Aberystwyth, 1989–95. He has written over twenty books on modern British and Welsh history, of which the most recent are *Modern Wales: Politics, Places and People* (1995), *Callaghan: A Life* (1997) and *The People's Peace: A History of Britain since 1945* (new updated edition, 1999). He was a close colleague of David Jones, as was his late wife, Dr Jane Morgan.

Peter Stead is a writer and broadcaster and a former Senior Lecturer in History at the University of Wales, Swansea. He is the author of *Film and the Working Class* and biographical studies of Richard Burton and Dennis Potter. In 1998 he was joint editor of *Heart and Soul: The Character of Welsh Rugby* and co-author of *Ivor Allchurch MBE*. His father, Superintendent John Stead, was an officer in the South Wales Constabulary.

Dorothy Thompson, wife of the late E. P. Thompson, taught history at the University of Birmingham. Specializing in late modern British social and labour history, her many publications include *The Chartists* (1984) and *Outsiders: Class, Gender and Nation* (1993).

Introduction

DAVID W. HOWELL AND KENNETH O. MORGAN

This memorial volume has been prepared as a fitting tribute to a Welsh scholar who made a massive contribution to our understanding of later modern British society. By the time of his tragic death at the age of only fifty-three he had become an outstanding practitioner of his craft. He displayed rare skills of historical judgement, always informed by knowledge of the theory and practice of criminology and other related social sciences. He wrote with scrupulous objectivity, yet always with a warm, humane sympathy for the poor and underprivileged. Born in 1941, he was from a rural working-class Montgomeryshire family, the son of an agricultural labourer in Llansanffraid-ym-Mechain by the Severn Valley and never anything but radical in his political and social outlook. His choice of historical subject, the poorer sorts and classes of people, social victims all, was almost predictable. Those very credentials of relatively humble origins and radical credo equipped him with an instinctive understanding of his chosen themes. As a historian he wrote of the sons and daughters of Rebecca. That he would have marched with them shoulder to shoulder at the time cannot be in doubt.

He went to the local grammar school in Welshpool and then in 1959 to the University College of Wales, Aberystwyth. Here, his early attraction to the 'crowd' as a historical theme on the lines illuminated by George Rudé at the time, received a setback when his choice of special subject became unavailable owing to Richard Cobb's absence on sabbatical leave. But the consequence for David was momentous. Instead, he turned to Welsh social history and thus came under the direct formative influence of two great pioneering, if contrasting, scholars, David Williams and Gwyn A. Williams, who jointly supervised him for his doctoral thesis on 'Labour Disturbances in Wales between 1792 and 1832', which he completed in 1965. It was at this period that David discovered the riches of court records as a source for tracing the processes of social change, notably the gaol files of the Welsh Courts of Great Sessions, and his love for legal records proved to be abiding and central to much of his later work.

After a year's teaching at Grove Park School, Wrexham, he was appointed in 1967 to the history department at the University College of Swansea. Here, under the inspired leadership of Glanmor Williams, a vigorous school of modern Welsh social, political and labour history was now under way. David found the atmosphere of innovative inquiry into the Welsh *mentalité* deeply stimulating. He played a major role in the progress of the department in many scholarly articles of fundamental importance, through his first book, *Before Rebecca* (Allen Lane, London, 1973), and through his support in the early 1970s for exciting research developments like the SSRC-sponsored south Wales coalfield research undertaken by Hywel Francis and Dai Smith, and taken forward by *Llafur*, the Society for Labour History in Wales of which he was the founding secretary.

It was in the mid-seventies that David developed the self-confidence to branch out into wider areas of British history, although, as Dorothy Thompson's personal portrait indicates, working outwards from a Welsh base. His total mastery of the intricacies of Welsh Chartism had been on display at an important Welsh Labour History conference held at Swansea in 1971, published in the *Welsh History Review* as a special issue in June 1973. His wider study of British Chartism bore fruit in his *Chartism and the Chartists* in 1975. This strategy of working outwards and eastwards from his Welsh base – while never neglecting the important Irish dimension either – was equally apparent in his studies, from the mid-seventies onwards, of crime in the community, rural and industrial.

Winning a SSRC one-year award in 1974 for a project on Crime in Nineteenth-Century Wales, he and his full-time researcher, Alan Bainbridge, carried out a comprehensive survey of Welsh sources relating to crime, the fruits of which were presented in a two-volume report for the Research Council. Intellectually excited by this new range to his work, David went on to examine the acts of arson by rural labourers in East Anglia in the early 1840s, a project which led to his prestigious publication in the first issue of the journal *Social History* (1976) of an article 'Thomas Campbell Foster and the rural labourer: incendiarism in East Anglia in the 1840s'. Again, directly resulting from the Welsh crime Project came the experience and confidence to branch into a broader study of crime and policing in Britain as a whole. A series of case studies, including amongst other themes the Victorian poacher, the criminal vagrant, Merthyr's famous 'China' and the evolution of crime and the police in Manchester was published in 1982 under the title *Crime, Protest, Community and Police in Nineteenth-Century Britain* and became widely acclaimed by fellow scholars.

The study of Welsh crime in the mid-1970s also part inspired him to revisit Rebecca. In the preface to his widely admired *Rebecca's Children* (1989) David Jones wrote:

> My own interest in the story was rekindled some years ago when I was working on a project on crime and protest in the nineteenth century. It seemed to me that there was a case for seeing the Rebecca riots in the wider context of illegal activities and in a longer chronological perspective, not least because strands of the movement were present before and after the middle decades of the century.

David's mentor, Professor David Williams, in his magisterial *Rebecca Riots* (1955) had, in his characteristically cautious fashion, recognized the endemic turbulence in Welsh rural communities – 'The daughters of Rebecca were certainly not unused to violence.' But this theme, one somewhat suppressed by nonconformist Liberals of the Henry Richard school later in the century, was only to be highlighted and shown in its full significance in David's fourth chapter 'Crime and Deviance'. Quiet country communities like the lower Teifi Valley were shown to be the unexpected domain of the 'lords of misrule'.

The crime-historical harvest was to ripen to its fullest in his last books, *Crime in Nineteenth-Century Wales* (1992) and – in a work most bravely completed when he knew that his health prospects were not good, and published posthumously through the devotion and loyalty of his wife, Gwenda – *Crime and Policing in the Twentieth Century: The South Wales Experience* (1996). The former work, which combines luminous studies of crimes of different categories with, among other things, a capacity to master and interpret the available statistics, reflects the work of early modernists in the field. It can only be speculated what a contribution he might later have made to the study of crime in early modern Welsh history, now that the relevant records have been so superbly catalogued by the manuscript department of the National Library of Wales, Aberystwyth. Just as the methodology and approach to his studies of English popular movements and of forms of crime were tested in a Welsh laboratory, so his knowledge of the wider British context was in turn to enrich his specifically Welsh subjects. Nowhere was this more in evidence than in what some considered his finest book, the study of the Chartist uprising in Wales in 1839, *The Last Rising*, published by Oxford University Press in 1985. He was explicit about this in the preface: 'I am also interested in the Chartist movement throughout Britain and this has helped me to understand that moment in time in November 1839.' By the same token, his writing on both urban and rural Wales was to sharpen his understanding of the distinctive character of each region – though, he would have insisted, not their separateness. In a particularly perceptive passage in *Rebecca's Children* (p.vi) he recognized that

> the lines between rural, urban and industrial [Wales] in the mid-nineteenth century were more blurred than we imagine. Ideas and beliefs, of Paineite radicalism, Liberal Dissent and much else, ran across geographical boundaries. Whether one lived in Llandysul or Merthyr there were patterns of language, thought and action which were familiar. The reader will find that there were people who moved to and fro across south Wales and, more bewilderingly, from one type of protest to another.

That David's prolific writing allowed him also to build up a fine reputation as a stimulating teacher is testimony to his professional commitment. Both a special subject on 'Chartism, Society and the State' and an optional course on 'Crime and Policing in Britain, 1760–1914' were always oversubscribed. Those many research students who worked closely with him during their postgraduate studies – including Owen Ashton, Angela John, Neil Evans, Brian Davies, Keith Strange and Audrey Philpin – were not only to respect his scholarship and drive, but also to become devoted and loyal friends in the years to follow. They – like all of us – were drawn to him by his charm, modesty and quiet sense of humour, not to mention the patient resignation of his support for Swansea City (he had been a fine footballer himself in his youth). As a teacher, he was passionate to explain and to be understood. As Professor Ralph A. Griffiths reflected in his moving obituary in the *Welsh History Review*, one of David's key phrases, in the lecture room or seminar class, was 'D' you know what I mean?' It was a simple question, deeply felt and invested with human sympathy. Equally, his colleagues respected his occasional obstinate but always principled stands, expressed quietly with the countryman's reflective calm which always characterized him. David was always his own man.

All the contributors to this book enjoyed personal and academic links with David, and believe it is important in a memorial volume that this should be the case. Some Festschrifts and memorial works aim for a disciplined conceptual and thematic coherence. We have deliberately followed a different course. This work is intended to reflect the range and scope of the work of the colleague to whom it is dedicated. He contained multitudes, perhaps even contradictions at times, and it is important to us that this aspect of his writing and personality be brought out. The choice both of contributors and of topics attempts to span David's early interest in the 'crowd', in the moral economy of rural society, his later study of the history of crime and judicial authority, and by the same token his investigations of both Welsh and broader British history.

We appreciate that an overall appraisal of his importance as a scholar is difficult to achieve, given his wide range of interests and approaches, but Dorothy Thompson's appraisal offers an individual perspective by one distinguished and honoured scholar of a key aspect of David's work and its importance – Chartism and popular movements. Her judgements about David's standing in this field have a central place in this volume, given the high regard David had for both Dorothy and the late Edward Thompson, a feeling that was warmly reciprocated. We have emphasized in this introduction David's major contribution to Welsh social and labour history. Kenneth Morgan's chapter examines a theme (new to him) of the dualism of Consensus and Conflict in modern Wales and its historiography from the early nineteenth century to the present time. Particularly with regard to the nineteenth century, leading scholars like David Williams, Gwyn A. Williams and Ieuan Gwynedd Jones would each have to confront this dialectic of dispute and deference. This chapter tries to locate David Jones's important place in this recurring historiographical polarity with reference both to his earlier writing on popular movements and his later contributions on the policed society.

The other essays reflect aspects of the two overriding themes of popular protest and of crime and policing respectively, roughly in chronological order even though they infuse the entire volume. Popular protest is the direct theme of three of the essays. David Howell's study of riot and disorder in eighteenth-century Wales, which examines among many other disturbances the corn and anti-militia riots in the years before the 1790s, relates directly to David Jones's initial research interest in popular protest in Wales in the years 1792–1832. The division generated in Chartist circles over the enthusiasm some felt for continental revolutionaries was discussed by David in *Chartism and the Chartists*: he cited the republican W. E. Adams's observation that 'Old Chartists looked askance at our proceedings'. The essay by Owen Ashton, himself a research student supervised by David as we have noted, extends his own earlier study (1991) of this 'second-line Chartist' by examining his specifically republican activities. Meanwhile Neil Evans's investigation of the south Wales marches against the means test in 1934–6, and the light they shed on Valleys communities and their public projection during the depression years, focuses on a major aspect of twentieth-century social protest. The memory of the grim marches of the Chartists on Newport gaol in early November 1839 was openly evoked by the leaders of the means test marches a century later. History was indeed close to these men and women.

The other major theme – crime, punishment and policing – is reflected in four other essays. David's lectures introduced students to the importance of the Italian jurist Cesare Beccaria's *Essays on Crimes and Punishment* (1764), providing them with valuable background for their more specialized study of the work in Hugh Dunthorne's course on 'The Enlightenment'. In this volume, Dr Dunthorne's essay on Beccaria and Britain points to his importance in persuading English reformers that improvement of the legal system necessitated moderating the harshness of the penal code and administering the laws with greater certainty and humanity. In fact, frequent pardons had been granted in British courts in the face of so many offences carrying the death penalty. It was a theme taken up by David in his analysis of the precise reasons for the 'frequent resort to reprieve and pardon' in early modern Wales in his article 'Life and Death in Eighteenth-Century Wales' in *Welsh History Review*, 10, 4 (1981). David's studies of the role of the Victorian poacher in both the Welsh and the English countryside is given an added dimension by John Archer's essay on game-preserving and poaching in nineteenth-century Lancashire, in which a number of contrasts are drawn by the author between the situation there and what obtained in the well-documented stereotype of hunger-motivated poaching carried on in East Anglia.

Conversely, the essays by Clive Emsley and Peter Stead deal specifically with the police. David had noted in his first chapter in *Crime, Protest, Community and Police* that 'one neglected aspect of historical study has been the relationship between the police and the people'. Professor Emsley and Peter Stead take up this theme in their respective essays. The essay by Clive Emsley explores the extent to which the cosy image of the English police – nurtured by contemporary politicians and senior policemen, and embraced by later Whiggish historians – seen as the friend of the public, deriving their authority and legitimacy from the people locally and thereby contrasting fundamentally with the continental gendarmerie run by the central government and imposed on the community, is a reliable one. It is a theme of fundamental significance for the study of public order on a comparative basis. David Jones also always recognized the importance of the media in reflecting and feeding popular interest in crime and policing. He observed in *Crime and Policing in the Twentieth Century* (p. 282): 'The press, radio, television and cinema, as well as popular and serious fiction, are saturated with stories of crime and policing, and public opinion surveys leave us in no doubt as to the extent of people's interest and anxiety.' Peter Stead's essay on dramatizing the police examines a key aspect of media treatment by analysing the changing presentations of the police – amounting to a virtual reinvention – from the long-running *Dixon of Dock Green* to *The Sweeney*, *The Bill*, *Taggart* and *City Central*. For good or ill, the police have become central to our culture.

One disadvantaged group in society important to David is not reflected here, purely through mischance. Dorothy Thompson notes that he was 'amongst the first historians to look at the place of women in popular movements and to publish [in 1983] one of the first essays on women in the Chartist movement'. David was similarly concerned within the Welsh context to point to the involvement of women in the 1790s corn riots and the Rebecca disturbances. His analysis of crime and deviance in *Rebecca's Children* makes a particular point of this. Women criminals are powerfully discussed (pp.171–5) in *Crime in Nineteenth-Century Wales*. He points out the manifest unreliability of the statistical evidence in this area. As our Foreword indicates, the planned chapter on women and crime in Pembrokeshire was not completed owing to the sad death of Mrs Audrey Philpin. Despite this, however, we trust that the volume as it stands does show that this major strand of David's work is not neglected.

Finally, David's publications have been listed by Dwyryd W. Jones of the history department at the University of York. He was a wholly appropriate choice. Both Montgomeryshire men, David and Dwyryd entered Aberystwyth in 1959 to read History. Of all his fellow students, David stood most in awe of Dwyryd for his academic brilliance and prodigious dedication to his work. They shared a room in hall in the first year there and were to remain close friends over the years. It is fitting that this volume, and indeed this introduction, should end on such a note for a work devoted to the most comradely and collegial of scholars. We mourn his death, but celebrate and rejoice in his massive, if incomplete, achievement. Not only academic history but life itself would have been so much poorer without our having known him.

David Jones: An Appreciation
DOROTHY THOMPSON

By the time of his too early death, David Jones was established as, in the words of Clive Emsley, 'one of the best historians not only of nineteenth-century Wales, but also of the people of early nineteenth-century Britain' (*Welsh History Review*, 15 (1990–1), 300). He was writing in years during which some of the best social history of the century was being written in Europe and America before rather arid 'theoretical' arguments among social historians led students away from the archives or back into traditional forms of political history firmly based on *Hansard* and the papers of the party politicians.

David was an innovative and stimulating scholar whose work influenced older historians among his contemporaries as well as those of his own and later generations. He was always generous both in the sharing of ideas and material and in his recognition of the achievement of younger historians. In a letter in July 1976 I find him both sending references for my husband's work on wife sales and praising the work of some of his former graduate students – 'Whenever I meet them I get the feeling of walking backwards . . . '

I must, as will be apparent, declare a personal interest here. I was a friend and colleague of David's from the time he first began to publish. I have been very much influenced by his work and his approach, and I find them sympathetic to my own in very many ways. We often exchanged information, compared courses and recommended graduate students to each other. During the sixties, seventies and eighties indeed Chartist studies became in some ways a kind of club or network. Undergraduate courses on Chartism were offered at half a dozen major universities. Graduates were working on Chartist subjects in many more on both sides of the Atlantic. Theses were appearing which added significantly to local and specialist understanding, and articles appeared in British history journals in such numbers and of such quality that one publisher in the early seventies seriously considered producing a journal of Chartist studies. David's publications and his work in research and in teaching were an important part of this intellectual activity. The footnoting to his work and to that of other scholars in the field gives some indication of the continual interaction that was going on. One result, however, of the way Chartist studies developed in those years may perhaps have been the development of a network of correspondence, seminars and conferences from which some scholars working more on their own felt excluded. Seminars and conferences on Chartism and British popular movements generally tended to discuss problems which had arisen within the network. Work was familiar through seminar papers and informal discussion long before it was published. To give an example from my own experience, when I was desperately trying to reduce my own general work on Chartism to a manageable single volume, I deliberately took out a closer study of the Newport rising because I knew that David's book-length study, which had been in preparation for some years, was of far greater depth and complexity than any work I had done and would soon appear. Most of the arguments about the nature and extent of the movement had been rehearsed at seminars in Britain, Europe and the USA before they appeared in published form. My assessment of David's work therefore must inevitably be based on a general approach to the writing of history which he shared with me and my husband and with this wider network of scholars.

David's work in some ways epitomizes that of historians of a whole generation. The late 1930s had seen in the work and the teaching of G. D. H. Cole, H. L. Beales, H. A. Marwick and David's own teacher David Williams, the beginning of new approaches to the study of popular movements – approaches based not simply on ideology and the assessment of leadership figures, but on the examination of trades, communities and localities. The social history of the forties and fifties moved away from narrative history to a more socially directed examination of themes, communities and *mentalités*. The most important work on Chartism in the period, *Chartist Studies* with the two key essays by its editor Asa Briggs, emphasized the importance of the study of the movement in the localities and of moving away from a simple analysis based on political theory towards a more complex understanding of the areas in which the movement took hold. This was an approach that appealed to David, laying as it did emphasis on the importance of the study of Welsh experience within the wider context of a more general understanding of the conflicts in industrializing Britain. He did not in fact abandon narrative history, but offered a more sophisticated form of non-linear examination which took in many of the insights of the social sciences. Like others among the innovative historians in Europe and America in the fifties and sixties he came increasingly to use new techniques of research and analysis to interrogate the records of the past. His mature work shows an understanding of social anthropology, sociology and the assessment of rhetoric and of public expression. He had a particularly fine ear for the language of the anglophone Welsh. An example to which he drew my attention was the letter from a Welsh Chartist collier protesting against the evidence published in the *Morning Chronicle* about the way of life of Glamorgan colliers. It starts in correct journalese: 'Probably I am better acquainted with the morals and the mode of living of the working men of this district, being one of that order myself, than the Reverend John Griffiths, the vicar of Aberdare who furnished the commissioners with this false and calumnious report.' But at this point he slides inevitably into the demotic – 'I am of the opinion this said Reverend J. Griffiths is in the habit of living rather greasy himself.'

David's decision to stay and work in Wales was made in spite of what must have been quite tempting offers of posts in other parts of Britain. But although he did work and publish on British history other than Welsh, his main interest was always in the Principality, and as his work progressed and deepened over the years he showed an unrivalled understanding of the life and society of the Welsh people. He rejected many of the dichotomies on which some contemporaries and most historians had insisted between rural and urban, chapel and pub, physical force and moral force, trade loyalties and community loyalties among the Welsh people. Going back to a closer scrutiny of the writing, speeches and activities of the people, he was able to demonstrate the extent to which such facile categorizations had too often obscured the real narrative.

Like many British post-war social historians, David was first attracted to the moments of violence and confrontation which occurred in the nineteenth century. Chartism in particular was an episode richly documented in its own and in the hostile press, in the legal and criminal record and in reminiscences and contemporary accounts, more so indeed than any earlier movement. Many of the questions it raised about urban and rural responses to industrialization and the modernizing of the machinery of control and policing have risen again over the years in the developing world of the nineteenth and twentieth centuries. Perhaps because of its apparent relevance to contemporary labour politics, Chartism had until the 1950s been more than most episodes in recent history allocated by historians a place in one or other of the dominant historical teleologies. In the Whig picture it represented a premature attempt to gain access for some excluded classes to the parliamentary system; for Marxists it was seen as the first expression of the specific class-consciousness of the developing industrial proletariat; for modernization theorists it represented a complex series of responses to the emergence of the modern, centralized nation state and the growth of national and international markets. The working class was generally recognized as being a powerful force in the massive industrial change which the nineteenth century witnessed – even if some historians preferred to use the plural and to emphasize differences of outlook based on skill levels or the variations of local industries. Whether the workers were to adapt to industrial society by accepting the role of partners to capital or by expropriating the expropriators and establishing a classless society, their role in the confrontations of the early industrial years was rarely questioned. Behaviour that belonged to earlier non-industrial or rural social forms was disregarded or seen as irrelevant or at best marginal in the interpretation of the movement. David's short book on *Chartism and the Chartists* (1975) was one of the first studies to break away from the totally political or the economically determined picture of Chartism to present a picture of a lively and many-sided movement, and to show some of the optimism and creativity which informed it.

In his earlier work done mainly in the sixties and published in *Before Rebecca* (1973), David had examined the outbreaks of violence in the Welsh communities in the pre-Chartist years. This close and detailed study of forms of protest including food riots, anti-tithe demonstrations and the demonstrations and riots at the time of the 1830–2 Reform agitation presented a new picture of the 'pre-industrial' Welsh crowd and began the work which was to lead to his major reinterpretations of the Newport rising and the Rebecca riots.

Perhaps the cross-dressing involved in the Rebecca episodes led to his being among the first historians to look at the place of women in popular movements and to publish one of the first essays on women in the Chartist movement, 'Women and Chartism', *History*, 68, 222 (February 1983). But any consideration of the crowd action of the first half of the century was bound to cast doubt on the theoretical categorizations that underlay many of the early studies. The neglect of the women and the marginalization of the role of country people and of the migrant and unskilled among the labour force had been among the reasons for the misreading by many historians of the Merthyr and Rebecca riots and of the events at Newport. David's great contribution to the history of the nineteenth century was his re-examination of these episodes and their insertion, through major and definitive studies, into the history of the Welsh people. He was not alone, of course, and other studies of the same and related subjects must be added to his, but his work stands out even in a period rich in the rediscovery of the early industrial communities.

In the preface to his study of the Rebecca protests David wrote:

> The riots are a part of the history of every Welsh man and woman. Until recent times we lived on the land, and the process of removal from it has been a painful one. At the time of this story, thousands of people were marching out of one past and into another. Of course, they ultimately became different people, but the lines between rural, urban and industrial in the mid-nineteenth century were more blurred than we imagine.

Throughout his work, on political movements, protest movements and social questions from criminality to gender roles, he was, like most of the creative social historians of those years, constantly examining the restrictive categories which generations of writers have imposed on the material. Some of these categories stand the test of this examination, even without the teleological presumptions, and David was, for example, always prepared to use the language of social class, though in a descriptive rather than a prescriptive way. Interestingly he found in the words of a contemporary Chartist writer the kind of sharp rejection of the rural and traditional elements in social protest which was to characterize the treatment of turbulence and violent actions by most later historians. It was Bronterre O'Brien who asked, at the time of the Rebecca riots in 1843, whether 'middle-class farmers' on horseback and in women's clothes had ideas in their heads (*Rebecca's Children*, p.vi).

The movement away from the Procrustean process of fitting violent behaviour into a pattern imposed by historical theory has been a liberating one for labour and social historians. The new patterns which emerge pose different questions. Most social historians studying a particular episode come across elements which lead in apparently unrelated or tangential directions. David found himself becoming interested in crime. In the opaque societies of industrializing Britain, old forms of authority were breaking down or had never come into existence. The protest movements, which were the starting-point of many studies, lapped over into forms of crime. Some – like arson, houghing and 'traditional' forms of public shaming – were often directed against unpopular local figures or people who transgressed accepted forms of behaviour, whether by insisting on landlords' rights, impinging on accepted and customary common rights or transgressing the sexual or familial mores of the communities. Other forms of crime were specific to types of community, or represented changes in customary expectations. And of course there was violent crime – rape, murder, theft from the person, as well as the theft or destruction of property – which had very little connection with social values. How crime was measured and assessed, the forms of detection and punishment adopted by the authorities at different times, the light which the definition of crime and the punishments meted out throw on the morals and values of the period – these and other questions led to publications dealing with crime and its historiography and measurement between the beginning of the nineteenth and the middle of the twentieth centuries.

The reconstruction and reinterpretation of the actions of the Welsh people has produced a large body of lively and stimulating historical studies in the last half-century. In the same years Welsh politics have taken their own course, different in significant ways from those of other parts of Britain. Welsh nationalism has never taken as prominent a part in actual political organizations as that of Ireland or even of Scotland. Nevertheless the history that has been written has been suffused by the unique qualities of the Welsh nation. The greater understanding of the Welsh quality in popular history has helped to throw light on the nature of other ethnic and regional aspects of British history in the period. David Jones's work has been in the fore both in the delineation of Welsh history and in relating it to that of the rest of the British Isles. The liveliness of his last work and the new directions it was taking in its examination of crime in the years since the Chartist movement indicated how much more he had to offer as a historian and particularly as a Welsh historian. His death was a tragedy for his family and friends. It was also a serious loss to the profession to which he belonged.

Consensus and Conflict in Modern Welsh History

KENNETH O. MORGAN

David Jones, in his brief but brilliant career, played a pivotal role in Welsh history's coming of age. When he graduated at Aberystwyth as a young man of twenty-one in 1962, there was scant awareness in the British historical world that Wales in the modern period had a history of its own. Most of the major literature, after all, focused either on early medieval Wales, prior to the English conquest in 1282, or else on the rule of the Tudors. Debates on the significance of the Act of Union loomed large. David Williams's pioneering studies of Welsh Chartism (1939) and the Rebecca riots (1955) were isolated achievements which stood almost alone. A journal called the *Welsh History Review* had come into being at Swansea only two years earlier; the seminal, if greatly contrasting, work of Gwyn A. Williams and Ieuan Gwynedd Jones was just beginning to appear. The building blocks of Oxford University's history syllabus were three compulsory papers on English (certainly not British) history, heavily political and constitutional in emphasis. The ghosts of Stubbs and Tout stalked the land. Continental novelties like the French *Annales* school need never have been. At that time, British history like British government was centralist and metropolitan in emphasis. There was in 1962 no Welsh Office, no Sianel Pedwar, certainly no vision of devolution. Plaid Cymru was a small minority which lost nearly all its deposits with monotonous regularity. The impact of Saunders Lewis's BBC lecture *Tynged yr Iaith* that February had still to be measured. The Welsh appeared to be relatively marginalized in British public and political life. To adapt the title of a famous stage review of the day, these Celts seemed almost beyond the fringe. Their modern history was similarly disregarded.

By the late 1980s, when David Jones was in full flow as an author, an extraordinary transformation had taken place. In the previous twenty-five years, history had become one of Wales's major growth industries. In particular, Welsh history in the nineteenth and early twentieth centuries, since the era of industrialization, had been done justice at last. David himself had been a dominant figure in this process. Between 1964 and 1989 he had written five major monographs, along with a score or more of learned articles, almost all of them concerned with Welsh popular protest in the early nineteenth century. But indeed the sixties, seventies and eighties were a time of extraordinary vitality for almost all aspects of the writing of the history of Wales, from the age of Hywel Dda to that of David Lloyd George and well beyond. It was one of the great success stories of British historiography in the post-war period. An array of imposing and acclaimed books and articles had poured forth in a mighty torrent. By 1987 four volumes of a six-volume *Oxford History of Wales* had been published. The *Welsh History Review* was striding confidently towards its fourth decade. It had been joined by innovative newer journals, notably *Llafur* which aimed successfully, as a journal of labour history, to create links between the academic community and the world of work. It straddled the great divide between scholarly writing and a wider social memory. All the Welsh university colleges had schools of graduate students; the staid gatherings of the Board of Celtic Studies in Gregynog were humming with life. Journals and scholars in England, Ireland, North America and the Commonwealth were also showing a new awareness of the centrality of the experience of the Welsh and their history; indeed, the fact that Wales, a classic 'unhistoric nation', had emerged as a community and as a nation but not as a nation state, made its history all the more fashionable. The historians' concern with regionalism and nationalism, with comparative cultural and linguistic pluralism, with the nature of *mentalité*, with 'history from below' penetrating beneath the formal veneer of the public archives and the records of government, made modern Welsh history appear fresh and relevant in quite new ways.

It was an intellectual development that interacted with the public in Wales, aware of massive processes of historical change with the closure of coal, new processes of secularization and the growing awareness of national identity. Movements of social and political protest loomed especially large in historical writing, perhaps reflecting the ideological preferences of most Welsh historians. Television and radio series in both English and Welsh, popular journals and magazines, well-attended day schools, the impact of the Open University, all spread the word amongst the general public. The history of Wales was entrenched, after a struggle admittedly, on the schools' core curriculum. Welsh history books, indeed, sold remarkably well (many of the volumes in the Board of Celtic Studies' monographs' series, 'Studies in Welsh History', went rapidly into paperback) perhaps because so many of them were attractively written in that extraordinary pungent literacy typical of so much Anglo-Welsh writing. Welsh history was, supremely, a branch of literature, not an arcane scholastic discipline for a limited group of specialists, still less an offshoot of computer science. A remarkable breakthrough had been made, and David Jones was one of the towering figures in its achievement.

This extraordinary renaissance, however, was the product of a remarkably small group of scholars. Welsh historians were a thin red line of a few dozen at most; their very productivity masked their meagreness of numbers. Cuts into higher education in the Thatcher and post-Thatcher periods had their impact. They greatly reduced the number of graduate students in the humanities, cutting back almost to zero the researchers working for the Board of Celtic Studies, reducing severely the budgets of the university and school libraries which purchased the new books and journals, delaying technical electronic advances even in the National Library of Wales. The range of active scholars became smaller still. They were also growing old together. Diminishing human resources had been masked, in part, by the continuing industriousness and zeal of active Welsh historians who kept on producing major work into their seventies or even eighties. Welsh history had no real 'schools' since it was so much a minority interest.

Now this situation certainly has had its distinct advantages. Limited numbers have given historians of Wales a rare sense of fraternity, of intellectual and other comradeship. They have been a convivial (overwhelmingly male) group, enjoying each other's company in the National Library or the university, or in colloquia at Gregynog. Their attitude towards each other, informally and in the formality of book reviews, has always been supportive and encouraging; feuds of the Taylor v. Trevor-Roper type appear in

Wales to be unknown. But the down side is that Welsh history has the problem sometimes of appearing too cosy and inbred. The scholars at work know and like each other almost too well, and perhaps review each other too often. When apparent disparities in interpretation appear – for instance between Gwyn A. Williams's depiction of south Wales as a revolutionary pressure cooker with the lid about to blow off, and Ieuan Gwynedd Jones's account of that same society twenty years later as stable and secure in reconstructing the basis of its institutional and religious life – there has been no open disagreement. It is very likely that both may be right, but at least the disparity is worth examination. A sign of the maturity of Welsh history, therefore, may be the emergence of argument, of dissent. The present writer is a peaceful man, as harmonious as his fellow members of the guild, with no wish to make war, even cold war, amongst his colleagues. But it appears not an inappropriate tribute to as creative a friend and as galvanizing a scholar as David Jones to suggest at least one area where the contours of argument might begin.

A major theme of David Jones's work is that of conflict and consensus in modern Wales. It chimes in with the main features of all mature societies – the balance between change and continuity, between upheaval and stability. Historians of Britain since 1945 have especially been caught up in it, in considering whether post-war Britain was marked by an overall consensus about public priorities. Political scientists like Dennis Kavanagh have been well to the fore here.[1] The theme has especially attracted the attention of American historians, ever fascinated by present-day resonances or the usability of their nation's past. In the early years of this century, US historians tended to see their history in terms of sectional and class conflict. Quite apart from the momentous disjuncture of the Civil War and the gulf over slavery, American historians were heavily influenced by the Progressive movement and its positivist impact upon the humanities and the emerging social sciences. Thus men like Charles Beard and Frederick Jackson Turner saw the key to American history to lie in conflict – the struggle between creditor/mercantile elements in the northeast and a producer society, between an industrializing east and a debtor south and west. Perhaps one of the last studies of this kind was Arthur Schlesinger Jr's *Age of Jackson* in 1945, the work of a young man who saw in Jacksonian Democracy of the 1830s a farmer–labour coalition that anticipated Franklin Roosevelt's New Deal a hundred years later. Indeed, Schlesinger's multivolume *Age of Roosevelt* years later deliberately replayed some of the old tunes. It was American academia's inverted version of a Whiggish interpretation of history.

But from the 1950s onwards, this well-established view came to be seriously challenged. Scholars like Louis Hartz or perhaps a more conservative figure like Dan Boorstin saw their nation's history as one of broad consensus. Hartz saw the key in an abiding liberal ideology reflecting the fact that America had no tradition of feudalism. Boorstin preferred the view that Americans were a pragmatic breed who had no real ideology at all.[2] By the sixties, some American historians, well aware of current tensions relating to blacks, gender and youth issues, and the war in Vietnam, were deeply alarmed at an anti-ideological brand of conservatism that seemed to be capturing their discipline – seeing America, in John Roche's words, as 'a quaker meeting moving through time'. It was, many feared, a backlash from the sterilities of the Cold War and the threat of McCarthyism.

Richard Hofstadter, my old mentor and perhaps the most intellectually dynamic of them all, somewhat hovered between the conflict and consensus scenarios. His *American Political Tradition* (1948) suggested long-term continuities, perhaps of an unattractive variety. His *Age of Reform* (1955) propounded conflict, at least between the rural Populists and the urban Progressives, a view shaped by Hofstadter's own reaction to racist, paranoid, rural McCarthyism. In his last major book, *Anti-Intellectualism in American History* (1963), Hofstadter focused on the topic more obliquely, namely the philosophical and political elements in American history that kept challenging radical intellectuals and placing them on the defensive. In an important essay published in 1968 shortly before his dreadfully premature death, Hofstadter reviewed the argument and tried to create a bridge between the two approaches.[3] He did, however, observe that a society marked by four years of terrible civil war and a fundamental ongoing rupture on the role of black Americans could hardly be deemed consensual in any firm sense.

American historians, then, reached a variety of conclusions. Not surprisingly, a consensus about consensus in their history was almost impossible to achieve. But at least they were debating and arguing amongst themselves. Now the history of Wales, in fact, implicitly raises many of the same themes. As noted, it is embedded in the very divergent view of early nineteenth-century Wales taken by Gwyn A. Williams and Ieuan Gwynedd Jones, a difference of temperament perhaps but also of scholarship. It has, however, been given spectacular public prominence. Again Gwyn A. Williams is the central exhibit. Indeed his writing throughout his career has been the embodiment of the conflict thesis. In *When was Wales?* (1985), as in many previous monographs and later television series, he saw Welsh history as the product of schizoid turbulence, social fractures and (a favoured phrase) 'brutal ruptures'. It was specifically put forward as an alternative, non-establishment interpretation. Welsh history for him was full of revolutionary moments, led invariably by unsuccessful revolutionaries, marginal men from Macsen Wledig through Owain Glyndŵr and Iolo Morganwg to Noah Ablett and David Irfon Jones in the present century. His thesis came out most vividly in *The Dragon has Two Tongues*, a series of memorable television confrontations (rather than programmes) with Wynford Vaughan Thomas.[4] They were to embody conflict and consensus in exaggerated form. Revolutionary turbulence and consensual inertia were personalized in the tiny, voluble Valleys Marxist who argued with (or shouted at) the gentle elder pillar of the establishment. It reached almost absurd lengths of visual imagery. In the first programme, Gwyn physically embodied revolutionary movement as he was alternately thrust down the main shaft of Blaenavon's Big Pit and then hurtled aloft in a helicopter a few minutes later above the Uffington horse on the Berkshire Downs. Meanwhile, Wynford was to be observed chugging gently along the Neath canal on a sunny afternoon, apparently settling down over a gin and tonic.

It was in many ways a contrived study in joint exaggeration, and also unreal. Gwyn Williams, after all, was a distinguished and learned creative academic scholar; Wynford Vaughan Thomas was by trade a very distinguished radio outside broadcaster but not a serious historian at all. The series was designed to entertain, provoke, perhaps shock, and it succeeded. It surely helped persuade a generation of Welsh schoolchildren to find the history of Wales challenging, dramatic, intensely exciting; videos of the programmes were used for university recruitment by history departments. Gwyn himself, the marvellous illuminator of Madoc and other myths, found himself hailed as the source of a new myth, the diminutive apostle of 'impossible revolutions', lauded by radicals and nationalists as a 'people's remembrancer' in a way that other middle-class Welsh historians who appeared on television were somehow not. But clearly the series also opened up a wider theme of consensual and conflict images of Welsh history which are of great importance.

As it happens, David Jones himself embodies these two viewpoints throughout his work. He was, as emerges in Dorothy Thompson's foreword, a superb analyst of Welsh history as social protest. His work for most of his career concerned popular upheavals in both rural and industrial Wales – corn riots, enclosure protests, the Scotch Cattle and their 'black domain', the Merthyr rising and the martyrdom of Dic Penderyn, the bloody suppression of Chartism, the Rebecca riots. All of them he studied with impeccable scholarship but also a quiet passion. He was aware always of the social and human roots of the movements he described. His study of the Rebecca disturbances and the attacks on the toll-gates was more emotionally and politically committed by far than that of his old Aberystwyth mentor, David Williams. The latter had indeed seen the riots as the product of a rural society in crisis, but his account of the troubles was detached, the work of a disenchanted disciple of the sceptic Voltaire, even ironic as he described 'the sordid events' with Shoni Sguborfawr and his mates weaving and wenching their way down the valleys. David Jones invested them all with humanity and a kind of heroism. Similarly whereas David Williams had cast doubt on the revolutionary intentions of John Frost and the Gwent Chartists of 1839, David Jones saw them as intent on direct action, launching a mass uprising in south-east Wales perhaps to link up with Chartist groups throughout England. To him, 'moral force' and 'physical force' Chartism seemed to blend into one.

And yet there was another theme in David Jones's work. He was scrupulous in seeing these popular uprisings as all explicable and ultimately transient. He also documented the very rapid passing of the revolutionary moment of Wales's frontier years, amidst the Victorian respectability and self-help of Wales in the 1850s and 1860s. He noted how the Liberal pacifist, Henry Richard, looked back on Chartism in 1866 with 'undisguised repugnance and horror'.[5] In David Jones's later work, on crime and policing, indeed, the theme of consensus emerged all the more clearly. The rate of crime in nineteenth-century Wales was indeed relatively low by comparison with England. The crime-free land of the white gloves, 'gwlad y menig gwynion', while open to serious qualification, was not wholly a myth. This was partly because local crimes and misdemeanours were sorted out locally and informally, without involving the rigours of the criminal law, even amongst incorrigibly turbulent groups such as the coracle fishermen of the Tywi and Teifi. Police were thin on the ground in rural Wales and socially acceptable (the son of one of them became principal of Aberystwyth). There was an element of consensual social self-regulation which made the law almost redundant.[6] Self-advancement and greater prosperity in the later Victorian period strengthened the process. More and more of the Welsh had something to preserve.

David's posthumous work on crime and policing in south Wales in the twentieth century in its way further emphasized this theme of consensuality in Welsh society. David noted in passing the fierce eruptions of industrial conflict in Wales from the Penrhyn strike of 1900–3, through Tonypandy down to the unemployed marches of the 1930s, with a posthumous echo in the miners' strike in 1984. Yet in south Wales, too, there was something of Robert Reiner's English 'golden age of policing' down to the 1960s, dangers to public order were very few, and relations between police and public generally good. Despite the marked upsurge in criminal offences after 1960, the Welsh were still felt to be generally 'well-behaved', with less drinking than earlier in the century and with fewer indictable crimes than England as late as 1989.[7] By the 1990s, relations with the police were edgy as elsewhere, but the rapid growth in crime by individuals was explicable in social terms similar to those in England, and as abhorrent to the general community in Wales as elsewhere. David Jones, therefore, placed himself scrupulously on both sides of the consensus–conflict argument, according to his theme, and we may deal with each in turn.

The conflict thesis emerged amongst Welsh and other historians with particular force in the 1960s and 1970s. It was no doubt in part a product of the intellectual stimulus of movements in England, the impact of Marxist writers like E. P. Thompson and

Raphael Samuel rescuing obscure popular movements, leaders and led, 'from the enormous condescension of posterity', and the rise of the History Workshop and other agents of radical scholarship. Intellectually it was an attempt to assert the importance of ideas, a reaction to the fifties, to Namier 'taking the mind out of history' and Oakeshott and the linguistic school doing the same to philosophy. It was an emphatic denial of Daniel Bell's pronouncement that the Cold War had meant 'the end of ideology'. It also reflected the wider social and cultural turbulence of the permissive sixties, the 'youth revolt' so-called, and in Wales the particular impact both of class-conscious labour militancy and of a nationalist upsurge. It had a special impact on the earlier issues of the journal *Llafur* and the interest in labour and working-class history. Modern Wales, it seemed, should be viewed above all in terms of revolt and protest: a popular GCSE course with colourful documents attached was concerned with nineteenth-century Wales from the Merthyr rising in 1831 to the tithe riots in the 1880s. It was entitled 'People and Protest'. Less spectacular or more stable periods of Welsh history such as the constitutionally-minded Liberal ascendancy of the years 1870–1914, the period of county councils and county schools, and the passion expended on the unlikely theme of the disestablishment of the Church of England, attracted less attention in the media, although Lloyd George perhaps bestrode both worlds to some degree.

Welsh history was seen, especially in the era since the advent of industrialization, in terms of *Stürm und Drang*, class or sectional. It was a story of often violent confrontations, from the Scotch Cattle and the Merthyr rising through the labour troubles of 1910–26 down to the attempted arson of Penyberth aerodrome by Saunders Lewis and his fellow nationalists in 1936. Gwyn A. Williams's *When was Wales?* (1985), following on a memorable charismatic BBC annual lecture under that title, brought many of those themes together. In particular, he focused on the marginal men, the Jacobins of the 1790s, the syndicalists of the Plebs League in 1912, the Marxist dissidents of National Left. Gwyn Williams's book, however, a product of the high noon of Thatcherism, was marked by a deep and growing pessimism as Wales's succession of impossible revolutions proved to be impossible indeed. His Wales was being destroyed by Toryism, capitalism and acid rain. All that was left was a fractured consciousness and a state of mind. On the other hand, a lively collective volume somewhat in the same vein, *A People and a Proletariat,* edited and with a sparkling introduction by Dai Smith (1981), was more pluralist and also more buoyant. Many of its contributions, perhaps a reflection of the comparative youth of many of the authors, were distinctly upbeat. Something of an exception is a Marxist lament on the management of the coal industry by Kim Howells, but he was the exception that proved a kind of rule.[8] He was later to emerge in the 1990s as a strongly Blairite MP and New Labour minister who called for the repression of ideas of socialism, indeed almost of ideology altogether.

The conflict thesis took hold amongst Welsh historians not only because it was colourful and dramatic but because in so many ways it was true. I was and am much drawn to it myself. The history of Wales in the past 200 years has been shot through by confrontation at many different levels. There has been, for instance, ample evidence of political conflict, Liberal and Tory before 1914, Labour and Conservative thereafter. No doubt this is true of virtually all developed societies in the democratic era. But it has taken a particularly vehement, even virulent, form in Wales, reflecting the class and other polarization of Welsh society. The first county council elections in England in 1889, for instance, were not much of a change. In rural areas respected landed gentry returned to head the new authorities: the success of descendants of the Marlborough dynasty in semi-feudal Woodstock, for instance, was only to be expected. But in Wales, from Anglesey to Monmouthshire, these elections saw a massive political revolution, with Liberals and nonconformists dancing on the political graves of a despised, fading squirearchy. More than other parts of the United Kingdom, the Welsh from the 1860s onwards drove on the left. It was not surprising that Keir Hardie, rejected successively by the voters of West Ham, Bradford East, North Aberdeen and Preston, should in 1900 find safe haven in the radical stronghold of Merthyr, where voters still cherished memories of Chartist clubs and the triumph of the pacifist Henry Richard. The fact that Hardie stood for Merthyr as an anti-war candidate amidst the jingoism of the Boer War, and shortly after Mafeking, defended by the allegedly Welsh Baden-Powell, was relieved, did his campaign relatively little harm.

Throughout the years of Liberal ascendancy down to the First World War and then the long march of Labour down to 1945, the Welsh found belligerent political champions. Lloyd George startled the English establishment with the passion of his onslaught on the landlords and the Randlords: privately he was a most pugnacious man, as is shown by the prevalence in his correspondence of the verb 'to smash'. Aneurin Bevan was in his day thought to be a socialist extremist; he notoriously celebrated the launching of the National Health Service in July 1948 by declaring the Tories to be 'lower than vermin'. Of course, Welsh politics threw up many more moderate men, Tom Ellis or Jim Griffiths perhaps; but it was the more extreme practitioners who captured the public attention. In Wales, as in Clydeside in Scotland and most of Ireland, the tone of politics appeared to be particularly bitter. It was noticed in the 1930s that migrants from south Wales to Dagenham, Slough, Coventry or Oxford brought with them a new tone of class-conscious militancy, sometimes from within the Communist Party. It was the Welsh in Oxford's car works who led the first strikes in Pressed Steel and Morris Motors in the early thirties. Another car manufacturer, Herbert Austin in Longbridge, condemned the Welsh for their 'bloody-mindedness'.[9]

Political conflict was underpinned by religious. As social life became politicized in the 1840s and 1850s, Welsh religious life was consumed by sectarian bitterness. Nonconformists began a prolonged campaign against the Church of England for national equality. So they did also in England, but in Wales the warfare was more intense and overlaid by national or nationalist overtones. Radical journalists like Samuel Roberts of Llanbrynmair and the especially pugnacious and dialectically unscrupulous Thomas Gee, publisher of *Baner ac Amserau Cymru* over many decades, drew on the latent passion once released in Chartism or the Rebecca disturbances. They openly encouraged acts of lawlessness like the Llanfrothen burial dispute which gave the youthful Lloyd George his first national platform, or the agitation and accompanying riots for the non-payment of tithe, or the clearly illegal non-implementation of the 1902 Education Act by the Welsh county councils which foreshadowed the role of Clay Cross and other Labour local authorities in the 1970s. Welsh bishops like Bishop John Owen might proclaim the indissoluble role of the Church in the historical identity of the Welsh people from medieval times, but to nonconformists bent on civic status and political victory, this seemed antiquarian nonsense. Sectarian conflict poisoned prospects of consensus on other issues, for instance in university education where the inflexible approach of Lampeter kept it for seventy-five years removed from the national university. The long campaign for disestablishment of the Church, reaching its subdued climax in 1919 when a Welsh prime minister was otherwise engaged at Versailles, gave a virulent tone to Welsh denominational religion. The nonconformists and Anglicans seemed almost concerned more with undermining each other than with spreading the Word: they focused more on statistics of each other's falling numbers in the religious census of 1906, not the 55 per cent of the population who attended no place of worship at all. The tone was captured by Sir Henry Jones's verdict on the Commission on the Welsh Churches after his resignation in 1907: 'I learnt for the first time how much ill-feeling religious men can entertain towards one another. Such an atmosphere of distrust, suspicion and pious malice I never breathed before or since.'[10]

Linguistic conflict may seem a phenomenon of very recent years, since the formation of Cymdeithas yr Iaith Gymraeg in the summer of 1962. So in many ways it was. It was only after the First, and especially the Second World War that the Welsh language was felt to be under terminal threat: Liberals before 1914 were remarkably complacent about the clear evidence of growing Anglicization especially in the industrial south. Yet it was their language and culture that underlay the Welsh campaign for national equality. It was the wholesale condemnation of both by the Education Commissioners of 1847, 'Brad y Llyfrau Gleision', which stung Welsh nationalism awake. It first awakened the radical fires of popular publicists like S.R. and Gwilym Hiraethog. Cultural renaissance, the emergence of major new poets like T. Gwynn Jones and Silyn Roberts, the work of a popularizing littérateur like Owen M. Edwards, the revitalization of the national eisteddfod, were pivotal to the Edwardian years prior to 1914. Cymdeithas yr Iaith and even more the direct-action members of Meibion Glyndŵr in their arson attacks on English-owned property, drew strength from early traditions of Welsh lawbreaking, often of a violent kind. Linguistic conflict, irresponsibly fanned by senior politicians like Leo Abse, underlay the tensions over devolution in 1979 and helped to lead to its massive rejection. Without an accommodation and far greater tolerance, devolution would never have received even the very narrow endorsement it won in 1997. Wales could have been consumed by the linguistic violence of Catalonia, Belgium or French Quebec.

Social conflict of all forms has often taken a particularly frightening form in modern Wales. It need not be discussed at length, since most of its manifestations have emerged in the work of David Jones. He and others focused on mass disturbances in both rural and industrial areas, on the Newport march, on the co-ordinated flouting of the law in the Rebecca disturbances, on the folk symbolism of the uprising of the Scotch Cattle or the significant ritualistic reappearance of the *ceffyl pren*. It should be added that conflict in the countryside returned in the 1880s, a period somewhat later than that in which David Jones chiefly worked. There was class tension comparable with that of Ireland in the confrontation between landlords and the Welsh Land League. It emerged fiercely in the Carnarvon Boroughs by-election in April 1890 fought between the youthful agrarian radical, David Lloyd George, and Ellis Nanney, the squire of Gwynfryn Castle. Earlier, the protests against payment of tithe to an alien Church led to ugly incidents in normally tranquil farming communities in Clwyd and Powys. At Meifod in Montgomeryshire in June 1887, the county militia was brought in and the Riot Act had to be read. Fifty civilians, many of them farmers, and thirty-four police were injured. Wales, it seemed, had its own version of the Irish 'Plan of Campaign'.

After the turn of the century, this tradition spread to industrial areas. The south Wales coalfield, for micro-economic and also geological reasons, was the most torn by conflict and class hatred. In Tonypandy there was loss of life; contrary to his later disavowals, Churchill as Home Secretary (admittedly with much reluctance) had to send the hussars to the mining valleys. Troops dealt with demonstrators in Pontypridd with fixed bayonets. The trouble spread elsewhere in the coalfield to other industries. In the national rail strike of July–August 1911, several men were shot down and killed in Llanelli; detachments from the Worcestershire and Sussex regiments patrolled the town, but no inquiry followed. In the intensified industrial conflict after the end of the war, with mass unemployment rising especially fast in a traditionally exporting coalfield like south Wales, confrontations mounted. In the traditionally more peaceable anthracite coalfield of Welsh-speaking west Wales, there was massive violence between striking miners and the police at Ammanford in 1925, remembered for decades afterwards.[11] A similar story came with the 'stay-down' stoppages at Abertillery in 1935, and in the handling of demonstrators from south Wales in the means test and unemployed marches around the same period.[12] Even in the far less troubled years after 1945, the 1984–5 miners' strike replayed some of the old themes in south Wales. A passing motorist lost his life inadvertently, while Norman Willis, general secretary of the TUC, was greeted by an audience at Port Talbot with a gallows rope symbolically strung down from the public gallery. Nor was rural protest dormant either. Welsh farmers turned to direct action in the 1980s and 1990s as their livelihood collapsed around them, notably in furious protests over the handling of 'mad cow disease' in 1996, and picketing shipments of meat due to be landed at the port of Holyhead.

The continuing common theme was that of violence. In the coalfield the Welsh seemed to be in perpetual turmoil. In violent confrontation they led the way, from the Merthyr uprising and its brutal suppression, to the popular martyrdom of Saunders Lewis, another Dic Penderyn *avant la lettre* in 1937, which led even the anti-nationalist David Lloyd George to an explosion of wrath (admittedly from the safe and comfortable haven of Montego Bay).[13] Detailed study of aspects of Welsh society have reinforced this view. My late wife, Jane (a close professional associate of David Jones who contributed a fine chapter to her memorial volume), found in her study of the police and industrial conflict that, even more than Liverpool or Glasgow, it was south Wales that provided her with the major examples of conflict.[14] She cited a contemporary account of Tonypandy when Churchill sent in the hussars: 'With a dervish yell and batons drawn they dashed out between 80 and 90 strong from the colliery yard ... The two sides were in furious combat ... Scores of the rioters were struck down like logs with broken skulls and left on the ground.'[15] One man (Samuel Rays) was left dead, 500 were injured amongst the rioters, along with 40 per cent of the foot constables and sixteen mounted men. The rioting continued intermittently in 1911;

meanwhile the local constabulary, the feared 'Glamorgans', turned their acquired experience of manhandling strikers to other fields, notably in battering into submission the clay workers of hitherto peaceful Cornwall in the St Austell area in 1913.

After 1920, things were just as bad. Captain Lionel Lindsay, long-term chief constable of Glamorgan who had first seen service in suppressing the Egyptian fellahin under Sir Garnet Wolseley, was fully embattled. The government used the Emergency Powers provision to send in troops, warships to patrol the port of Cardiff and even (for surveillance only!) the air force to force the miners in south Wales into submission. Nor was this violence confined to the industrial south. Just as the Chartist movement had first erupted in deeply rural Llanidloes, so the Penrhyn Quarry stoppage of 1900–3 was also marked by massive confrontations. As Merfyn Jones has shown,[16] Lord Penrhyn's regime (with its prohibition of trade unions which had originally provoked the strike) saw the massive use of auxiliary police, of cavalry and infantry in a manner astonishing to the quiet slate villages of Caernarfonshire. There was intense personal bitterness towards Penrhyn himself. For a generation or more of industrial conflict, from the turn of the century down to the mid-thirties, this pattern of physical confrontation was to continue. Violence, said in the sixties to be 'as American as cherry pie', appeared rather to be as British as Welsh rarebit.

Is this, then, the true face of modern Welsh history? Were the Welsh always roaring boys, always a race apart? Was their social history a saga of rioting and striking, knocking down toll-gates and enclosure walls and burning down aerodromes, in eternal conflict with the official forces of the law? Has Wales since 1800 been in a state of continual sub-revolutionary turmoil simmering just below the surface, the cockpit of the western world?

Clearly this view would, in fact, be a parody. These episodes did indeed take place, but they were only part of the story, as David Jones's work recognized, especially when he wrote on the policed society. Compared, for example, with the multiple tragedies of modern Ireland, from the time of Cromwell down to atrocities such as that of Omagh in early 1998, Wales has been by contrast the model of constitutionality. Its representative folk symbol is not the nation in arms but the committee man in the council chamber, armed not with an armalite but with his Bangor or Aberystwyth BA. There is nothing remotely like the Irish tradition of long-term communal violence. There was no Welsh Ulster, no Welsh Provisional Sinn Fein or IRA. The Welsh Land League was far less aggressive than the Irish and the countryside infinitely more peaceful. There was no mass movement for a republic. There was no Welsh de Valera or Michael Collins, let alone Gerry Adams. In time, even social conflicts as intense as those of the Rebecca years in the 1840s or the industrial clashes of 1910–26 gradually faded away, and a more constructive phase took their place. Welsh history over the past 200 years is one of conflicts, actual and potential, but then of their being invariably resolved.

There are many social explanations for this. Gradual economic prosperity neutralized points of conflict: unlike Ireland, labourers from the countryside, surplus to economic needs in marginal rural areas, found employment within Wales itself. Indeed, they found it possible to live harmoniously in the Valleys with thousands of other immigrants from England and Ireland (or, indeed, in Cardiff from North Africa and the Middle East). In rural areas, socio-economic unrest usually concerned small property-holders, conservative with a small 'c' if seldom with a large one. Welsh tenant farmers, politically antagonistic towards their landlords as they may often have been, were nevertheless small entrepreneurs, who owned their tools and stock and whose common interest with their labouring force was limited. At the turn of the century, as depression in the countryside eased and marketing and transport facilities improved, rural tension rapidly diminished. Lloyd George's land crusades seemed to be by 1914 somewhat out of date. Very few Welsh farmers endorsed the nationalization of land advocated by the far-left Revd E. Pan Jones in *Y Celt*, published in Mostyn in deepest Clwyd. In any case, David Howell has argued, tenurial relations in rural Wales were never that hostile. Even in the worst depths of agricultural depression in the late nineteenth century, the social structure remained organic, closely knit and deep-rooted.[17] After 1910, Wales experienced its own 'green revolution' when tens of thousands purchased their freeholds. Their subsequent financial difficulties found them locked in conflict not with remote Anglican landlords (a pathetic rump by now) but with local banks.

In industrial Wales, revolt was neutralized by many factors. There was a robust strength to community life in the Valleys, the product of a range of agencies from the nonconformist chapels to the mass of local rugby or other sporting clubs. The Tonypandy rioters in 1910 made a point of leaving alone the chemist's shop of Willie Llewellyn, a famous rugby international. One important element was the spread of house-ownership, a rapid development widespread in mining communities after the turn of the century.[18] 'Building clubs' and, later, building societies found profitable and harmonious fields for their operations in industrial south Wales, while the leasehold property owned by the Bute family and others in Cardiff, Barry and Newport did not create mass friction at this time. Here and elsewhere, Welsh society was becoming less polarized, especially as public education created a new generation of social leadership through the county schools and the national university. Even Welsh women, long subjugated, found professional and other openings, notably through the schoolteaching profession. Bangor Normal and Trinity College, Carmarthen, entered after 1900 upon halcyon years.

Perhaps the most pivotal figures in Welsh life after the turn of the century are not the combatants but the bureaucrats. A new generation of bourgeois conquerors was created, the committee men who ran the new councils and commissions, public servants like Thomas Jones, Alfred Davies, John Rowlands, Percy Watkins or later Ben Bowen Thomas or Elwyn Davies.[19] Thomas Jones, a constructive Fabian, embodies the new ethos of 'administrative Wales' hailed as such in the monthly *Welsh Outlook* (which for a time he owned).[20] He was the supreme bureaucrat, running Welsh health and insurance, active in the university world, sponsoring local economic initiatives, launching adult education – most notably in Coleg Harlech in 1927. In Wales, as at Downing Street in the service of his fellow Welshman Lloyd George, he was 'the fluid person moving amongst persons who matter'.[21] In London this could seem an irritating symbol of close-quarter patronage; in Oxford where Jones operated at All Souls alongside members of the 'Cliveden set' of appeasers of Hitler, stronger language could and would be used. In Wales, by contrast, Jones was a constructive, healing, idealistic figure, helping to bind the nation's earlier wounds, finding solutions and persuading his countrymen to pursue the path of peace.

A major factor in this move towards consensual approaches was without doubt the advent of democracy. Unlike Ireland, where democracy has so often foundered on irreconcilable social and sectarian divisions, especially in Ulster, Wales has found politics a panacea. It has spawned the triumphalism of the committee man. In the mid-Victorian era, that 'age of equipoise' so cogently analysed by Ieuan Gwynedd Jones, the years Walter Bagehot called the 'day after the feast',[22] modern Wales was reborn. New national and local institutions were created under the aegis of the new Liberal ascendancy. An almost unbroken string of peaceful victories followed – the capture of almost all the Welsh parliamentary constituencies at elections, the domination of the county councils (especially their crucial education committees), the ascendancy of a broad national/Liberal culture spanning chambers of commerce and trade unions, the nonconformist chapels, the editorial offices, the shops and the schools, even to a degree the local rugby clubs. In the Edwardian era, this consensual ascendancy had an immense variety of representative symbols, from the epoch-making victory over the New Zealand All-Blacks in December 1905 to the subtly inclusive investiture of Prince Edward at Caernarfon castle in July 1911. Lloyd George and Bishop A. G. Edwards, two old polemical adversaries but two supremely serpentine Celts, were amongst the orchestrators. David Lloyd George was being denounced by Unionists in England as a wild man, a dangerous, divisive force, taxing the rich, threatening the Lords, threatening dire consequences like a latter-day John Knox for 'golfers, motorists and all those miserable sinners who happen to own anything'. In Wales, by contrast, he seemed to have transcended political divisions; he was the greatest living Welshman, the cottage-bred embodiment of *y werin* in power, the pride and joy of his countrymen.

At first, the First World War and his premiership made this supra-party symbolism all the stronger. After all, he could now appear as the ultimate champion of Liberal, national values, the passionate defender of gallant little Belgium, gallant little Serbia and Montenegro – and, by implication, gallant little Wales.[23] The old conflicts therefore simply melted away as somehow irrelevant. The martyred evicted farmers of 1868, turned out of their holdings for having dared to vote Liberal, had been avenged long before. The Welsh squirearchy had long held up the tattered flag of surrender, taking refuge in such activities as becoming lords lieutenant or high sheriffs, or else chairing local history societies.

At the first sign of a Rorke's Drift or Little Big Horn, the squires turned tail. The bishops were to follow. The disestablishment of the Welsh Church in 1920, the age-old aspiration of nonconformists over the generations, thus seemed a monumental irrelevance. The long march of Welsh Liberalism ended not with an emotional bang but with the most anti-climactic of whimpers.

Democracy also helped to make consensual the Labour movement. Through social and political advance, Labour created its own constructive élite – in local government, in the world of the WEA and of adult education, in the deeply entrenched Co-operative Society, and always in the world of the trade unions. The miners and other workers created their own local leadership often as miners' agents. In place of firebrands like the proto-Fascist C. B. Stanton,[24] the Fed generated moderate leaders like Vernon Hartshorn or Charles Edwards or Arthur Jenkins, father of a famous Welsh centrist politician. The older pre-war Lib-Labs of the Mabon type passed away, but the militant advocates of direct action were gradually marginalized, too, especially after the general strike. Arthur Cook, the Somerset man who was the most charismatic of them all, ended his days sadly undermined by alcoholism, a feeling of class betrayal and fleeting sympathy for Sir Oswald Mosley.[25] Noah Ablett, the inspirational Marxist rhetorician of the Plebs League, also disappeared into the shadows. Meanwhile, Major David Watts Morgan, CBE DSO MP, 'Dai Alphabet', spoke of a new Labour respectability. The great Labour figures of twentieth-century Wales have all believed in the agency of democratic power. That was self-evidently true of Jim Griffiths, perhaps the most characteristic symbol of consensualism in the Welsh Labour movement. But it came to be true of Aneurin Bevan, too, who foreswore his early sympathy for forms of direct action like the workers' 'Defence Corps' and became dedicated to the pursuit and mobilization of democratic power.[26] Both Griffiths and Bevan, different in personality and outlook as they were, ended up as Cabinet ministers with great social achievements to their credit, and as national statesmen. At the time of Suez, Nye Bevan was hailed as a workers' patriot, morally superior to the Wykehamist traitor, Gaitskell. The Labour ascendancy after 1945, as deep-rooted as the Liberal ascendancy before 1914, defused any prospect of any kind of workers' revolt, even under the extreme provocation of Thatcherism in the 1980s. Great titans at the local level, of whom Llew Heycock in Glamorgan was the outstanding example, provided communal forces of stability and penetration after 1945, as they had fought to keep local services going during the harsh years of the means test and mass unemployment in the thirties. For all its semi-revolutionary antecedents and occasional Marxist flourishes, Labour Wales was part of the consensus and of the establishment.

So, it may be remarked, was the Communist Party in its way. In the twenties, it threatened to be a focus of radical and industrial protest of a quite new kind, as disillusion with parliamentary politics set in. Gwyn A. Williams cast affectionate eyes on the role of David Irvon Jones, who had to seek refuge in South Africa in the end.[27] But in the thirties, Arthur Horner, much the most important Communist, became president of the South Wales Miners' Federation; later on he worked closely with the National Coal Board in producing the 'Miners' Charter'. The old poacher was close to becoming gamekeeper.[28] After his time, another distinguished Communist, Dai Francis, could move on from a career confined to the union to becoming an active participant in the movement for Welsh devolution.

Democracy had its emollient effect on nationalism also. Since the 1960s, Welsh Nationalists have become politicized. In effect, the irreconcilable outlook of Saunders Lewis has been replaced by that of Gwynfor Evans, and even more that of Dafydd Wigley. Instead of becoming instruments of protests, of expressionist politics, nationalists have mainly pursued consensual strategies, notably in enabling the two linguistic communities to work together in the setting up of Welsh-language schools. Advocates of direct action, still more fringe movements such as the arsonists of Meibion Glyndŵr, have been totally marginalized, as Plaid Cymru has grown in confidence, the Scottish Nationalists have continued to thrive, and the prospects for inclusive co-operation within the Welsh Assembly have opened up. Plaid Cymru has certainly become far more politically aware than in the early sixties, and also no doubt more aware of its opportunities as the heady possibilities opened up by strong by-election votes in Rhondda West and Caerphilly in 1967–8 later reappeared. But the main democratic achievements have lain not in political but in cultural nationalism, in the way that Welsh culture has become more harmonious and able to play a fuller part in the revival of popular culture, design and artistic life (notably in the cinema) that the period following the 1997 referendum result appears to have witnessed. Of course, in this nationalists have gone with the grain of the movement for national recognition in Wales, an urge for equality and fair treatment within the United Kingdom, rather than the separatism relentlessly sought by the Irish. But it is hard to see Welsh Nationalists as being more successful through militant methods under any circumstances. Even compared with the Scots, they have been subdued, in accordance with the modest nature of any kind of Welsh separatism. Owain Glyndŵr, potent symbol though he may be, is no Wallace or Bruce. He has never yet inspired a Welsh *Braveheart*.

The more rhetorical versions of conflict as the abiding theme of recent Welsh history must, therefore, be rejected. The Marxist diagnoses of Wales popular in some circles in the 1980s collapsed with the Berlin wall. The dominant tendency in Welsh history is not a militant tendency. On balance, during the twentieth century, elements of conflict within Welsh society have steadily diminished. The ideological extremes have not struck long-term roots. The Welsh Labour movement was solidly centre-right: Communism made only localized headway. Any form of Fascism found less receptive soil in Wales than elsewhere in the British Isles. There have been no anti-Jewish activities in Wales since 1911 – and those events in Tredegar may not have been anti-Semitic at all.[29] Nor have there been any significant racial riots in the land since those in Cardiff in 1919.[30] For much of the century, Wales could be claimed to be more harmonious than England. In the years before 1914, George Dangerfield saw Liberal England in the process of undergoing a strange death, its civic culture undermined by violent strikes, militant suffragettes, near civil war in Ireland, and a widespread atmosphere of extremism. In Wales, at that very same period, there was a high noon of national unity and achievement. There was pride in the growth of the city of Cardiff, the commercial development of the new port of Barry, the eminence of cultural leaders like John Morris-Jones and Owen M. Edwards, in the golden age of Welsh rugby. Even Lloyd George, as has been seen, played very different roles in Wales and in England. In England he was an extremist, but in Wales almost a reconciler. Indeed, similar contrasts can be made throughout the century if a comparative method is used and Welsh and English are posed face to face. The conflict thesis, therefore, can be exaggerated. Yet consensus is hardly a satisfactory diagnosis of our historical experience either. In part, this may be simply a matter of semantics or of definition. Historians must consider such issues as consensus among whom, and at what level. Is it a consensus over the framework, over the policy, or is it a broader moral consensus? History in Wales, as elsewhere, is supremely the analysis of the process of change, of stress and its resistance. The study of the past is inherently a dialectic if not a materialist one.

Overt physical conflicts have been contained or set aside. But other forms of conflict keep emerging, even if historians, trained by their cloistered disciplines to seek harmonies in life, are sometimes too squeamish to acknowledge the fact. Even the gentle achievement of disestablishment of the Church in 1920, a wholly bloodless victory, was testimony to a major dislodging of traditional forms of authority. It helped to promote a wider disestablishment in Wales, notably that of the remnants of the landed gentry. Lloyd George, brilliant and brutal, was probably nearer the political realities than the gentle and philosophical Tom Ellis. And as one historic conflict was being resolved, it merely uncovered other forms of conflict based on class, culture, gender or generation. A new environmental radicalism, dimly prefigured in the Tryweryn controversies over water supplies in the fifties, might transform the nature of Welsh protest yet again. And Wales is, of course, deeply affected by pressures from outside, especially in an age of televisual imagery and the revolutionary impact of information technology. Earlier conflicts down to the 1960s were moderated because of faith in the British social order and constitutional system, in the civil service, in local government, in the rule of law, so fascinatingly underlined in David Jones's later work on the police in south Wales. From that time on, Wales like much of the rest of Britain has seen an erosion in that earlier Fabian confidence, a declining faith in Parliament, in the justice system, in the monarchy itself. Just as the nationalist protests in Wales in the sixties had links with events in the Sorbonne and Berkeley, so inherent conflicts at the end of the millennium reflected wider pressures from outside, notably a Europe with which Wales was inseparably entwined.

The Wales of whose history David Jones was the incomparable chronicler was, then, a complex society and a fluctuating concept. It is not surprising that parts of his work may be located in the camps both of the consensualists and of the apostles of conflict. It showed the difficulties with the simplistic dualism (created, it should be said, by the television series, not by the participants) of *The Dragon has Two Tongues*. Ultimately, though, David Jones depicts a people that has held together in the modern period, and indeed become more confident of its identity as the pressures have mounted. Richard Hofstadter spoke of a society like the United States keeping intact despite the massive disruption of a civil war because of what he called 'comity' – 'a sense that community life must be carried on after the acerbic issues of the moment have been fought over and won'.[31] He contrasted American society positively in this respect with Spain at the time of the civil war in 1936.

In Wales, much of the comity of its recent history has come from the character of its nationhood. This has been expressed in terms of the idea of nationality rather than the aggressive doctrine of nationalism. It has thus been incremental rather than divisive. It could lead, as Rees Davies has brilliantly shown,[32] to Owain Glyndŵr becoming a protean figure in social memory, a looming hero for all moods and all seasons. It has not led to a Welsh Ulster, let alone a Welsh Bosnia being created from the fires. Welsh nationhood, however ill-defined, has thus enabled an inclusive form of self-expression to emerge. It has created a power of integration, in a form of Welshness increasingly acceptable to the English-speaking majority from the eisteddfod to Sianel Pedwar and Welsh-language schools. Nor is it merely the cult of a bourgeois Welsh-speaking élite in the Cardiff suburbs. The Welsh trade unions, for long the class-conscious advocates of solidarity for ever, now flaunt their Welshness. This kind of nationhood had also encouraged an increasingly positive and intelligent response from outside over many decades. In that sense, to see the entire span of Welsh history from the 1880s to our own time as 'the rebirth of a nation', rather than a people crushed into embittered oblivion by the processes of global capitalism, is wholly justified. The advance of national equality for Wales is an erratic but consistent story from Gladstone in the late Victorian era down to politicians of all parties in the 1980s and 1990s. Even under Mrs

Thatcher, that stern, unbending champion of British unionism, the Welsh Office developed mightily as the symbol of an active new Welsh territoriality. Even Thatcherism added an important ingredient to the awareness of identity. So, ironically, does an increasingly regional Europe, which the Mrs Thatcher of post-Bruges days regarded as anathema.

The impact of a devolved elected Welsh Assembly from May 1999 is hard to foresee. Its economic powers are very limited and this may lead to friction. It may reproduce the kind of parochial bickering that has made the federal University of Wales less of a national institution than it could have been. It may, however, create a different style of inclusive social leadership which will both have wider implications for the working of the British Isles and help evolve that sense of citizenship (perhaps in Europe as well as in Britain) that the Welsh have conspicuously lacked since the Tudor Act of Union. Nationality was not a theme in any of the social protests David Jones analysed: he was not Welsh-speaking and his view of devolution is not formally recorded. But it may be that its achievement could blur the disunities of his Wales. It could temper still further at least some of the stresses of a tormented society of which he was the wise and gentle remembrancer.

Notes

I am much indebted to Professor Ralph Griffiths for many helpful comments on this article.

1. E.g. Dennis Kavanagh and Peter Morris, *Consensus Politics from Attlee to Thatcher* (Oxford, 1989).
2. Louis Hartz, *The Liberal Tradition in America* (New York, 1955); Daniel Boorstin, *The Genius of American Politics* (Chicago, 1953).
3. See particularly Richard Hofstadter, 'Conflict and consensus in American History', in his *The Progressive Historians* (New York, 1968). It should be compared with the essay on Hofstadter by Arthur Schlesinger Jr in Marcus Cunliffe and Robin Winks (eds.), *Pastmasters: Some Essays on American Historians* (New York, 1969).
4. Shown in Harlech TV, January–March 1985.
5. David J. V. Jones, *The Last Rising* (Oxford, 1985), 228.
6. Idem, *Crime in Nineteenth-Century Wales* (Cardiff, 1990), 201ff.
7. Idem, *Crime and Policing in the Twentieth Century: The South Wales Experience* (Cardiff, 1995), 65ff.

8. Kim Howells, 'Victimisation, accidents and disease', in David Smith (ed.), *A People and a Proletariat* (London, 1980), 181–9.
9. Kenneth O. Morgan, *Modern Wales: Politics, Places and People* (Cardiff, 1995), 16.
10. H. J. Hetherington (ed.), *The Life and Letters of Sir Henry Jones* (London, 1924), 95.
11. See Hywel Francis, 'The anthracite strike and the disturbances of 1925', *Llafur*, 1, 2 (May 1973), 15–28.
12. See David Smith, 'The struggle against company unionism in the south Wales coalfield, 1926–1939', *Welsh History Review*, 6, 3 (June 1973), 354ff.
13. Lloyd George to Megan Lloyd George, 9 December 1936, in Kenneth O. Morgan (ed.), *Lloyd George: Family Letters, c. 1885–1936* (Oxford and Cardiff, 1973), 213–14.
14. Jane Morgan, *Conflict and Order: The Police and Labour Disputes in England and Wales, 1900–1939* (Oxford, 1987).
15. Ibid., 156, citing the contemporary account of the *South Wales Daily News* journalist, David Evans.
16. Merfyn Jones, *The North Wales Quarrymen, 1874–1922* (Cardiff, 1981), 246ff.
17. Peris Jones Evans, 'Evan Pan Jones – land reformer', *Welsh History Review*, 4, 2 (1968), 143–59; David W. Howell, *Land and People in Nineteenth-Century Wales* (London, 1977), esp. 148ff.
18. See P. N. Jones, *Colliery Settlement in the South Wales Coalfield 1850 to 1926* (Hull, 1969).
19. An invaluable work on this theme is Percy Watkins's memoirs, *A Welshman Remembers* (Cardiff, 1944).
20. See the admirable biography by E. L. Ellis, *T.J.: A Life of Dr Thomas Jones CH* (Cardiff, 1992).
21. Thomas Jones to his wife, 12 December 1916 (National Library of Wales (NLW), Thomas Jones Papers, X/7).
22. Ieuan Gwynedd Jones, *Explorations and Explanations* (Llandysul, 1981), and idem, *Communities* (Llandysul, 1987). For Bagehot's view, see W. L. Burn's unjustly neglected book, *The Age of Equipoise* (London, 1964), 55ff.
23. Lloyd George's speech at the Queen's Hall, London, 19 September 1914, reprinted in *From Terror to Triumph* (London, 1915), 1–15.
24. Cf. Eddie May, 'Charles Stanton and the limits to patriotic labour', *Welsh History Review*, 18, 3 (1997), 483–508.
25. See Paul Davies, *A. J. Cook* (Manchester, 1987), 159ff.
26. Hywel Francis and Dai Smith, *The Fed* (London, 1980), 192ff.
27. Gwyn A. Williams, television programme on 'David Irvon Jones', 1992.

28. See Arthur Horner, *Incorrigible Rebel* (London, 1960).
29. A rare proto-Fascist was the Swansea businessman, W. Mainwaring Hughes: see Peter Stead, 'The Swansea of Dylan Thomas', in *Dylan Thomas Remembered* (Swansea, 1978), 8–24. For the anti-Jewish disturbances, see W. D. Rubinstein, 'The anti-Jewish riots of 1911 in south Wales: a re-examination', *Welsh History Review*, 18, 4 (December 1997), 667–99. The author concludes that, if anything, the Welsh were philo-Semitic.
30. Neil Evans, 'The south Wales race riots of 1919', *Llafur*, 3, 1 (1980), 5–30.
31. Hofstadter, 'Conflict and consensus', p.454.
32. Rees Davies, *The Revolt of Owain Glyndŵr* (Oxford, 1995), 338–42.

Riots and Public Disorder in Eighteenth-Century Wales

DAVID W. HOWELL

It is difficult to reach a safe conclusion about the level of public order in eighteenth-century Wales. That the dependent, vulnerable and impoverished lower orders were reduced to a large measure of obedience and servility through a mixture of kindly paternalism, threats and bullying on the part of local gentlemen and aristocrats there can be no doubt. Again there is no mistaking the strength and succour of kinship within communities, the reciprocal ties between neighbouring farmers, the fellowship between farmers' families and their menservants and maidservants, the folk customs and religious beliefs, and the distribution of poor relief, all of which served as a prop to community stability and harmony. Yet this notion of peaceful neighbourhoods is just one side of the picture. Court cases above all, but an array of evidence besides, point to a violent, unsqueamish, brutal society easily given to lawlessness and physical affray, a breakdown in public order which the magistrates and their helpers for all their often brave intervention were unable to do much about. Indeed, a significant amount of the lawbreaking and resort to violence involved rioting justices themselves. David Jones was right to point to the tradition of violence which underlay the society which spawned Rebeccaism.[1]

The rural community had its own standards and sense of right and wrong which often conflicted with statutory law. Corn riots were sanctioned by the poor as a legitimate defence of a traditional right to purchase food at a 'fair' price, and likewise smuggling, wrecking, poaching and the exercise of a whole range of common rights were cherished by the lower orders as customary rights succouring them in their struggle for survival. Attempts to interfere with the enjoyment of these rights on the part of the authorities led to conflict. In particular, new forces afoot in the eighteenth century, such as the engrossing and forestalling of the market by profiteering middlemen and the reassertion of manorial franchises as their perceived legal right on the part of manorial lords, would inevitably spark riot and disorder on the part of the poorer sorts of people. The crop of militia laws, too, that came on to the statute book from the mid-eighteenth century were injurious to the meaner ranks of society and met with determined resistance. Another irritant to the countless traditional, highly localized neighbourhoods that made up Welsh rural society was the intrusion of strangers from outside into their midst. As a manifestation of this we shall scrutinize the violent race riot just outside Denbigh in September 1754. Finally, public disorder was the frequent product of the strong partisanship inflaming both parliamentary election contests and borough politics.

Food riots were a frequent occurrence in different parts of Wales, as in England, throughout the eighteenth century. Recognizing this, David Jones commented: 'the riots from 1793 to 1801 were therefore remarkable only because they were so numerous'.[2] Corn riots thus took place in earlier decades in 1709, 1713, 1728, 1740, 1752, 1757–8, 1766, 1778, 1783 and 1789, all years of scarcity and high prices, such disturbances demonstrating the working population's heavy reliance upon bread as a staple food. Labourers' meagre budgets in Denbighshire and Merioneth in 1788 indeed saw between 60 and 63 per cent of weekly expenditure going on the purchase (symptomatic of the poorer areas of north and west Britain) of barley or oatmeal.[3] This impoverished working population scraped a living in normal times, but a bad harvest meant local famines, out-of-reach prices and awful deprivation. Typically, the winter of 1739–40 experienced 'the great frost' in north Wales which, lasting from 23 December 1739 to 10 February 1740, saw prices for corn rise and food riots erupt in May, and again the food disturbances in Anglesey in 1757 and 1758 occurred against the backdrop of the 'remarkable' season of 1756–7, which produced 'dearth and scarcity' in corn.[4]

As mentioned, this fragile situation arising from the vagaries of the harvest was rendered worse throughout Britain by the increasing tendency over the course of the century for corn factors, badgers, millers, large farmers and others to seek to engross and forestall the market. Testimony as to the harmful impact on ordinary people of this practice is ample. In August 1741 Mary

Richard and Humphrey Griffith Owen, both of Dolgellau parish, Merioneth, were prosecuted at the Great Sessions for having in the previous June engrossed 200 bushels of barley at Llanelltud parish and sold it at a profit in Dolgellau market, 'which illegal practice ... tended ... to the enhancing of the price of corn at Dolgellau and several other places in Merioneth to the very great prejudice of several of the inhabitants of the said county'.[5] In similar vein, Haverfordwest Corporation in March 1757 noted that

> several large quantitys of all sorts of corn and grain have since last harvest been bought up from time to time in county Pembroke and shipped off for other parts of this Kingdom by which means the prices on all corn brought to the marketts of this town and of the county of Pembroke are raised to so considerable a height that the poorer sort of people are already greatly pinch'd and much distressed thereby.[6]

It is not surprising that at periods of bad harvest labouring people should have turned their anger against those who were making the situation worse by buying up grain for export. As Edward Thompson so forcefully argued, at these moments of crisis the working population resented what they perceived to be illegitimate behaviour which did violence to the old moral economy of the lower orders with its notions of a fair or just price for bread as a traditional right. Corn riots, while certainly sparked off by hunger or fear of hunger, were informed by this popular consensus of traditional rights and the need to defend them.[7] Such attitudes extended to other vital provisions, and at times of deprivation the people also stole butter, cheese and beans and prevented their export. The years 1757 in north-west Wales and 1795–6 in Pembrokeshire, in particular, saw high prices for butter which led to disturbances in those areas. In the light of Sir Thomas Mostyn's letter from Gloddaeth (Caernarfonshire) in early December 1756 that 'Butter wch our *Country people live on* is very dear' (my italics), it is small wonder that riots in north-west Wales in 1757 and 1758 were as much concerned with its exportation as with corn.[8]

It was this anger over the export of grain and, on some occasions, other foodstuffs from local areas in times of scarcity which partly determined the location of disturbances. Food riots frequently occurred in the coastal and riverine ports of England and Wales and in the market towns that supplied London and the new manufacturing centres.[9] In the years before the corn riots of the 1790s and 1800–1 in Wales, disturbances which early engaged David Jones's attention, food riots erupted in and around Wrexham in spring 1709, at Loughor and Swansea in February 1713, at St Asaph and elsewhere in Flintshire and at Beaumaris in summer 1728, at Pembroke, Denbigh, Rhuddlan, Rhyl, St Asaph and Prestatyn in spring 1740, at Caernarfon in April 1752, at Holyhead, Laugharne and Carmarthen in early and mid-1757, at Redwharf, Llanbedr-goch and Beaumaris (all in Anglesey) in winter 1757–8, at Caernarfon, Conwy and Pwllheli in early 1758, at Flint in 1778, at Aberystwyth in 1783 and across the entire north Wales coalfield in 1789.[10] That the riots flared up more frequently in north Wales than in the south can be explained by the proximity to the manufacturing and commercial centres of Lancashire and Cheshire.

Perhaps as important in giving rise to food riots in Wales, as in England, was the presence in the disturbed areas of groups of industrial wage-earners like colliers, lead miners, slate quarrymen and the like and of craftworkers like shoemakers, tailors and weavers.[11] These groups were all exposed to the sharp price fluctuations in the open markets of the towns and, as such, were far more vulnerable than agricultural labourers, who enjoyed greater protection from the harsh realities of local markets. Moreover, by 'the force of custom' the latter were more deferential to their masters than were the non-agricultural workers. Roger Wells's insistence that the majority of eighteenth-century food riots did not include rural agricultural workers is well-taken, although some of the industrial workers in Welsh riots were living in rural townships and parishes.[12] Colliers were a very important group in many Welsh corn riots: it was they who removed corn from vessels at Loughor and Swansea in February 1713; colliers from local pits rioted at Pembroke in May 1740; only colliers were involved in the riots at Laugharne and Carmarthen in 1757; colliers from the coalworks at Mostyn and Bychton comprised the hard core of the rioters ransacking Rhuddlan in May 1740; an important element in the crowd in the three days of rioting at Denbigh on 28, 29 and 30 May 1740 was 'an outrageous mobb of miners, colliers around Denbigh', and coal miners rioted at

Flint in 1778 and across the north Wales coalfield in 1789.[13] Again, lead miners rioted at Aberystwyth in 1783 in protest at the high corn prices. Likewise, slate quarrymen were prominent in the riots at Caernarfon in spring 1752 and in early 1758. Craftsmen and artisans, also, were prominent in the food disturbances in Denbighshire and Flintshire in May 1740. Of the 130 people arraigned before the Flintshire Great Sessions in August 1740 for taking part in the riots at Rhuddlan and its vicinity in May, apart from the fifty-three colliers and miners there was a strong contingent of shoemakers, weavers, carpenters, blacksmiths, tailors and the like.[14] Shoemakers and tailors were likewise prominent in the assault perpetrated by Denbigh people on the parishioners of Llanfydd parish on 30 May over the exportation of corn.

In their determination to stop shipments of corn and other produce sometimes vessels would be boarded and the cargo stolen, as at Beaumaris in late June 1728, at Pembroke on 23 May 1740 and at Lawrenny creek in Milford Haven on 16 February 1757.[15] The following winter, 1757–8, indeed witnessed the theft of 'several shiploads' of corn, butter and cheese about to leave Anglesey.[16] On other occasions specific houses were visited by perambulating groups intent upon stealing corn destined for export. Friday 23 May 1740 saw men break into several private dwelling houses at Rhuddlan and destroy as well as divide among themselves large amounts of corn intended for shipment. Similarly on Thursday 29 May 1740 a group of people from around Denbigh made for the house of John Morris of Launt in Denbigh parish, a miller , and took away about three hobbets of wheat. Likewise, a mob broke into a house at Rhydbont, Anglesey, on Tuesday 3 January 1758 intent upon stealing the butter and cheese of Edward Rimmer of Warrington, maltster, and proceeded to break up the cheese butts into pieces and share them among themselves (estimated to be about 100 persons). That the sole motive of the rioters, as Edward Thompson has demonstrated, was not just to obtain desperately needed food but sometimes merely to express outrage at the violence being done to traditional moral assumptions by greedy middlemen and to punish them is reflected in two of these instances cited, for at Rhuddlan corn was destroyed, and the corn stolen from Morris of Launt was left 'some in the high road and some in the fields' near his house.[17]

Yet many of the same mob that visited Launt had the previous day, Wednesday 28 May, stolen five hobbets of wheat already sold for export from John Edwards of Henllan parish, a farmer, and the next morning one of their number proclaimed at the Denbigh cross that its price was to be 10s. a hobbet, at which level it was sold that morning. The proceeds were then divided among the group, each receiving 3s. In all this we glimpse the complexity of food riots: the corn stolen at Launt was simply left, but the same group earlier in the day had set the price, albeit the money they received was not returned to the original owner, John Edwards. Lowering the price was again in evidence in the Caernarfon riot of February 1758, William Morris informing his brother on 13 February that local quarrymen had the previous week made for the town, broken open the storehouses and sold the corn, butter and cheese at reduced prices. Likewise, in Anglesey, of the shiploads of corn, butter and cheese stolen in the winter of 1757–8, 'the greatest part of it [was] never sold at all and what was sold was next to nothing – Barley at 1s. a Pegget, Butter 1d. a pound and some for $^1/_2d$. a pound and cheese at the same rate'.[18]

In a couple of instances certain townspeople, without resorting to actual riot, resisted the high prices in difficult years by seeking to control market prices, as was likewise to occur in the corn riots in south-west England in 1800–1. Late May 1740 thus saw various people who went to Bala market (Merioneth) to buy oatmeal being forcibly taken before Charles Vaughan of that town, styled by his accomplices 'recorder', and being allowed to take their oatmeal home only on swearing on oath that they had not purchased it for export or to be sent out by sea. Having paid variously 2d. to 4d. for their oaths, they were handed tickets signifying they had been sworn which had to be produced at the outskirts of the town as a condition of their being able to leave unmolested. Community solidarity was shown in Pembroke town in early 1796 when the townspeople entered an agreement among themselves not to buy anything till the prices fell, resolving that they would not give more than $4^1/_2d$. per lb for beef or mutton or $9^1/_2d$. for fresh butter.[19]

Edward Thompson's claim that provision riots had specific aims and that these were pursued in a disciplined manner sometimes holds true within a Welsh context throughout the century.

Many of the riots were free from random, indiscriminate looting and wanton destruction of property or physical assault.[20] Lowering the price on some occasions and, again, as Glyn Parry indicates, the scrupulous behaviour of the Denbigh rioters on 28 May 1740 in taking corn from any one place only if the quantity there exceeded three hobbets is testimony to the specific aims shared by the rioters in Wales, as was the case elsewhere in Britain and western Europe.[21] Yet, following Bohstedt, food riots in Wales were often 'disorderly' in the sense that on many occasions food was taken from the owners without payment. Even when a lowering of the price occurred – and this was far from being general – there is some evidence, as in the case of theft from John Edwards of Henllan, that the proceeds of the sales were not returned to the owners.[22]

In addition, physical violence was by no means a rarity. To some extent of course the propensity for violence was related to the size of the assembly. Many riots were small affairs, ranging from just a handful of people to twenty or so. Others were much larger: a crowd variously estimated at between 700 and 1,300 rioted at Rhuddlan on Friday 23 May 1740, and some 400 the following day; the Denbigh mob who marched on Llanfydd parish on 30 May 1740 numbered no fewer than thirty and perhaps as many as 150; an estimated 150 people marched from Beaumaris and Llanerchymedd to Holyhead in January 1757, and on 17 June 1758 around a hundred colliers raided a Carmarthen storehouse. It was among these big crowds that discipline sometimes fragmented. The Rhuddlan disturbances in May 1740 certainly got out of hand when on 23 May the 'infatuated' mob ransacked the houses of three merchants who were too frightened to enter the town. The mob, indeed, carried five pikes with them, boasting that four were to carry merchant George Colley's quarters and the other his head, and they also swore that they would pull magistrate David Ffoulkes 'limb from limb and his house about his ears'.[23] The march of the Denbigh 'gang' on Llanfydd led to a fracas in which one Llanfydd man was shot dead by a member of the gang, Thomas Evans, a Denbigh shoemaker. After breaking open storehouses in Caernarfon in February 1758 and selling corn, butter and cheese for low prices the quarrymen got drunk 'and played misrule'.[24] In the ensuing scuffle with the authorities several rioters were shot, one mortally. Highway robbery and theft of money on the part of six men occurred during the course of the Denbigh food riot on 1 April 1795 and three magistrates were assaulted. These last instances should certainly caution us about too readily thinking in terms of orderly crowd behaviour even within Bohstedt's 'small agrarian villages' of up to 3,000.[25]

E. P. Thompson pointed to some particular provocation sustained as the likely explanation for the collapse of crowd discipline.[26] In the case of Rhuddlan in 1740, merchant Colley's action on the first day, 21 May, in apprehending five rioters and the follow-up by David Ffoulkes, Esq., in placing them under arrest inflamed the situation. But political party rivalries, too, played some part in this riot. K. Lloyd Gruffydd has persuasively argued that with the approaching parliamentary elections of 1741 there was an element of political faction at work ready to take advantage of the economic crisis: the Tory Sir Thomas Mostyn's colliers were prominent participants at Rhuddlan, chanting on their arrival 'A Mostyn', and arms were provided for the rioters by John Wynne, the steward of Sir Thomas, at Mostyn Hall itself. Significantly, magistrate Ffoulkes observed on 25 May that the mob were 'encouraged and have money given them by gentlemen around Holywell'.[27] Similarly, in the politically turbulent borough of Carmarthen it is possible that the collier-rioters in June 1757 were stirred up by one of the factions.[28]

That troops were called in on many occasions suggests on the face of it that the authorities were responding unsympathetically. Yet it may have been as a last resort, for they knew that the local popular resentment that would build up against such troops would not quickly evaporate. Again, as the fiasco at Carmarthen in June 1757 highlighted – when the mayor stood trial at the Assizes for having ordered troops to fire on rioting colliers, killing five of them, but not before reading the Riot Act and several times asking them to disperse – the very uncertainty of the magistrates' proper course of procedure in forcefully encountering the mob discouraged them from acting resolutely. The want of reliability on the part of local constables and local military, as David Jones demonstrated, was sometimes shown during the years 1793–1801, and was another constraint upon magistrates looking to call in troops.[29] In the south-west of England in 1800–1, at the beginning of the riots the authorities took a pacific stance. Whereas at Rhuddlan in spring 1740 three magistrates were for promptly calling in the military, the sheriff and justices preferred to meet the mob on Monday 26 May to try to pacify them. Some gentlemen, perhaps many, throughout the century clung to the old paternalist model and were conscious that the malpractices of corn factors, badgers, farmers and the like were harming the poor.[30] Efforts were made on their part to prevent corn from being exported; thus at the behest of the local justices corn was not cleared from the mouth of the River Conwy in March 1757. Glyn Parry has shown that such magistrates were warmly praised by the people, one contemporary ballad acclaiming that Humphrey Meredith from Pengwern would have 'a proper lodging in the kingdom of Heaven' for his vigilance in stopping corn exports. Contrariwise, those who neglected to do so were subjected to verbal attack, even physically assaulted, as were six justices at Llanerchymedd in Anglesey during the provisions crisis in 1757.[31] On occasions, too, magistrates were intent upon punishing forestallers. The Anglesey justices were certainly siding with the people in the crisis of 1757, William Bulkeley recording in his diary on 8 February 1758:

> The new Justices viz. – Sir Nicholas Baily, Jones of Henllys, Brisco the Collector of Beaumaris, Lloyd of Hirdrefaig and Wangle of Llwydiarth are greatly suspected to encourage and set them on, that ever since last Hillary Quarter, they have adjourned the Quarter to the Shire Hall, Beaumaris, every week ever since, where all the farmers that have sold any corn and those that bought it have been several times summoned to attend at the peril of their lives from a mob of 200 to 300, who fill the Hall and insult and abuse all those attending there upon their Summons who are kept there to answer the same questions asked over and over again by those threatening inquisition who from the Bench bully them, while the rude mob behind insult and abuse them, when between threats, noise and insults they at last are tired and confounded that they confess on themselves and are accordingly convicted and unmercifully fined.

By contrast, during the recent corn riot in Anglesey in January 1757 the authorities had acted leniently towards the rioters, for of the sixty-five or so prisoners arrested from an estimated mob of 150, all but the 'General' were set free the following day.[32]

Such unwillingness to bring them before the courts chimes with 'the reluctance to prosecute, or at least to arraign suspects on capital charges' on the part of the magistrates of south-west England in 1800–1. Overall, however, no general conclusion can be reached about the nature of the sentences imposed on the rioters in Welsh courts. Whereas sentences ranging from a 6*d*. fine and a day's imprisonment to 1*s*. fine and a week in gaol were meted out by the Caernarfonshire Great Sessions on the men and women who stole barley at the parish of Llanbeblig on 7 February 1758, seven rioters, two of them man and wife, were sentenced to transportation for seven years for their part in the riots in May 1740 at Rhuddlan and the surrounding countryside. At the same time, it is impossible to ascertain the sentences passed on their numerous fellow rioters arraigned before the courts of both Denbighshire and Flintshire in 1740 (some 130 names appear in the Flintshire gaol files alone). Whatever the reason for the stiff sentences meted out to the Rhuddlan seven, the harsh punishment of three or four years' imprisonment together with sureties for seven years' good behaviour imposed by the magistrates on some six men for their part in the Denbigh corn riot in 1795 arose from their assaulting a magistrate and unlawfully imprisoning him. Similary, in the wake of the serious corn riot at Merthyr in September 1800, two were hanged, in this case doubtless to warn against any future large-scale damage to property.[33]

Even if a number of magistrates were sympathetic, order had to be restored. Troops were thus used on a number of occasions, some coming from outside the area as, for example, troops from Cheshire during the Denbighshire and Flintshire riots of 1740 and the Old Pensioners from Chester Castle during the Caernarfonshire troubles in February 1758.[34] A riot or the *threat* of one also saw the raising of subscriptions to buy large quantities of corn to be distributed at cheap rates to the poor become a familiar response of the propertied classes, especially in the 1790s and 1800–1. Similar if less frequent action was taken earlier in Welsh counties. Such conduct on the part of the Haverfordwest Corporation in 1757 was looked upon as a necessary means to avoid 'dreadful consequences' and, significantly, the county remained quiet in that tumultuous year.[35] Again, subscriptions were raised in Denbighshire and Flintshire in early 1783 when grain prices were exceedingly high in consequence of the bad harvest of 1782. Here, as in the case of the subscription raised towards allaying the corn crisis in Monmouthshire in 1800, an added consideration beyond charitable concern or mere self-preservation motivated some landowners, namely, their political and local standing and the danger of being wrong-footed in the charity stakes by their opponents.[36] The threat of disorder, too, on one occasion at least brought greedy farmers to their senses, those about Pembroke in early December 1795 having 'become alarmed and promised a constant supply'.[37] There is some evidence, too, that in the wake of the riots coal owners mended their ways towards their workforce. Thus within weeks of the riot at Pembroke on 23 May 1740 the duke of Newcastle was informed that 'such care is now taken by ye owners of ye collerys to supply ye men with corn and to keep 'em in order yt no disturbance can happen for ye future'. Again, following the disturbances in the county in 1795, Pembrokeshire coal owners supplied their workforces at reduced prices.[38]

As for England and Wales in general, it is difficult to discover precise gender involvement in the food riots under discussion. Edward Thompson argues that the 'sexually-indeterminate' vocabulary like 'rioters', 'the mob', and 'the poor' frustrates specific gender identification.[39] Nevertheless there is some evidence of the presence of women and children at a number of the riots in Wales as elsewhere in Great Britain. A crowd of 400 men, women and children made for Rhuddlan on 21 May 1740 where they prevented a wagonload of wheat from being exported, while on 6 June 1740 a crowd comprising mainly women unloaded wheat from a vessel about to sail from Flintshire.[40] According to one account, the fracas at Llanfydd on 30 May 1740 ended with 'Denbigh men, women and children persuaded to return to Denbigh'. When two days earlier twelve men visited the house of John Edwards of Henllan, five or six boys, the youngest about thirteen, accompanied them.[41] Giving evidence in court on 29 March 1758 concerning a food riot, John Hughes of Llanwenllwyfo, Anglesey, stated that in December 1757 he saw 'a great multitude of people, some women amongst them, coming to Redwharf in Anglesey armed with clubs and staves'.[42] There is difficulty in relying on gender differentiation emerging from an analysis of legal indictments for it is possible that, apart from cases where women played a leading role, there was rather more willingness on the part of the authorities to prosecute men than women.⁴³ The indictments brought before the Great Sessions for the Welsh circuits suggest that this was so. Of the 130 people indicted for rioting at Rhuddlan in May 1740, just six were women (one of whom, with her husband, was transported); in the Denbigh riots of May 1740 some sixty males, but no female, were indicted (yet we hear elsewhere of women present at Llanfydd on 30 May!); some eighty males and eight females were indicted for riot in the Anglesey disturbances in early 1758; and there was just one female indicted as against some fifty-five males for theft of food before the Caernarfonshire Great Sessions in 1758/9. A somewhat larger contingent of females was to be found among the corn rioters tried before the Welsh courts between 1793 and 1801 for, reveals David Jones, of the total of 103 people indicted and convicted at the Great Sessions some fourteen were female.⁴⁴

In most Welsh as English food riots, women were certainly not more prominent than men. In so far as Wales was concerned, in all probability men were to the fore in the majority of cases but at the same time women constituted a significant presence in a number of them, no doubt as Bohstedt suggests 'partly because they were essential partners as bread-winners in the household economies of pre-industrial society and partly because bread riots were still effective politics in stable small-to-medium-sized traditional towns'. Moreover, at Haverfordwest on 18 August 1795, at Hay on 23 August 1795 and in the marches from Llangyfelach to Swansea in February 1793 and from Llangattock to Beaufort in March 1800 women were prominent participants even if the leaders of the last two marches were men.⁴⁵

For all the threats made to fire Pembroke and Rhuddlan in 1740 and to cause physical harm to the gentlemen of Rhuddlan, these, as for similar outbursts across Britain, were so much rhetoric.⁴⁶ It seems that certain gentlemen called forth particular resentment towards themselves, because of what was perceived as their overzealous activity in arresting leading culprits. At both Rhuddlan and Pembroke in 1740 and at Conwy in February 1758 those arrested were forcibly released and David Ffoulkes, Esq., in Rhuddlan and Mr Justice Holland in Conwy came in for hostile treatment.⁴⁷ Even so, there was no general undercurrent of antigentry ideology present in the riots before the 1790s – albeit at times the mobs were the tools of political faction. The riots were grounded in the hunger of the people and their resentment towards unfair profiteering at their expense. At Rhuddlan the people's wretchedness had reached such depths that they would rather be 'Hanged than Starvd' and the local JP William Price distilled the essence in observing: 'We must attribute the Comotion to ye necessity of the People.'[48] A perceptible change in the chemistry of food riots was to occur in the 1790s for, with the heightening of radical consciousness, food riots in Wales as elsewhere in Britain were sometimes driven, in part at least, by Jacobinical sentiments.[49]

Militia riots occurred in late eighteenth-century English and Welsh communities following the Acts of 1757, 1762, 1769 and 1796.[50] Undoubtedly rural communities experienced financial loss and hardship arising from the militia laws. Thus in May 1778 it was being claimed that the absence of Brecknock men serving in the militia meant that poor rates in their native county were mounting:

> Within this week I have received no less than 40 letters of complaints from the miserable objects we have left behind, we have one drummer that has a wife and six children / the eldest not 10/ *now pennyless* who depended entirely upon his Labour and Pay.[51]

In the wake of the Act of 1769 which attempted to tighten up on defaulters,[52] a riot broke out in Chirk (Denbighshire) on 3 March 1770 on the occasion of a subdivision meeting for Chirk Hundred at which the constables were to prepare lists of all men fit to serve in the militia. Upon the constable of Llanrhaeadr-ym-Mochnant being called into the Hand public house – where the magistrates had convened the meeting – to present his list, the noisy 400–500-strong mob gathered outside, armed with knotted ash clubs, pitchforks and rakes, broke the window of the room occupied by the magistrates and declared they would take away their lives if they persisted in the execution of the warrants to ballot for militia men. When the justices went outside to reason with the people their efforts proved in vain. It fell to John Evans of Llanrhaeadr, a blacksmith, to bargain with John Edwards of Glynn, Denbighshire, one of the magistrates, that the people should be given a discharge from militia service for the remainder of the three years. The matter did not rest there, however, for shortly afterwards Thomas Roberts of the parish of Llanrhaeadr, 'after stating all the hardships he and his neighbours had endured by the militia laws', informed Edwards that a discharge for three years was not enough and demanded they must have a discharge for ever. Upon Edwards responding that under the law he could not permit this and exhorting them to go home, they soon dispersed, but only after warning that next time the authorities should meet for the purpose they would come down with ten times the number and kill all of them. During the course of the disturbance the militia lists from the several parishes were forcibly taken from the constables and torn into pieces or burned.[53]

Mobilization of the militia led to riots in Merioneth in 1779, when in early summer about 300 to 400 people so abused the magistrates and deputy lieutenants that they were unwilling to raise the militia without having some regular troops or militia at their disposal to keep the mob quiet.[54] The impassioned face-to-face confrontation between people and magistrates that took place during these latter riots at Chirk and in Merioneth as on countless other occasions underlines the fragile equilibrium that obtained at this time between deference and defiance.

As David Jones indicated, the 1790s saw a heightening of hostility towards balloting of men for the militia, for now the war situation saw a mergence of all the grievances against high taxation, rising food prices, the Navy Act of 5 March 1795 and the Act of 11 November 1796 for augmenting the militia. On 1 April 1795 there was a serious riot at Denbigh against the Navy Act and balloting for the militia, when significantly the ringleaders were alleged to be 'seditious men' seeking to stir up 'Discontent amongst the Ignorant'. Later, in November and December 1796, anti-militia disturbances broke out in Carmarthenshire, Merioneth and Flintshire. In these militia riots, as in the case of food riots, we often see, as Bohstedt demonstrates, 'local political bargaining' being played out. Riots, then, 'were quintessentially local politics'.[55]

Resistance in Welsh neighbourhoods was often directed at 'strangers' who were perceived as constituting a threat to order, harmony and tradition in the community. One interesting manifestation of this was the fight between Welshmen and Englishmen in Henllan parish near Denbigh on Sunday evening, 1 September

1754, the affray taking place during the journey home from Cappel wakes where people from the town of Denbigh and the parish of Henllan had spent the day drinking. Some ritualistic posturing and menacing behaviour preceded the 'promiscuous hott fight', in the form of both sides holding sticks and staves above their heads, shouting and bawling, and crying out 'Dinbech' (some using the Anglicized 'Denbigh') and 'Henllan' respectively. In the subsequent trial a Denbigh sawyer alleged that when he attempted to quieten both sides, the Welsh people answered: 'We are not for [i.e. against] the Denbigh people but for [against]the Englishmen.' A further Denbigh witness, likewise attempting to cool tempers, addressed the country people (allegedly in pursuit of the Denbigh contingent) as follows: 'For God's sake be quiet, let the Strangers alone, for the Factory people pay sixty pounds a week wages and the people / meaning the Factory people / spend it all in the Country.' It is clear that the resentment of the Welsh-speaking country people of Henllan parish was aimed at the English strangers, the 'Factory' people, of the neighbouring town.

The attempts at containing the situation failed. In the ensuing mêlée John Ffoulke, a Henllan blacksmith, who had at the outset declared 'he would have the Englishmen beaten before they went from thence', was knocked down with a stick and subsequently died from the wound. Perhaps of significance is the fact that in the evidence taken from both sides not a single witness claimed to have seen who struck the mortal blow, the nearest form of identification using the following words: 'he was knocked down by a tall person who had a stick or stake in his hand and who then was either in his shirt or waistcoat without sleeves'.[56]

Professor Dodd likewise reminds us how the north-east Wales colliers in the eighteenth century 'were ever resentful of the intrusion of strangers'. Thus on 3 October 1776 riots broke out for half an hour on Harwood mountain when colliers objected to the employment of Englishmen in the collieries in the Wrexham district.[57] An unusual manifestation of this suspicion of and resistance to strangers was instanced in Dolgellau at the close of the eighteenth century when pandemonium broke out over the arrival there of a gentleman with a black servant. Such was the level of antagonism displayed towards the servant wherever he went by the townspeople on this their first experience of a coloured person in their midst that the two were forced to leave the place sooner than intended.[58]

Perhaps the most frequent dispute in eighteenth-century Wales, and hardly surprising given the vast areas of open moorland, occurred over manorial rights, particularly rights of common. Both private and crown manors witnessed clashes between the lords of those manors and the general body of the rural community, the latter including freehold or customary tenants of those manors as well as the numerous propertyless poor, over what each party perceived to be their 'rights'. As the century progressed there was a perceptible and growing insistence on the part of manorial lords on their legal rights of property in the face of what they deemed to be an increasing erosion of their manorial franchises by local freeholders and the propertyless alike. Not only were they concerned over encroachment and enclosure of commons but also over the making of bricks upon the commons, the digging and burning of lime and the cutting of turves without the lord's permission. Manorial lords saw part of the trouble of such encroachment on manorial franchises as stemming either from past neglect on the part of agents in enforcing rights like the collection of commortha rents – perhaps in part owing to the 'obstinacy and perverseness of the inhabitants' – or the wish on their own part to be popular, the resulting leniency giving rise to rights being but perfunctorily enforced, if at all.[59] The attempt – increasingly so from the mid-eighteenth century – to arrest the decay of manorial franchises and to lay claim to concealed and lost rights was met with hostility by the rural populace who, perceiving their 'rights' to be grounded in customary usage and traditional practice, accused the manorial lords of harassment and oppression and offered resistance in the form of petitions, resort to legal action, or riot.[60]

One compelling reason for manorial lords to pay greater attention to their manorial franchises over the course of the century was the growth of industrial enterprise, mineral rights accordingly taking on a whole new significance. Bitter and protracted disputes consequently arose between lords of manors and freeholders over the right to work these mineral deposits. Fiercely contested during the 1740s and 1750s was the Duke of Beaufort's reassertion of his mineral and other rights in the lordship of Gower, local gentlemen-tenants of the seigniory like Thomas

Price of Penllergaer, Robert Popkin of Forest and Richard Dawkins of Kilvrough denying the duke's right to coal and claiming for themselves rights to the waste and to work coal mines therein. Grievances were aired by the gentlemen-tenants as a body – at least thirty of them – at a meeting at the Guildhall, Swansea, on 8 December 1747, Thomas Price opening the proceedings by directly attacking the duke's rights.[61] Later, in August 1749 some twenty-two tenants of the manor of Oystermouth petitioned the duke that they were customary freeholders rather than copyholders – so giving them the right to work mines under their lands – and the same claim was to be made in June 1755 by tenants of the manor of Pennard, who filed a Bill towards establishing this mode of tenure.[62] While tenants of Pennard and Trewyddfa claimed that their reduced status as copyholders had been an innovation of recent years, the duke's formidable agent, Gabriel Powell, disputed this, having earlier contended in 1742 that 'it seems to be a settled rule amongst the tenants to rob the Lord as much as they can'.[63]

Disputes of a much more violent nature occurred over the mining of lead ore within the Crown lordships in Cardiganshire, occasioned by Lewis Morris, deputy steward of the Crown lands there, attempting at mid-century to reassert the Crown's right to ore lying under the open wastes against the often blatantly illegal claims and encroachments of private owners like the squires of Nanteos, Gogerddan and Crosswood, who viewed such open lands as part of their freeholds. So, aided and abetted by rioting justices at the head of their dependent, subservient but loyal countrymen, violence surged unchecked, the most spectacular outburst occurring on 23 February 1753 when a group of Cardiganshire freeholders, including the defiant owners of Crosswood and Nanteos, stormed and took over the Crown lead mine of Esgair-y-mwyn.[64]

Mineral disputes apart, resistance to the lords' attempts to recover lost rights after a spell of slackness or to assert their right to making the most of their manorial property was a familiar occurrence. The Morgans of Tredegar House encountered resistance in the 1780s from Brecknock freeholders over Charles Morgan's attempt to recover his perceived right of collecting commortha rents in the manor of Brecon, through the neglect of agents not collected since 1752. Unwilling to reach any accommodation with Morgan, the freeholders entered a combination of allegedly 150 or more to try the right at law.⁶⁵ Waxing 'warm' on both sides in 1784, the whole matter was complicated by considerations of the approaching parliamentary election, Bowyer of Lincoln's Inn advising the Morgan camp on 6 December: 'It therefore behoves Mr. Morgan to proceed with circumspection and to be on safe ground before he attacks so formidable a Confederacy, and particularly as he is member for the County and many of the Bondsmen [the Combination members] are freeholders.'⁶⁶ Morgan, as Crown lessee, also fell foul of the freeholders of Devynock Hundred in the late 1770s and 1780s over his insistence on the right of depasturing strange cattle from different counties like Glamorgan on the Great Forest of Brecon in order to make up the Crown rent, the freeholders as borderers on the Forest claiming an exclusive right to the pasturage thereon. Their protest took the form of impounding the strange or 'foreign' cattle and refusing to release them on 'fair' terms, which in turn led to lawsuits. While for their part the Devynock freeholders informed Morgan: 'we would fain believe that as we are both your tenants and constituents we are entitled to indulgences of that nature more than strangers have a right to expect', Morgan in reply defended his actions thus: 'I hope you and they [i.e. his "friends" within his political interest] think better of me than to suppose I would give the preference to strangers or that anybody should be indulged before my tenants and constituents but at the same time I also hope you cannot object to my maintaining my right as tenant of the crown and whereby no injury will be sustained by the tenants.'⁶⁷

In similar vein, John Morgan of Tredegar House in November 1791 was anxious to maintain his right to cutting timber on Coedmoeth Common in the parish of Bedwellty (Monmouthshire) in the face of the parishioners claiming such a right as belonging to themselves and their ancestors 'time out of mind'. Morgan's response to their twenty-one-strong petition was typical of the resistance put up by lords of the manor to claims to rights of common by neighbouring inhabitants, his agent replying:

> he will accede as far as he can to your request therein [not to cut timber into cordwood on the common]; and that as you do not claim the said wood, or the cutting of them, as a matter of Right,

but of Favour only; He will oblige you so far as to order the cutting of them as favourable as possible to your Interest; I mean so as to leave a sufficient quantity for the purpose you mentioned remaining – for the value of them is not his whole object in cutting them, but the maintenance of his undoubted Right therein and thereto as Lord of the Soil.[68]

Much community conflict arose, too, over manorial lords resorting to eviction or rent increases in an effort to put a stop to the growing numbers of trespasses by cottagers on the open wastes. Again, two opposing views of 'legal' *vis-à-vis* 'customary' rights were in collision. The right to dig turf led to many disputes. Thus from time to time the Lloyds of Bronwydd (Cardiganshire) as lords of the manor were in dispute with people encroaching on their commons to dig turf. Summer 1718 thus saw trespassers on the Cemais Commons within the lordship of Cemais (Pembrokeshire) being summoned to appear before the lord's court to clear themselves or to acknowledge their trespass; significantly, those making such acknowledgement were to be 'kindly used', but those refusing to appear would be prosecuted with rigour by both the lord and other gentlemen having right of common.[69] Lords of the manor, private and Crown alike, were also concerned at prosecuting those who made encroachments of small parcels of land on the commons, the rising population from mid-century witnessing a growth in the practice. In the late 1760s, for example, the lessee of the Crown lordship of Cantremelenith in Radnorshire, in order that the king should 'reap the benefit of his own lands', sought to make the great number of those who had erected cottages and made small enclaves on the commons turn tenants upon pain of having ejectments served on them. Such ejectments were indeed found to be necessary, John Lewis of Harpton, the Crown agent, commenting in 1768 on 'the natural dispositions of people being averse to turn tenants and acknowledge any Lord'. Freeholders as well as small cottagers were involved, and the former petitioned in 1773 against the claims of the Crown's lessee, 'who now terribly harasses your petitioners having sued several of us as trespassers for privileges which we have heretofore peaceably enjoyed'. By 1779 the efforts to assert the crown's rights had proved ineffectual, for despite having served several ejectments and brought three successful trials at Hereford 'the commoners have immediately prevented his [John Lewis, the agent] possessing the recovered land by throwing down their inclosure and claiming their common'.

As was the case with the Morgans of Tredegar, this dispute over manorial rights was seen as having possible damaging political repercussions. Thus in election year, 1768, John Lewis was anxious as to the political fall-out consequent upon his work as Crown agent (though in the event he triumphed over his opponent, Edward Lewis) and again in 1774 he was urging that the unjust and false representations being made against him as Crown agent should be gainsaid.[70]

Encroachments on to wastes by cottagers were disliked by freeholders and their tenant farmers, and so landowners along with manorial lords were anxious to put a stop to such 'depredations'. Significantly, those same freeholders of the manors of Gower Suprabosaus and Pennard who were challenging the duke of Beaufort's mineral and other rights in the seigniory of Gower, drew up a remonstrance in 1747 intended to be sent to the duke complaining of the 'numberless encroachments of the commons ... by erecting multitudes of cottages and making divers enclosures thereon within a few years past'.[71]

Various responses to this colonization of the wastes by the poor were instituted. Thus freeholders, often in response to the complaints of their tenant farmers, banded together to throw down the cottages and small enclosures of the squatters, the latter in Cardiganshire and seemingly elsewhere believing, it was stated in 1797, 'that cottages erected on the waste with each a portion of land annexed to them cannot be pulled down'.[72] Given this notion it is not surprising that concerted efforts by landowners at throwing down enclosures were by no means invariably effective. In March 1759 William Owen of Porkington (Shropshire) was informed:

> There are great complaints made by your tenants of Dolbenmaen and Penmorva [Caernarfonshire] against several cottages and enclosures erected lately on the common called Garn Dolbenmaen. I've waited on purpose upon Mr. Wynne of Wern and Mr. Lloyd of Gessel, who has a Right there, Mr. Wynne said he had been to throw down some of them. But it proved to no purpose for they were soon repaired, and for that reason he thinks it better to have them indicted and he will join in it.[73]

On some occasions, landowners were careful to act legally in their efforts to demolish encroachments. At the request of the Grand Jury of the county Assize Court, a large body of Montgomeryshire freeholders met at Welshpool on 5 May 1787 to enter an agreement to throw down all recent encroachments on the wastes and to prevent future ones. Towards this goal the meeting appointed a committee which was to draw up proposals for a subscription to be made 'for supporting in a legal manner' the Rights of the freeholders to the wasteland.[74] Thus fortified, gentry and freeholder subscribers proceeded to level several recent encroachments, whereupon the great landlords, as lords of the manor, fearful of the mounting crisis, set their faces against the scheme. Seemingly this led to its collapse.[75] Westwards, in Cardiganshire, lords of the manor and freeholders were by 1797 so anxious about 'this growing evil' of encroachments that legal advice was sought as to how best to put a stop to them and how best to effect the demolition of cottages already built.[76]

Enclosure of common lands on the part of the burgesses within certain Welsh boroughs met with riotous opposition from the poor,[77] who justifiably felt cheated of their right of common. Carmarthen borough, especially, witnessed a number of disturbances, demolition of enclosures occurring in 1726, 1786 and late March 1789, when a mob broke down all the enclosures of the commons about the town. Of the latter, Anne Philipps of Cwmgwili reflected nervously: 'I am afraid it will end seriously if there is not a stop put to it soon, the first Rebellion that ever happened in Carmarthen was about enclosing the Commons. I hope it will not end as it did then.'[78] Disputes occurred in other boroughs. Five labourers and one gentleman were indicted at the Glamorgan Spring Assizes 1768 for having on eleven separate occasions between 6 and 25 April 1767 entered a piece of ground in Swansea called Goat Street, otherwise 'the waste', in possession of the burgesses for the previous ten years, and destroyed the ground and removed the burgesses from their possession.[79] On occasion, substantial landowners would challenge the enclosing burgesses. Thus spring 1783 saw landowners possessed of estates about Carnarvon Borough enter an agreement to be at joint expense in taking steps towards preserving their right of common called Rhospadrual, enclosed by the corporation.[80]

Enclosure by Act of Parliament did not witness the same degree of friction and resort to rioting as occurred over encroachments on to the wastes by squatters. Rioting in Flintshire on 22–3 April 1793 over the Hope enclosure Act of 1791 was exceptional not only for its violence but because the poor were allegedly incited by their leaders to 'murmur against all order and to be dissatisfied with their situation'.[81] However, if actual violent resistance to parliamentary enclosure was rare, there may well have been much ill-feeling engendered.[82] Certainly this was the case with regard to the enclosure of Narberth and Templeton commons in 1787. Isaac Callen of Monkton parish, yeoman, swore an affidavit in early summer 1787 condemning the harshness of the main landowner-beneficiary of the Act, Mr Knox of Slebech: 'Oh! my heart does still ach for the oppression that people have suffer'd by the tyranny of the Irish wolf' [Knox was born in 1732 in County Monaghan] who had not 'the least right for such tyrannical barbarous proceedings ... And the hard hearted wretch obliged 'em to put away all their sheep from these mountains.' Consequently, he averred, about eighty people had fallen ill so that they could not labour to support themselves. Another strident critic was Thomas Davies of Narberth, gent., who had a case brought against him at the 1789 Autumn Assizes for Pembrokeshire for insinuating that the three local enclosure commissioners had acted 'illegally and unjustly' in the execution of their offices.[83]

The nature of the electoral system meant that eighteenth-century politics in Britain were shot through with violence in the form of the threat of eviction as a means of persuasion, physical intimidation of voters and rioting.[84] Riots occurred at Llanidloes on 26 December 1721 in the build-up to the 1722 election for the Montgomery boroughs seat, and at the Carmarthenshire election of the same year.[85] The most spectacular disorder arising from political faction, however, was to occur in Carmarthen Borough at mid-century, the fierce struggle between Whigs and Tories there from 1746 culminating in the Tory-gentry-sponsored riots and mob violence of 1755 which reduced the town to fire, smoke and tumult.[86] Violence also frequently characterized borough politics, gentry factions paying scant attention to public order. The Leet Court or Sheriff's Tourn of Haverfordwest held in October 1740 before the mayor and sheriff saw the outbreak of a 'scandalous and notorious riot' by several persons who leapt on the table of the court, broke the cryer's staff and insulted the mayor and sheriff for half an hour, misbehaviour leading to the disenfranchisement of nine burgesses.[87] Pandemonium was to occur during the election of mayor for Cardigan in 1761 between the partisans of John Lewes, gent., and Benjamin Davies of Clydey parish, Pembrokeshire.[88] Vanity and a prickly sense of parochialism meant that at least on one occasion local officials fell out in public as to the area of their respective authority. Fair days were times of heavy drinking and often fighting, and in the evening of the Cardigan fair of 25 March 1729 a riot broke out in the street, several persons beating one another with cudgels. John Morgan, Esq., a JP for Cardiganshire, required the Peace, and with the help of two other county magistrates attempted to seize the cudgel of the ringleader, Charles Thomas John, a yeoman of the town. The latter, resisting, was with the help of others conveyed to the gaol. But standing at the door was the deputy mayor, William Jones, mercer, who declared nobody should put any man in gaol in his corporation, proceeded to rescue the prisoner and, upon the latter mounting a bench and brandishing a staff at the justices who had arrested him, took to 'embracing and caressing' him. Challenged a little later by Morgan to explain his conduct, Jones replied: 'No Justice shall intermeddle in my Corporation. I'll wipe his Commission in my Backside.' The riot went on for nearly another hour, and for half an hour none of the constables of the town intervened.[89]

Public disorder was also manifested when neighbours came to the defence of one of their number who was being taken into custody by a local official. In Welsh communities as elsewhere society was in a very real sense 'ungovernable'. Certainly Prendergast on the outskirts of Haverfordwest then, as later, was something of a 'no-go' area for the authorities: the attempted taking into custody in late 1771 of one William White of Prendergast, butcher – to answer to a suit of debt brought at the Court of Exchequer – on the part of the prosecutor John Mathias, a farmer, with the help of special bailiffs, ended in failure. Following his arrest in a public house, the woman who kept it quickly raised a mob who surrounded the house and threatened to murder Mathias and the bailiffs 'and that their bones should be carried home in bags' if they attempted to arrest White. In the uproar the latter shouted that neither they 'nor all the devils in hell' should get him from thence and that 'Prendergast was not easily managed'. Frustrated on that occasion, a second attempt on Friday 20 December 1771 at 4 a.m. to 5 a.m., backed by six special bailiffs and several other persons armed with guns, was likewise to no avail, the mob proving too strong for them.[90] Earlier, in March 1731, Edward Parry, a high constable of Bromfield Hundred in Denbighshire, having apprehended Phebe Leadbeter, spinster, on suspicion of felony, was forcefully robbed of his prisoner by being knocked down by William Barber – whom he had just before charged to assist him – 'having a great mob of women about him' at the time Barber attacked him.[91] Women here were clearly coming to the stout defence of their own gender.

Other officials were the victims of crowd violence in the course of carrying out their duties. The long coastline of Wales was an open invitation to smuggling and wrecking, and the authorities were frequently attacked when attempting to apprehend the culprits. Thus a riot occurred at New Quay, Cardiganshire, on 5 August 1704 when salt smugglers were waylaid at 3 a.m. by eight Aberdovey customs officers. Three boats laden with salt were approaching shore and about 150 men and 200 horses standing by to convey it inland. Upon their seizing five bags already landed, the country people attacked them with stones and sticks, and the officers, firing in their defence, hurt several, one seriously. Remarkably, at daybreak the 'rabble' left the shore, only to return quickly with several constables who arrested two officers and carried them before a local JP. One, Remarke Bunworth, was bound over to appear before the Assizes, the 'rabble' charging him with seriously wounding one of their number![92] Likewise, at night-time on 19 May 1741 several people assembled in a 'riotous and tumultuous' manner at Dinas creek on the north Pembrokeshire coast in order to carry off salt from an Irish vessel. Intervening, two customs officers were violently assaulted, one of them fatally.[93] From the 1730s smuggling of tobacco, rum and brandy along the south Wales coast became so commonplace – allegedly because of the demand from local colliers for spirits – and the local people so openly defiant of the authorities that the few customs officers were helpless to do anything to stop it. For example, in 1759 a West Indiaman sailing for Bristol dropped anchor off Rhossili Bay, Gower, and in open daylight dispatched for shore quantities of rum, sugar and molasses. So big was the waiting mob – 'nigh on four hundred' – that the officers stood no chance of access to the beach.[94] On those occasions when officials attempted to intervene they were subjected to violence, as was Lord Cawdor of Stackpole Court, Pembrokeshire, and the Collector of Pembroke, when on Sunday evening, 1 November 1801, they were attacked on Freshwater East beach in attempting to arrest people engaged in receiving casks from a lugger anchored offshore. One Henry July was captured and imprisoned in a nearby house but later he was rescued by a mob of people who also stole some of the confiscated casks stored there.[95]

If, as has been claimed, the local people of south Wales 'considered smuggling a lawful and natural act against the penal duties imposed by a "foreign" government' is difficult to substantiate,[96] there can be no doubt that wreckers looked upon their booty as a natural right. Thus a customs officer present at the wreck of a ship off Anglesey in 1745 was told by some wreckers that they had as much right to be present as he had.[97] Writing in his *Tours in South Wales*, published in 1803, the Revd John Evans remarked upon the practice of wrecking along the Glamorgan coastline:

> when a wreck occurs, which they call a God send, looking upon it as a special favour sent to them in the course of providence, their nature seems changed, and they seize with rapacity, and defend with ferocity, what they conceive to be peculiarly their own.

To show the disregard for the forces of law and order, he cited the case of the *Caesar* bound from Bristol to Santa Cruz falling foul on a dark night of the rocks at Break-sea Point:

> numbers quickly flocked down to the coast for the purposes of plunder, ... some gentlemen in the neighbourhood came down with what strength they could collect, with a view to hinder their depredations; but showers of poplers, the large pebbles on the beach, soon convinced them, that to attack or defend was in vain, and that the safety of their own lives depended upon a precipitate retreat.[98]

Forestalling merchants and greedy farmers, manorial lords reasserting their lapsed rights, freeholders and tenant farmers insisting on guarding their rights to common land against the encroachments of cottagers, and notions among the peasantry as to what constituted their just and natural rights sanctioned by custom, all help to explain the remarkable degree of public disorder at this time, an incipient lawlessness often provoked and participated in by the ruling class. A number of the riots constituted collective popular political bargaining. In the light of such easy resort to physical violence and to verbal threats, insults and downright saucy conduct on the part of the lower orders, it is difficult not to conclude that deference could not be taken for granted; it had to be earned and was quickly withdrawn. Lawlessness was often fortified by drink and at times driven by the passionate attachment to one political faction or another, such friendship and reciprocal bonds embracing not just gentlemen and lesser freeholders but tenant farmers and dependants within the entire neighbourhood. There was scant hope indeed of any illegal acts being redressed by impartial justice when sheriffs who ran elections and decided on the complexion of juries were the creatures of a particular clique. Much of the lawlessness sprang from either painful hunger, or the wish on the part of the freeholders and peasantry alike to enjoy old usages, or trials of strength between overweening, vain gentry families, and there was no ideological underpinning to speak of. As David Jones made clear, that radical input to disturbances was to come only from the 1790s.

Notes

1. D. J. V. Jones, *Rebecca's Children* (Oxford, 1989), 150.
2. Idem, 'The corn riots in Wales, 1793–1801', *Welsh History Review*, 2 (1964–5), 323.
3. A. H. Dodd, *The Industrial Revolution in North Wales* (Cardiff, 1933), Appendix, 420–1, citing David Davies, *The Case of Labourers in Husbandry* (London, 1795).
4. F. V. Emery, 'Wales', in J. Thirsk (ed.), *The Agrarian History of England and Wales*, V, i, 1640–1750, *Regional Farming Systems* (Cambridge, 1984), 405, citing the diarist Owen Thomas; J. E. Griffith, 'Extracts from the diary of William Bulkeley, of Brynddu, Anglesey', *Anglesey Antiquarian Society Transactions* (1931), entry for 15 April 1757.
5. NLW, Great Sessions 4.299/1.

6. Pembrokeshire Record Office, Haverfordwest Corporation Records, 2143, fo. 52.
7. Edward Thompson, 'The moral economy of the crowd', *Past and Present*, 50 (1971), 78.
8. Clwyd Record Office, D/M 4289.
9. J. Stevenson, *Popular Disturbances in England, 1700-1870* (London, 1979), 95.
10. At Wrexham: Clwyd RO, D/E/539; at Loughor and Swansea: A. H. John, 'Glamorgan, 1700-1750', in A. H. John and Glanmor Williams (eds.), *Glamorgan County History*, 5: *Industrial Glamorgan*, 42; at St Asaph: University College of North Wales (hereafter UCNW) Library, Penrhos, i, 807; at Beaumaris (1728): UCNW Library, Penrhos, i, 367; at Pembroke: Public Record Office (PRO), SP.36/50, part 3, fos. 88-9; at Denbigh: NLW, Great Sessions 4.47/3; at Rhuddlan, Rhyl, Prestatyn and St Asaph: PRO, SP.36/50, part 3, fos. 92-7, and K. Lloyd Gruffydd, 'The Vale of Clwyd corn riots of 1740', *Flintshire Historical Society Publications*, 27 (1975-6), 38-9; at Caernarfon in 1752: W. H. Jones, *Old Karnarvon* (Caernarfon, n.d.), 135-6; at Laugharne and Carmarthen: D. W. Howell, *Patriarchs and Parasites* (Cardiff, 1986), 135, 161; at Holyhead, Redwharf, Llanbedr-goch and Beaumaris: G. Nesta Evans, *Social Life in Mid-Eighteenth Century Anglesey* (Cardiff, 1936), 185-6; NLW, Great Sessions 4.252/3; Griffith, *Diary of William Bulkeley*, entry for 8 February 1758; in 1758, J. H. Davies, *The Morris Letters* (Aberystwyth, 1909), II, 62, kindly provided in translation by Dr Prys Morgan; Caernarfon RO, M/1705: letter of Edward Bridge of Aberwheeler, Bodfari 21 February 1758; at Conwy: Caernarfon RO, M/1705; at Pwllheli: NLW, Great Sessions 4.273/1; at Flint and across the north Wales coalfield in 1778 and 1789: Dodd, *Industrial Revolution*, 400; at Aberystwyth in 1783: W. J. Lewis, *Lead Mining in Wales* (Cardiff, 1967), 277.
11. Stevenson, *Popular Disturbances*, 96.
12. Sir Frederick Eden, *The State of the Poor* (London, 1797), III, 904; Roger Wells, 'The revolt of the south-west, 1800-1', *Social History* (October, 1977), 740-1.
13. NLW, Chirk Castle MS E.87; Dodd, *Industrial Revolution*, 400.
14. Lewis, *Lead Mining*, 277; Davies, *Morris Letters*, letter of 13 February 1758; Lloyd Gruffydd, 'Corn riots', 42.
15. NLW, Great Sessions 4.816/3.
16. Griffith, *Diary of Willliam Bulkeley*, entry for 8 February 1758.
17. PRO, SP.36/50, part 3, fos. 92-7; NLW, Great Sessions 4.47/3; Great Sessions 4.252/3; Thompson, 'Moral economy', 114.
18. Griffith, *Diary of William Bulkeley*, entry for 8 February 1758.
19. Wells, 'Revolt of south-west', 726; NLW, Great Sessions 4.299/1;

NLW, MS 1352B, fo. 321, Dudley Ackland to Mr [John] Campbell, 10 March 1796.
20. Thompson, 'Moral economy', 112; David Jones made the same claim for the riots in Wales in the 1790s and 1800–1, 'The corn riots in Wales', 339; Wells, 'Revolt of south-west', 723.
21. Glyn Parry, 'Stability and change in mid-eighteenth century Caernarvonshire', unpub. MA thesis, University of Wales (1978), 105.
22. J. Bohstedt, 'Gender, household and community politics: women in English riots 1790–1810', *Past and Present*, 120 (1988), 105.
23. PRO, SP 36/50, part 3, fos. 94, 96.
24. Davies, *Morris Letters*, 62. The Welsh phrase used by William Morris in his letter of 13 February 1758 was 'a chware *mas y riwl*'; NLW, Great Sessions 4.64/4.
25. Bohstedt, 'Gender... politics', 106.
26. Thompson, 'Moral economy', 113–14.
27. Lloyd Gruffydd, 'Corn riots', 41; PRO, SP.36/50, part 3, fo. 94.
28. *Gentleman's Magazine*, 27 (1757), 591–2; A. J. Hayter, *The Army and the Crowd in Mid-Georgian England* (London, 1978), 17.
29. Thompson, 'Moral economy', 121–2; Jones, 'Corn riots', 339.
30. NLW, Clerk of the Peace Correspondence, Pembroke County Records, 1795–7: in February 1796 the Pembrokeshire magistrates resolved: 'all persons going from farm to farm to purchase up the corn storehousing the same in order to export it for profit in these times of scarcity are enemies in the country and the real authors and instigators of the riotous disposition of the people'. Wells, 'Revolt of south-west', 724, comments: that 'magisterial indifference to the claims of the free market was one of the reasons for the survival of the "moral economy"'.
31. NLW MS 12501E (Wigfair 101): letter of Robert Howard to Mr Wynn, 30 March 1757; Parry, 'Stability and change', 101.
32. Evans, 'Social life', 185–6.
33. Wells, 'Revolt of south-west', 743; NLW, Great Sessions 4.273/1; Great Sessions 4.1002/5; K. Lloyd Gruffydd, 'Corn riots', 40–2; Great Sessions 4.47/3; Great Sessions 4.64/4; my thanks to Glyn Parry for the reference to Merthyr. The hanging of the pig gelder for his part in the Caernarfon corn riot of April 1752 after a 'drum-head court-martial' held on the spot was perhaps done out of pique by the authorities at the effrontery of the riot taking place during the sitting of the Sessions. I owe this information and idea to a conversation with Glyn Parry, and for details see Jones, *Old Karnarvon*, 134–5.
34. Parry, 'Stability and change', 106; Caernarfon RO, M/1705.
35. Pembrokeshire Record Office, Haverfordwest Corporation Records, 2143, fo. 52.
36. NLW, Wynnstay MS 125, fos. 299, 317–18, 325; MS 128, fos.

167 and 253; NLW, Tredegar Castle MS 292: letter of 26 March 1800 of Henry Brown to Sir Charles Morgan.
37. NLW MS 1352B, fo. 310.
38. T. S. Ashton and J. Sykes, *The Coal Industry of the Eighteenth Century* (Manchester, 1929), 119; NLW MS 1412E (Henry Owen MSS), letter of Lord Cawdor, 5 April 1796, to Major Ackland.
39. E. P. Thompson, *Customs in Common* (Penguin, 1993), 308ff.
40. Lloyd Gruffydd, 'Corn riots', 37-9.
41. NLW, Chirk Castle MS E.4894; NLW, Great Sessions 4.47/3.
42. NLW, Great Sessions 4.252/3.
43. Thompson, *Customs in Common*, 327.
44. Lloyd Gruffydd, 'Corn riots', 40, 42; NLW, Great Sessions 4.47/3; NLW, Chirk Castle MS E.4894; NLW, Great Sessions 4.252/3; Great Sessions 4.273/1 and 273/3, Caernarfonshire gaol files, First Session 1758 and Second Session 1759.
45. Bohstedt, 'Gender ... politics', 89; W. Thwaites, 'Women in the market place: Oxfordshire c. 1690-1800', *Midland History*, ixl (1984), 35-6; Jones, 'Corn riots', 344-5, 350.
46. Thompson, *Customs in Common*, 246-8.
47. PRO, SP 36/50, part 3, fos. 88-9 for Pembroke; PRO, SP 36/50, part 3, fos. 92-3 for Rhuddlan; NLW MS 12501E for Conwy.
48. Lloyd Gruffydd, 'Corn riots', 38, 42.
49. Jones, 'Corn riots', 336-7, 343; Thompson, *Customs in Common*, 248.
50. J. R. Western, *The English Militia in the Eighteenth Century* (London, 1965), chs.6, 7, 8 and 9.
51. NLW, Tredegar Park MS 52/230, letter of Charles Powell, 20 May 1778, to Charles Morgan. For the financial burden in Anglesey, see D. J. V. Jones, *Before Rebecca* (London, 1973), p. 51; for the refusal of the overseers of Newchurch parish to relieve the family of an absent Carmarthenshire militiaman, see Carmarthenshire RO, Cwmgwili MS ii/379.
52. Western, *English Militia*, 197-9, 298.
53. NLW, Great Sessions, 4.57/3; PRO, SP 44/142, fos. 262-6.
54. PRO, WO 1/1005, fos. 927-8. I was directed to this source via Western, *English Militia*, 298.
55. Jones, *Before Rebecca*, 52-3; W. Lloyd Davies, 'The riot at Denbigh in 1795 – Home Office correspondence', *Bulletin of the Board of Celtic Studies*, iv (1928-9); J. Bohstedt, *Riots and Community Politics in England and Wales, 1790-1810* (Cambridge, Mass., 1983), 3.
56. NLW, Great Sessions 4.51/4.
57. Dodd, *Industrial Revolution*, 399; Ruthin RO, QSD/SR/267: Michaelmas 1776 Quarter Sessions.

58. H. Wigstead, *A Tour to North and South Wales in the year 1797* (London, 1799), 48.

59. NLW, Tredegar Park MS 66/166: 6 December 1784, concerning Charles Morgan's right to collect commortha rents in the manor of Brecon; Carmarthen RO, Vaughan MS 8029: letter of John Vaughan of Golden Grove, 28 December 1756, which talks of the lord's right having been 'shamefully neglected' in Golden Grove manors; NLW, Wynnstay Deposit, 1952, vol. I, concerning collection of fines and amerciaments in the manor of Cyfeiliog, 1763.

60. The whole complex problem of 'custom, law and common right' is the title of Edward Thompson's awe-inspiring chapter 3 in his *Customs in Common*. For a petition from a body of freeholders complaining of harassment on a Crown manor in Radnorshire from the 1760s see NLW, Harpton Court MS 1791.

61. NLW, Badminton ii, MS 1930: Gabriel Powell's answer, 15 February 1748.

62. Ibid., MSS 1455, 1457, 1458, 2061.

63. Ibid., MSS 2363-8, 1457, 2334.

64. O. Beynon, 'The lead mining industry in Cardiganshire', unpub. MA thesis, University of Wales (1937), 84–106 and Appendix, 18ff; S. R. Meyrick, *History and Antiquities of the County of Cardigan* (London, 1808), Appendix, nos. 18, 19; W. J. Lewis, *Lead Mining in Wales* (Cardiff, 1967), ch.5.

65. NLW, Tredegar Park MSS 70/226, 70/227, 66/166.

66. Ibid., MSS 70/266, 66/166.

67. Ibid., MS 119/624, 116/230, 114/526, 124/527.

68. Ibid., MS 64/29.

69. NLW, Bronwydd MSS, group i, MS 569; see also for a legal dispute in 1779 between Madam Lloyd and V. Thomas and his 'gang' over the right of cutting turf in Nevern parish, Bronwydd MSS, group i, MS 568.

70. NLW, Harpton Court MSS 1721, 1784, 1802, 1785, 1843, 1791, 1853, 1739, 1844, 1845, c/89.

71. NLW, Badminton ii, MS 1932.

72. NLW, Crosswood MS, i, 1174.

73. NLW, Brogyntyn, MS 1274.

74. *Shrewsbury Chronicle*, 7 April, 19 May 1787; NLW, Wynnstay MS 126, fos. 476, 487 and 499.

75. Melvin Humphreys, *'Crisis of Community': Montgomeryshire 1680–1815* (Cardiff, 1996), 139–40.

76. NLW, Crosswood MS, i, 1174.

77. See Thompson, *Customs in Common*, 121ff. for urban protests over common rights.

78. Carmarthenshire RO, Cwmgwili MS i/283; for a 1786 'Notice' drawn up by the Carmarthen rioters of that year see Carmarthenshire RO, Plas Llanstephan MS 337, cited in Jones, *Before Rebecca*, 40–1.
79. NLW, Great Sessions 4.621/3.
80. NLW, Wynnstay MS 128, fo. 173: letter of F. Chambre to Sir Watkin Williams Wynn, 1 April 1783.
81. Jones, *Before Rebecca*, 45–6; NLW, Leeswood MS 1758.
82. Roger Wells, 'Social protest, class, conflict and consciousness in the English countryside, 1700–1880', in Mick Reed and Roger Wells (eds.), *Class, Conflict and Protest in the English countryside, 1700–1880* (London, 1990), 155–6; J. M. Neeson, *Commoners: Common Right, Enclosure and Social Change in England, 1700–1820* (Cambridge, 1993), 280–1.
83. Pembrokeshire RO, Lewis of Henllan MS 1/83; NLW, Great Sessions 4.842/2.
84. For a lively discussion see Ian Gilmour, *Riot, Risings and Revolution* (Pimlico, 1993), ch.10.
85. T. M. Humphreys, 'The Llanidloes riot of 1721', *Montgomeryshire Collections*, 75 (1987), 107–15; P. D. G. Thomas, 'County elections in eighteenth-century Carmarthenshire', *The Carmarthenshire Antiquary*, iv (1962), 35–7.
86. Howell, *Patriarchs and Parasites*, 134–5.
87. Pembrokeshire RO, Haverfordwest Corporation Records, 2143, fo. 14.
88. NLW, Bronwydd MSS, group i, MS 519.
89. NLW, Great Sessions 4.889/4.
90. NLW, Great Sessions 4.819/5.
91. NLW, Great Sessions 4.45/2; for the difficult position of 'plebeian constables ... obliged to enforce an essentially patrician concept of order', see David Eastwood, *Governing Rural England: Tradition and Transformation in Local Government 1780–1840* (Oxford, 1994), 226–30.
92. A. S. Davies, 'Cardiganshire salt smugglers – an xviii century riot', *Archaeologia Cambrensis*, xci (1936), 312.
93. NLW, Great Sessions 4.813/3.
94. Graham Smith, *Smuggling in the Bristol Channel 1700–1850* (Newbury, 1989), 141.
95. NLW MS 1352B, fos. 361 and 367.
96. Smith, *Smuggling in the Bristol Channel*, 133.
97. J. Rule, 'Wrecking and Plunder', in D. Hay, P. Linebaugh and E. P. Thompson (eds.), *Albion's Fatal Tree* (London, 1975), 177.
98. Revd John Evans, *Letters on Tours in South Wales* (London, 1803), 112–13.

Beccaria and Britain

HUGH DUNTHORNE

I

Beccaria's essay *On Crimes and Punishments* was one of the great international best-sellers of the eighteenth century. First published by Aubert of Livorno in July 1764, in its original Italian the book went through five editions (including a couple of pirated versions) in less than two years, and translations soon followed into French (1766), English (1767), Swedish (1770), Spanish (1774), and German (1778).[1] As its anonymous English translator remarked, with only slight exaggeration, 'perhaps no book, on any subject, was ever received with more avidity, more generally read, or more universally applauded'.[2] The book was in demand from Scotland to Sicily and from St Petersburg to Philadelphia; and its author, though seldom named on the title page of these early printings, became a household word almost overnight. To his British readers, he was 'the celebrated Marquis Beccaria', 'the excellent Marquis Beccaria', 'the humane and benevolent Beccaria', 'that acute Reasoner', 'so able and liberal a writer', so 'ingenious' and 'elegant'.[3] And it comes as no surprise to find an English advocate of penal reform adopting the pseudonym of Beccaria Anglicus in order to lend authority and appeal to his writing.[4]

Yet such fame and success would have surprised Beccaria himself, who can hardly have been thinking of a broad international readership when he wrote *On Crimes and Punishments* in the early 1760s. At the time, he was associated with a group of young Milanese aristocrats – gentlemen intellectuals like himself, many of them with political ambitions – who met regularly at the house of the brothers Alessandro and Pietro Verri and whose passionate and reputedly violent discussions led to their adopting the name *Accadèmia dei pugni*, the academy of clenched fists. For a couple of years between 1764 and 1766 they published a monthly journal called *Il Caffè*, through which they sought to convert conservative Lombard society to their reforming point of view and to ingratiate themselves with the more progressive Habsburg administrators of Lombardy. Their aim was to replace their country's still semi-feudal form of social organization with one that would promote the security, well-being and happiness of all its members. And it was with this general aim in view (and with a good deal of encouragement from Pietro Verri) that the 25-year-old Beccaria composed *On Crimes and Punishments* during the nine months from March 1763 to January 1764. Attacking the system that he saw around him, an 'irregular, particularist and custom-bound legal system, based on hereditary rights and the personal rule of the monarch and nobility', he pleaded (in the words of his most recent editor) for 'a regular, centralised and rational system of justice that was equal for all and grounded in the rule of law'.[5] Moreover, the readers to whom Beccaria addressed these aspirations were primarily his fellow Italians – 'thinking men' and 'those who are charged with the public welfare' (pp.8, 3). His aim, he said, was to introduce his compatriots to the reforming ideas and initiatives that were being taken up elsewhere in Europe (p.30).

No doubt Beccaria hoped that his book would be read outside Italy too and particularly by philosophers, his fellow citizens in the international republic of letters. We know, for example, that he sent an early copy to David Hume.[6] But he cannot have expected the wide British readership that he got, still less that his book would have run through at least half a dozen English-language editions by the end of the eighteenth century.[7] Indeed, if Beccaria had Britain in mind at all at the time of writing his essay, it was not as a potential recipient of his ideas but rather as one of their sources and as a model of good sense and sound government. Bacon's *Essays*, which he had read in Latin, provided the characteristically cautious maxim which he placed on the title page of the book: 'In all negociations of difficulty, a man may not look to sow and reap at once; but must prepare business, and so ripen it by degrees' (p.1). And some of Beccaria's key ideas may have come from Bacon, too, including his insistence that there was little place for revenge and retribution in a just penal system.[8] Among more recent thinkers, he acknowledged Hume as one whose 'immortal works' had been his 'constant reading',[9] and his use of the idea of a social contract in explaining the origins of government and of the state's right to punish clearly owed something to Locke. The source of the famous principle that laws should promote 'the greatest happiness shared among the greater number' (p.7), a phrase used both by Beccaria and by Pietro Verri in his *Meditations on Happiness* of 1763, is more complicated. But it seems likely that it too derived from British writers – principally from Francis Hutcheson's *Inquiry into the Original of our Ideas of Beauty and Virtue*, which the *Caffè* group read in a French translation of 1749, and possibly from Bacon also.[10] Like other continental observers, Beccaria took a flatteringly rosy view of the inhabitants of Britain, 'a nation the glory of whose letters, the superiority of whose trade and wealth, and hence power, and whose examples of virtue and courage leave us in no doubt about the goodness of her laws' (p.42). And he commended the English system of trial by jury on the grounds that it promoted equality under the law (p.35).

All this praise for British writers and institutions (not to mention British periodical literature, which Beccaria acknowledged as the model for *Il Caffè*),[11] was flattering to British readers of course. But it is hardly enough to explain Beccaria's popularity in Britain, particularly as there is little evidence to suggest that his book was read simply because it appealed to British self-esteem. Given that the author's plea for penal reform was primarily directed at his own countrymen, his success in Britain seems surprising, and is worth investigating. The British, after all, have not often turned to foreign writers for advice about how to govern themselves. Why, then, did apparently so many of them turn to Beccaria's *On Crimes and Punishments*? What did they make of the book? And how did they put it to use?

II

One place to look for an answer to these questions is among the reviews of Beccaria's book that appeared in the London periodical press during the mid-1760s. The original Italian edition was noticed in the *Monthly Review* at the end of 1765, and within a couple of years the English translation had been reviewed in the same journal as well as in the *Critical Review*, the *London Magazine* and the *Annual Register*.[12] Judging from these early assessments, it seems clear that what initially attracted British readers to *On Crimes and Punishments* was not just the ideas contained in the book but the character and reputation of the author himself. Admittedly, not much was known in Britain at this time about 'the marquis Beccaria of Milan', and what *was* known was not always accurate. But it was sufficient for him to be seen, not as the timid and retiring individual that he really was, but rather as an embattled and even heroic figure, who had transcended the traditional Roman Catholic culture 'in which he was born and educated' and was not afraid to criticize 'the established laws of his country' and to speak out boldly for 'liberty' and 'the natural rights of mankind'.[13] In so doing, he was said to have provoked a conservative reaction among certain sections of Italian society, the kind of reaction that was to be expected in 'a country enslaved by civil and ecclesiastical authority'.[14] In 1765 his book was attacked in the Venetian press on grounds of impiety and sedition, and a year later it was placed on the papal Index.[15] But despite this opposition, he had succeeded in carrying 'the most intelligent part' of the Italian people with him, thus demonstrating that even Europe's most conservative countries were amenable to the power of reason. Moreover, as a contributor to the *Monthly Review* pointed out, Beccaria's success in his own country had wider implications. It showed

> that the time is not far off, when other nations, as well as ourselves, will become sensible that there are certain rights and privileges which all mankind inherit, and that no species of men, whether emperors, kings, parliaments or priests, have a right to tyrannize over their fellow-creatures.[16]

Here then, according to its first English reviewers, was a book which, though it had been written in Italy for Italians, nevertheless had a message for all countries, for the subjects of parliamentary regimes no less than those living under absolute monarchies. What is more, it was a message with a particularly strong resonance in Britain, since in several ways it harmonized with a debate on the reform of the country's criminal justice system that had been proceeding intermittently for a generation or more. A few reforming steps had already been taken. The use of torture in examining suspects, which Beccaria singled out for particular criticism (chapter 16, pp.39–44), was one feature of the old penal system which was now 'happily abolished in this nation'. As the Scots antiquary George Chalmers pointed out, it had not been used in England since 1620 nor in Scotland since the Treaty of Union.[17] But there were plenty of other 'evils' still lurking in the system and much remained to be done if a 'thorough reformation' was to be carried out.[18] So it is not surprising to find British reviewers quoting with approval from the general indictment of traditional laws which Beccaria placed at the start of his book, an indictment of laws haphazardly made in response to passing circumstances, of laws supporting the interests of a small and powerful social élite and doing nothing to promote 'the greatest happiness shared among the greater number' (Introduction, pp.7–8).[19] It was a charge that echoed similar criticisms made a quarter-century earlier by Samuel Johnson. At a time when there was growing alarm about rising levels of violent crime, especially in London, and when the House of Commons had recently set up a committee to report on 'the defects ... or amendment' of the penal laws,[20] Johnson had published a perceptive essay in the *Rambler* of 20 April 1751, showing how the natural inclination of human beings to rule 'by force rather than by persuasion' had led to the adoption in Britain of ever more 'vindictive and coercive' penal measures. Each new wave of robberies prompted new laws. But they were always laws imposed 'in the heat of anger' rather than being drawn up by legislators 'sincerely and calmly studious of human happiness'. And the result was a penal regime characterized by disorder and inconsistency, 'a confusion of remissness and severity'.[21]

Another part of *On Crimes and Punishments* which caught the attention of reviewers and was extensively quoted was the group of three chapters concerned with classifying and measuring crimes and proportioning punishments (chapters 6–8, pp.19–25). Beccaria argued that crimes should be measured by 'the damage done to the nation', not by 'the malefactor's intention', 'the rank of the injured party' or 'the gravity of the sin' (p.22). And he insisted that 'there must be a proportion between crimes and punishments' (p.19): 'if an equal punishment is laid down for two crimes which damage society unequally, men will not have a stronger deterrent against committing the greater crime if they find it more advantageous to do so' (p.21).[22] In saying this, Beccaria was not introducing a new principle into European legal thought. It had been recognized for some time that an indiscriminately savage system of penal justice could actually give men an incentive to commit new crimes in order to avoid the risk of being caught and punished for those they had committed already. In 1748 Beccaria's mentor, 'the great Montesquieu' (p.10), had anticipated his argument in favour of proportionality by contrasting the effect of using the death penalty selectively, as in China, with its more extensive use in Russia:

> In China, those who add murder to robbery are cut in pieces: but not so the others; to this difference it is owing that though they rob in that country they never murder.
>
> In Russia, where the punishment of robbery and murder is the same, they always murder. The dead, they say, tell no tales.[23]

And, two or three years after Montesquieu, much the same point was being made by advocates of penal reform in Britain, where a growing number of crimes (mostly crimes against property) were made capital offences in the course of the eighteenth century. By the 1760s, there were reckoned to be 160 capital felonies on the statute book.[24] Not only was such indiscriminate severity seen as an incitement to criminals to commit murder in order to conceal less serious crimes.[25] It was also argued – again anticipating a point that was to be made by Beccaria (chapter 33, p.87) – that by applying the same punishment to different offences the law was undermining what Oliver Goldsmith called the people's 'sense of distinction in the crime', a distinction which was 'the bulwark of all morality'.[26]

Underlying Beccaria's horror at the vindictiveness of Europe's penal systems and the disproportionate penalties that they often imposed was his conviction that the basic purpose of punishment was not revenge but deterrence: not to 'torment or afflict any sentient creature' or to 'undo a crime already committed', but rather 'to prevent the offender from doing fresh harm to his fellows and to deter others from doing likewise'. 'Consistent with proportionality', punishments should 'be so selected as to make the most efficacious and lasting impression on the minds of men with the least torment to the body of the condemned' (chapter 12, p.31).[27] This is not to say that Beccaria wanted to dispense with retribution altogether. As two recent commentators on his book have pointed out, he believed that while *legislators* should frame penal laws primarily with a deterrent purpose in mind, the role of *magistrates* in applying the laws to particular cases should be to ensure that the guilty are punished and that they pay the appropriate penalty for their misdeeds (chapters 3–4, pp.12, 14–15).[28] But in the context of his own time – when existing systems of justice were heavily retributive in character and when conventional legal theory insisted that their main concern was with 'the redressing of wrongs and the avenging of injuries'[29] – it was Beccaria's emphasis on deterrence that marked his work out. According to the first English reviewer of *On Crimes and Punishments*, the 'grand object' of the book was not only to put the case for proportional penalties but also to show that the primary aim of punishment should always be to deter, to ensure 'the prevention of future crimes'.[30] And on this matter, too, there was a similarity between Beccaria's ideas and some of the notions of penal reform that were already circulating in Britain.

The similarity can be explored by considering Beccaria's chapter on the death penalty (chapter 28, pp.66–72), a chapter that was extensively and approvingly quoted by a contributor to the *London Magazine*.[31] Interest in the chapter did not of course imply acceptance of everything that Beccaria said there, and certainly not of his radical conclusion that capital punishment should be abolished altogether. In Britain at this time, as elsewhere, very few people questioned the conventional assumption that for 'willfull murder ... the only proper punishment is the death of the offender': in such cases, as Adam Smith dramatically put it, the blood of the victim 'calls aloud for vengeance'.[32] Nevertheless, some of the arguments by which Beccaria reached his conclusion would certainly have been familiar to those who wished to see the use of capital punishment restricted to murder and a few other serious crimes.

In the first place, there was Beccaria's argument that the state had no *right* to put any of its own subjects to death. By means of a hypothetical 'social contract', men were deemed to have surrendered a small part of their freedom to a sovereign authority 'in order to enjoy what remains in security and calm' (p.9).[33] But this surrender, he maintained, could not logically have included giving up the right to kill oneself, since no one possessed such a right in the first place (p.66).³⁴ This was the very argument that Goldsmith had put into the mouth of the vicar of Wakefield when he argued that the death penalty was an unjust and unreasonable punishment for horse-stealing. The idea that there could be a tacit contract requiring 'that he who deprives the other of his horse shall die' was simply untenable, since 'no man has a right to barter his life, no more than to take it away, as it is not his own'.³⁵

But it was Beccaria's second argument against capital punishment which probably had most appeal for his British readers. This was the argument that as a *deterrent* the death penalty was manifestly less effective than penal servitude. For the public at large, he maintained, the execution of a criminal was a 'terrible but fleeting sight', impressive while it lasted but soon forgotten and therefore less influential than 'the long-drawn-out example of a man deprived of freedom who, having become a beast of burden, repays the society which he has offended with his labour' (p.67); while for the criminal or potential criminal, the prospect of sudden death on the scaffold ('one day of pain') was less daunting than that of spending 'many years, or even the remainder of his life ... in slavery and suffering before the eyes of his fellow citizens' (p.69).³⁶ Similar doubts had been expressed in Britain about the deterrent effect of the death penalty for some time, and particularly since the 1720s when Bernard Mandeville wrote his *Enquiry into the Causes of the Frequent Executions at Tyburn*. In Mandeville's view, the trouble with public executions was that they conveyed no moral message. The disorder and 'hurry' of these occasions made it impossible for even 'the best dispos'd Spectator' to 'pick out anything that is edifying or moving'. Besides, as a contributor to the *London Magazine* asked in 1766, in an increasingly godless age how many people really feared death and the 'dreadful consequences' that were supposedly waiting for them in the afterlife? To those for whom crime was the only means of escape from a life of destitution, the danger of ending it on the scaffold could easily seem a risk worth taking.³⁷

From arguments such as these the conclusion generally drawn by British advocates of penal reform was that while the death penalty ought to be retained for those convicted of murder, lesser offences should be punished by more effective and constructive deterrents.³⁸ Stealing, for example, was conventionally seen as the result of sloth and idleness. Rather than threatening thieves with execution, therefore, 'a more discouraging as well as a more adequate punishment', according to Bishop George Berkeley, would be to make criminals 'useful in public works' by sentencing them to 'servitude, chains, and hard labour for a term of years'.[39] The very visibility of this form of punishment was believed to be one of its advantages, since the guilty would be 'living, standing examples' to the community at large. For this reason, Berkeley and others rejected the alternative of transportation to the colonies (established by Parliament in 1718 as a regular part of the penal system and widely used in the 1750s and 1760s) on the grounds that putting convicts 'out of sight' rather than 'exposing them to public view' significantly reduced the deterrent effect of their punishment.[40] Moreover, as Dean Patrick Delany pointed out, confining an offender 'to labour at home' had the further advantage 'that the profit of his labour might be applied to repay the damages he did' and that by acquiring 'a habit of honest industry, ... instead of being cut off from the commonwealth as a nuisance, [he] might be preserved to it as a profitable member'.[41]

The arguments that Beccaria used against the death penalty, then, and particularly his criticisms of its effectiveness as a deterrent, were to a large extent already familiar in Britain. And the same went for other parts of the book which were quoted by reviewers. Like the writers mentioned above, Beccaria recommended hard labour as the most appropriate penalty for crimes of theft (chapter 22, p.53); and he too rejected transportation on the grounds that it was 'distant' punishment 'and so almost useless' as a deterrent (chapter 29, p.75).[42] It is true that he also went further than conventional opinion by suggesting that theft was the crime not so much of idleness as of 'poverty and desperation', the crime of 'that unhappy section of men' who were victims of the unequal and unnatural distribution of property in society (p.53). So long as the gulf between rich and poor and between strong and weak remained and was actively reinforced by harsh laws, it was only to be expected that the poor would resort to stealing simply in order to live (chapter 28, p.69) – just as poor unmarried mothers would resort to infanticide in order to avoid social disgrace (chapter 31, p.81).[43] These were offences stemming not so much from individual human weakness or wickedness as from a harsh social system, and Beccaria put the crime of adultery into the same category. So long as patriarchy ruled and arranged marriages were the norm, there would inevitably be adultery; whereas free marriages would increase 'conjugal fidelity' (chapter 32, p.80).[44] In all such cases, what was needed was not punishment but social reform by means of laws designed to promote the well-being and happiness of all members of society equally (chapter 41, pp.103–4).[45] Yet even these more utopian strands in Beccaria's thought had parallels in the more radical voices occasionally to be heard in mid-eighteenth-century Britain. At the end of his homily on penal reform, Goldsmith's fictional vicar of Wakefield looked forward to a time when the law, instead of reinforcing economic inequalities and 'drawing hard the cords of society', would loosen them and so become 'the protector . . . not the tyrant of the people'.[46] And there were real clergymen with a similar viewpoint, calling not for punishment but for more humane and socially responsible government as the most effective means of diminishing crime. 'Take away distress', said a preacher at Chester in 1766, 'and, as the apostle advises, he that stole steals no more.' In times of dearth, 'the skilful oeconomy of parishes' should look 'to their own poor'; and the government should pay less attention to the game laws and more to enforcing laws against corn monopolists. 'The welfare of a man' was more important than the preservation of landed property.[47]

It would be wrong to claim too much for the early English reviews of *On Crimes and Punishments* which we have been considering. They were competent pieces of journalism but no more than this, and none of them gave a full account of Beccaria's penal philosophy. What they showed, however, both in the passages which they selected for quotation and comment and in their general air of approval, was that Beccaria's ideas had struck a chord with the British reading public, or at least with its more progressive elements, with those who saw (and had seen for some time) that all was not well with the country's criminal justice system and that steps needed to be taken to reform it. Beccaria himself, of course, could hardly have been familiar with this growing body of British critical opinion. His knowledge of Britain was generalized and rather *un*critical and his reading of British authors was confined to such major philosophical texts as were available in Latin or French. So the affinity between his ideas and those of British writers on penal reform before 1767 stems not from any direct influence between the two but rather from the fact that both were drawing on a common stock of broadly enlightened, humanitarian and to some extent Christian thought.

III

But if there was an affinity between Beccaria and early British advocates of penal reform, there was also a difference. Before the 1760s, British pleas for penal reform tended to be occasional pieces, usually prompted by particular circumstances and dealing with some particular aspect of the problem; and they were scattered around in pamphlets, sermons, pieces for the periodical press, digressions in larger works, preambles to proposed legislation or the prefaces to legal textbooks. What Beccaria had done, by contrast, was to bring these ideas together within the covers of a single book, offering a concise, coherent and reasonably comprehensive synthesis of the case for penal reform. No book of this kind existed in Britain in the mid-1760s and there was a recognized need for one.[48] This explains why Beccaria's treatise was given such a warm welcome and why it could be hailed as 'one of the most original books which the present age hath produced'[49] – rightly so, since in form it *was* original, if not in substance. It also explains why the book was soon being emulated in a stream of English critical writings on England's penal system. The fourth volume of Sir William Blackstone's *Commentaries on the Laws of England* appeared in 1769 under the title *Of Public Wrongs*, William Eden's *Principles of Penal Law* in 1771, Henry Dagge's *Considerations on Criminal Law* in 1772, William Smith's *Mild Punishments Sound Policy* in 1777 (a couple of years after Jeremy Bentham had completed his *Rationale of Punishment*),[50] Menassah Dawes's *Essay on Crimes and Punishments* in 1782[51] and Sir Samuel Romilly's *Observations . . . on Executive Justice* in 1786. Of course these works differed from each other in length and originality, and to lump them together simply as imitations of Beccaria would be misleading. Nevertheless, they clearly shared Beccaria's reforming purpose, now transferred to the British context; and they would probably not have taken quite the form that they did, nor have been published in such numbers, without the prior example of *On Crimes and Punishments*. Beccaria's great innovation, as Bentham noted, was to have distinguished between studying the law *as it is*, which Bentham termed 'expository jurisprudence', and studying it *as it ought to be*, which he called 'censorial jurisprudence'. It was for opening up this latter approach that Beccaria could be styled, in Bentham's phrase, 'the father of censorial jurisprudence'; and what his book showed, more than anything else, was that laws must be framed on the basis of rational thought and analysis rather than being accepted unthinkingly as an inheritance from the past or imposed as a means of strengthening those in authority ('To the Reader', p.3; Introduction, p.7).[52] Thus Blackstone was laying down a fundamental Beccarian principle when he insisted, at the start of his fourth volume, that penal legislation 'ought not to be left ... to the passions or interests of a few' acting 'upon temporary motives' but rather should be

> calmly and maturely considered by persons, who know what provisions the laws have already made to remedy the condition complained of, who can from experience foresee the probable consequences of those which are now proposed, and who will judge without passion or prejudice how adequate they are to the evil.[53]

Similarly, in calling for 'a total revision and reformation of our penal laws', Romilly urged that the reform should be based on 'humane and rational principles' of jurisprudence and on the study of human psychology.[54] And it was with much the same Beccarian principle in mind that Sir William Meredith, during a parliamentary debate of 1777 on the introduction of a new capital statute, drew the attention of MPs away from the particular offence under discussion ('the wilful setting fire to merchants ships' while in dock) towards the wider and more fundamental problem of 'our whole system of criminal law' and 'our habit of thinking and reasoning upon it'.[55]

Emulating Beccaria and adopting his rational approach to the reform of penal laws inevitably led British writers to a fuller appreciation of his book. The earlier reviewers had been appreciative too, of course, but they had tended to treat *On Crimes and*

Punishments as a kind of anthology of humane opinions and 'striking paragraphs'. From the late 1760s onwards, however, the prevailing view of the book changed in some ways and it began to be seen much more as a unity, centred upon a single coherent argument. The argument was set out in two crucial chapters, neither of which had previously attracted much attention but which were now increasingly quoted: the twelfth, dealing with 'the purpose of punishment', and the twenty-seventh, on 'lenience in punishing'. Beccaria's starting-point, as has already been noted,[56] was that the purpose of punishment was not revenge but rather deterrence and the prevention of crime (chapter 12, p.31). It followed that punishments should be precisely laid down in the law, so that magistrates could impose them uniformly and consistently, and that degrees of punishment should be carefully proportioned so as to inflict just enough harm as to 'outweigh the good which the criminal can derive from the crime'. 'Anything more than this' – anything harsher than the minimum penalty needed to discourage a potential criminal – was 'superfluous and therefore tyrannous'. Indeed, it was likely to be counter-productive since disproportionately severe punishments would tend to be imposed intermittently and reluctantly by the courts and, as a result, criminals would actually be encouraged to commit crimes by the 'hope of not being punished at all' (chapter 27, pp.63–4; cf. chapter 3, pp.12–13).

Beccaria argued, in other words, that crimes were 'more effectively prevented by the certainty than the severity of punishment',[57] and it was largely on the basis of this principle that British reformers attacked the defects of their own country's penal system and sought to improve it. They pointed to the growing disparity between the letter of the criminal law, which was indiscriminately severe, and its execution, which was generally (though not consistently) much more moderate. Under laws enacted in the time of William III and Anne, for example, minor property crimes such as shoplifting and petty theft from a dwelling-house were punishable by death.[58] Yet, by the late eighteenth century, penalties of such 'obvious disproportion' were seldom imposed in practice.[59] 'Deterred by the severity of the law', victims of crimes were reluctant to press charges; and if cases came to court, juries were inclined to reach a 'compassionate verdict' and judges to recommend mercy.[60] At first glance, such leniency in administering the law might seem 'commendable'. But, as a contributor to the *Gentleman's Magazine* pointed out, it had 'pernicious consequences' for the deterrent effect of the penal system since it encouraged criminals 'to delude themselves' into overestimating their chances of escaping punishment.[61] 'As our laws are actually administered', Sir William Meredith told the House of Commons in 1777, 'not one in twenty' of those convicted of capital offences was executed, so 'the thief acts on the chance of twenty to one in his favour' and that 'confident hope of indemnity is the cause of nineteen in twenty robberies that are committed'.[62] To discourage crime, therefore, what was needed was to dispense with the confused mass of the existing 'bloody code', leniently and haphazardly applied though it was by the late eighteenth century, and to replace it with a series of clear and just laws, 'more merciful in general' but observing 'a just proportion . . . between the various degrees of crimes in the penalties appointed for them'[63] – laws which, precisely because they *were* just and 'moderate in degree', could be 'rigorously . . . and . . . invariably executed' with little or no discretion being left to the individual magistrate.[64] And they should be promptly executed too. For, as Beccaria had urged (chapter 19, pp.48–9) and as several of his British followers re-emphasized, the more quickly the punishment of a convicted and sentenced criminal could be carried out following his crime, the stronger would be the association in the public mind between the offence committed and the penalty which it necessarily incurred. In short, moderation, certainty and speed of punishment were all considered essential to strengthening the deterrent effect of the law.[65]

But the question remained as to what moderation actually meant in practice. What new kinds of punishment were to take the place of the law's traditional reliance on the death penalty? On this question Beccaria's *On Crimes and Punishments* was in some ways a rather less instructive guide than it was on broader matters of principle. Beccaria of course insisted that there should be proportion, and even analogy, between crimes and punishments: 'the punishment should, as far as possible, fit the nature of the crime' (chapter 6, pp.19–21; chapter 19, p.49). So he advised that 'assaults on persons . . . should always be punished with corporal punishment (chapter 20, p.50); that 'thefts without violence should be punished with fines' or enforced labour, thefts with violence with an appropriate 'mixture of corporal punishment and penal servitude' (chapter 22, p.53); and, in cases of debt, that 'innocent bankrupts' should be required to pay what they owed while only those convicted of fraud should be imprisoned (chapter 34, pp.89–90). Beyond citing these examples, however, Beccaria did not attempt any thorough or systematic explanation of the notion of proportionality, offering the excuse that 'this would demand immense and tedious detail' (chapter 8, p.24). Thus his advice, as Bentham remarked, was 'more oracular than instructive',[66] and it is doubtful if it had much influence on patterns of sentencing in British courts during the later eighteenth century. There is evidence from 1780s and 1790s that judges were now more concerned to match punishment to crimes, and for this purpose were drawing on a broader range of non-capital penalties, from whipping and fines to imprisonment with or without hard labour and forced recruitment into the armed forces. But this trend seems to have resulted from wartime legislation rather than from any more fundamental shift in penal policy. The Act of 1776, 'to authorize ... the punishment by hard labour', and the Penitentiary Act of 1779 were prompted by the need to find alternative penalties to transportation after it had been effectively brought to an end by the revolt of the American colonies; and it was under the terms of these acts that the sentencing powers of judges were enlarged.[67] What is more, the growing discretion now being exercised by the courts ran counter to a basic principle of Beccaria's, that the scale of punishments appropriate for different crimes should be precisely set down *in the laws* and not left to the subjective judgement of magistrates (chapters 2–3, pp.12–15).

But if Beccaria was reluctant to work out the principle of proportionality thoroughly, he had even less to say about another theme that featured prominently in the writings of eighteenth-century British penal reformers: the growing conviction that the proper function of punishment was not only to deter criminals but to reform and rehabilitate them. He was of course aware that the threat of punishment was not the only way of reducing crime. His remarks on the need for social reform have been mentioned already;[68] and towards the end of his book he included a short chapter on education, 'the surest but hardest way to prevent crime'. No sooner had he introduced the subject of education, however, than he dismissed it as 'too broad' and going 'beyond the limits which I have set for myself' (chapter 45, p.110). And these limits did not include considering education as a by-product of punishment either. When arguing against the death penalty and in favour of penal servitude, Beccaria's case rested squarely on the greater effectiveness of hard labour *as a deterrent* and ignored the moral benefits which prisoners might derive from such a regime (chapter 28, pp.67–8). Yet for a number of British reformers the moral dimension constituted an equally important part of the argument. As a writer in the *Gentleman's Magazine* put it, subjecting offenders 'to a certain term of laborious confinement' would not only serve as a discouragement to others but could actually 'reclaim' the criminals themselves: it would teach them to exchange 'habits of idleness and dissipation ... for habits of labour and application' and so 'renovate and restore them [as] useful citizens to the community'.[69] With its belief that punishment and spiritual instruction could be combined to turn bad men into good, this was a penal philosophy in some ways more optimistic and ambitious than Beccaria's, and certainly more overtly Christian. It received its fullest expression in John Howard's *State of the Prisons in England and Wales* of 1777, and it underpinned both the Penitentiary Act, with its emphasis on 'solitary imprisonment, accompanied by well-regulated labour, and religious instruction', and the new reformatory gaols established in Sussex, Gloucestershire and Lancashire during the 1780s and early 1790s.[70]

It is clear, then, that by no means all of the ideas about penal reform circulating in Britain in the later eighteenth century can be traced to Beccaria's treatise *On Crimes and Punishments*. Yet it would be difficult to deny the success which the book enjoyed and the influence which it exerted. Initially, that success derived from the fact that it seemed to confirm reforming attitudes already in circulation and to draw them together in a concise and coherent form. In the longer term, it was influential because it provided a model, a demonstration of how the criminal justice system could be rationally and critically examined, and because it argued convincingly that the key to improving that system lay in moderating the penal laws and administering them more rigorously. It took time, of course, for theory to be translated into practice and for Britain's old penal regime to be dismantled. When that happened, or began to happen, in the 1820s and 1830s, Beccaria had been dead for more than a quarter of a century.[71] But his book was far from being forgotten. In discussing the Mackintosh Committee's report of 1819, which was the immediate prelude to Peel's major programme of penal reforms in the following decade, a writer in the *Quarterly Review* recalled that it was now

> more than half a century since Beccaria published his Essay on Crimes and Punishments, one of the earliest works by which the attention of the world was much drawn to criminal jurisprudence, and in which the necessity of the infliction of death, in any case whatever, was first distinctly called in question.

It was a work marked by the time and place in which it had been written. But it also contained 'many acute and just general observations', and 'its principal value in the present day' consisted 'not so much in what the author has himself done, as in what he has taught others to do'.[72] If the British political establishment was now prepared to examine its criminal laws and procedures coolly and critically and to recommend their reform, as the Mackintosh Committee did, some of the credit at least should be given to the teaching of Beccaria.

Notes

1. Cesare Beccaria, *Dei delitti e delle pene*, ed. F. Venturi (Turin, 1965), viii–ix, 329, 545, 564, 597. Translations into Greek and Russian appeared early in the nineteenth century.

2. [Beccaria], *An Essay on Crimes and Punishments*, translated from the Italian: with a commentary, attributed to Monsieur de Voltaire, translated from the French (London, 1767), iii–iv.

3. *Annual Register*, 17 (1774), 219; William Turner, 'An essay on crimes and punishments', *Memoirs of the Literary and Philosophical Society of Manchester*, 2 (1785), 312n; William Godwin, *Enquiry concerning Political Justice* (1793; ed. I. Kramnick, Harmondsworth, 1976), 650; Patrick Colquhoun, *A Treatise on the Police of the Metropolis* (4th edn, London 1797), 260; Revd L. Wainewright, *A Vindication of Dr. Paley's Theory of Morals* (London, 1830), 12–13n.; Sir William Blackstone, *Commentaries on the Laws of England* (6th edn, 4 vols., Dublin, 1775), IV, 17, 357.

4. Beccaria Anglicus [Thomas Wright], *Letters on Capital Punishment Addressed to the English Judges* (London, 1807).

5. Beccaria, *On Crimes and Punishments and Other Writings*, ed. R.

Bellamy (Cambridge, 1995) (hereafter *OCAP*), xii–xv. Richard Bellamy's introduction to this edition offers an excellent account of the intellectual milieu in which Beccaria wrote his book. In the present chapter, all quotations from *On Crimes and Punishments* are taken from this translation, which is based on the fifth Italian edition of March 1766, the last to be authorized by Beccaria himself. Page numbers and, where appropriate, chapter numbers are given in brackets in the text after each quotation or reference. Another recent English edition which is well worth consulting, not least for its valuable editorial notes, is the translation made by David Young, also based on the Italian edition of March 1766, available in the Hackett Classics series (Indianapolis, 1986).

6. D. F. Norton and M. J. Norton, *The David Hume Library* (Edinburgh, 1996), 30, n. 55.

7. Besides the four 'numbered' editions recorded in the *Eighteenth-Century Short-Title Catalogue* and a fifth which appeared in 1801, a 'new edition' in cheap duodecimo format (the 'paperback' of its day) appeared in Edinburgh in 1778 and a 'new corrected edition' from the same publisher ten years later. Except for Italy itself, where thirty-one editions of Beccaria's *On Crimes and Punishments* were issued during the eighteenth century, no other country published as many as Britain. Further English-language editions were printed in New York (1773) and Philadelphia (three editions between 1778 and 1809). For the international publishing history of the book, see Venturi's edition of *Dei delitti e delle pene*, cited above n. 1, his *Italy and the Enlightenment* (London, 1972), 160, and L. Firpo, 'Le edizione italiane del "Dei delitti e delle pene"', in Beccaria, *Opere* (4 vols., Milan, 1984–90), I, 369–623.

8. *Essays*, iv: 'Of Revenge'. Beccaria did not, however, wish to eliminate retribution altogether from the legal process: see above pp.78–9.

9. Beccaria to André Morellet (the French translator of his work), Milan, 26 January 1766: *OCAP*, 121. Other intellectual debts which Beccaria mentions in this letter are to Machiavelli, Galileo and Giannone, and to the leading figures of the French Enlightenment, tactfully including Morellet himself.

10. R. Shackleton, 'The greatest happiness of the greatest number: the history of Bentham's phrase', *Studies on Voltaire and the Eighteenth Century*, 90 (1972), 1466–73; cf. *OCAP*, xviii–xix. In *The Advancement of Learning*, which Beccaria and his friends would have known in its Latin version as *De augmentis scientiarum* (1623), Bacon had written that 'the end and scope which laws should have in view, and to which they should direct their decrees and sanctions, is no other than the happiness of the citizens': *Works*, ed. J. Spedding (7 vols., London, 1857–9), V, 89. The phrase was taken up in France, too, around the middle of the eighteenth century, so it is likely that Verri and Beccaria

would also have come across it in their reading of authors such as Maupertuis and Helvétius.
11. Letter to Morellet, 26 January 1766: OCAP, 123.
12. *Monthly Review*, 32 (1765), 532–5; 36 (1767), 298–9, 382–7; *Critical Review* (April 1767), 251–5; *London Magazine* (June 1767), 306–8; *Annual Register*, 10 (1767), 316–20. All the reviews were anonymous or pseudonymous. Those in the *Monthly Review* have been attributed, respectively, to William Kenrick and the naturalist John Berkenhout: see B. C. Nagle, *The Monthly Review First Series 1749–1789: Indexes of Contributors and Articles* (Oxford, 1934), 4, 23, 97, 104. The review in the *Annual Register* has been attributed to Edmund Burke (see L. Radzinowicz, *A History of English Criminal Law* (5 vols., London, 1948–86), I, 745), though I have been unable to find any evidence to confirm this attribution.
13. *Critical Review*, 23 (April 1767), 252, 254; *Monthly Review*, 32 (1765), 533; 36 (April 1767), 298.
14. *Monthly Review*, 36 (April 1767), 298.
15. Father Ferdinando Facchinei, *Note ed osservazioni sul libro intitolato 'Dei delitte e delle pene'* (Venice, 1765); Beccaria, *On Crimes and Punishments*, ed. H. Paolucci (Indianapolis, 1963), xi. Several English reviewers repeated the story that Beccaria had been threatened with prosecution and 'for fear of the consequences' had 'been obliged to leave Italy' for Paris: *Monthly Review*, 32 (1765), 532n; *Critical Review*, 23 (April 1767), 252; *Annual Register*, 10 (1767), 316. The truth was that Count Firmian, the enlightened Austrian governor of Lombardy, had actually defended Beccaria against his conservative critics and later secured his appointment to the professorial chair of cameral sciences at the Palatine School in Milan. Furthermore, although Beccaria did indeed leave Milan for Paris in October 1766, he did so at the invitation of the French Encyclopaedists and not in order to escape prosecution. A reluctant traveller who hated being lionized in the Paris salons, he cut short his visit to the French capital after less than a month and returned with relief to Milan, which he never subsequently left. For a sketch of Beccaria's character and career, see the introduction to Paolucci's edition of *On Crimes and Punishments*, cited above, and O. Chadwick, 'The Italian Enlightenment', in R. Porter and M. Teich (eds.), *The Enlightenment in National Context* (Cambridge, 1981), 96–9.
16. *Monthly Review*, 36 (April 1767), 298.
17. *Critical Review*, 23 (April 1767), 254; *Scots Magazine*, 55 (1793), 391–3. Cf. Blackstone, *Commentaries*, IV, 321; J. H. Langbein, *Torture and the Law of Proof* (Chicago, 1977), 134–9.
18. *Critical Review*, 23 (April 1767), 252.

19. Quoted *Critical Review*, 23 (April 1767), 252, and *Annual Register*, 10 (1767), 317.
20. J. M. Beattie, *Crime and the Courts in England 1660–1800* (Oxford, 1986), 520–1.
21. *The Rambler*, ed. W. J. Bate and A. B. Strauss (3 vols., New Haven, 1969), 114 (20 April 1751), II, 241–7.
22. Quoted *Critical Review*, 23 (April 1767), 252–3, and *Annual Register*, 10 (1767), 318–20.
23. Montesquieu, *The Spirit of the Laws*, trs. T. Nugent (London, 1750), bk 6, ch.16. Cf. *OCAP*, ch.27, 63: 'The harsher the punishment and the worse the evil he faces, the more anxious the criminal is to avoid it, and it makes him commit other crimes to escape the punishment of the first.' Though not quoted by Beccaria's English reviewers, the importance of this passage was recognized later: see J. Bentham, *Rationale of Punishment*, in *Works*, ed. J. Bowring (11 vols., London, 1838–43), I, 400; W. Smith, *Mild Punishments Sound Policy* (2nd edn, London, 1778), 7–8; Turner, 'Essay', 307–8.
24. Blackstone, *Commentaries*, IV, 18. By the turn of the century the number of capital offences was over 200: J. A. Sharpe, *Judicial Punishment in England* (London, 1990), 30.
25. Johnson, *Rambler*, 114 (1751), 244; *London Magazine*, 35 (April 1766), 203.
26. Goldsmith, *The Vicar of Wakefield* (written 1760–2; published 1766), in *Collected Works of Oliver Goldsmith*, ed. A. Friedman (5 vols., Oxford, 1966), IV, 151. The same argument had been developed earlier by Sollom Emlyn in his preface to *A Collection of State Trials* (2nd edn, 6 vols., London, 1730), I, quoted L. Radzinowicz, *History*, I, 266; and by Johnson, *Rambler*, 114 (1751), 244.
27. Considering its importance, it is surprising that this key chapter on 'the purpose of punishment' was not quoted by any of Beccaria's English reviewers. Its importance was to be recognized later: see above pp.85–6.
28. *OCAP*, xxi–xxiii; D. Young, 'Cesare Beccaria: utilitarian or retributivist?' *Journal of Criminal Justice*, 11 (1983), 317–26. For a general discussion of deterrence and retribution, see Sharpe, *Judicial Punishment*, 6–13.
29. 'On the principles of criminal justice, as unfolded in Lord Kames's Essay on the History of the Criminal Law [1758]: with an examination of the theory of Montesquieu and Beccaria', in A. F. Tytler, Lord Woodhouselee, *Memoirs of the Life and Writings of the Honourable Henry Home of Kames* (2nd edn, 3 vols., Edinburgh, 1814), III, 120; see also Adam Smith, *The Theory of Moral Sentiments* (1759), ed. D. D. Raphael and A. L. Macfie (Oxford, 1976), 69–71, and *Lectures on*

Jurisprudence [1764], ed. R. L. Meek et al. (Oxford, 1978), 104, 475. For a perceptive comparison of Beccaria's legal thought with that of Kames and Smith, see Ferenc Hörcher, 'Beccaria, Voltaire and the Scots on capital punishment: a comparative view of the legal Enlightenment', paper delivered at the Eighteenth-Century Scottish Studies Society meeting in Grenoble, July 1996: I am grateful to Professor Hörcher for kindly sending me a copy of his paper in advance of publication.

30. *Monthly Review*, 32 (1765), 534.
31. *London Magazine*, 36 (June 1767), 307–8.
32. *Lectures on Jurisprudence*, 106; *Theory of Moral Sentiments*, 71; see also Woodhouselee, *Kames*, III, 143–9. Goldsmith likewise accepted that 'in cases of murder' governments had both a right and duty 'from the law of self-defence, to cut off that man who has shewn disregard for the life of another': *The Vicar of Wakefield*, 149.
33. Quoted *Monthly Review*, 36 (April 1767), 298. The term 'social contract' occurs at the beginning of ch.3; Beccaria probably borrowed the expression from Rousseau, whose *Du contrat social* had appeared in 1762. His debt to Rousseau had been noted by an English reviewer of the original Italian edition of *Dei delitti e delle pene*: see *Monthly Review*, 32 (1765), 533.
34. Quoted *London Magazine*, 67 (June 1767), 307.
35. Goldsmith, *Vicar of Wakefield*, 151. The same argument was also used in an anonymous letter on capital punishment published in the *London Magazine*, 35 (April, 1766), 203–4, a year *before* the publication of the first English edition of *On Crimes and Punishments*.
36. Quoted *London Magazine*, 67 (June 1767), 307.
37. Mandeville (1725) quoted in I. A. Bell, *Literature and Crime in Augustan England* (London, 1991), 75–6; *London Magazine*, 35 (February 1766), 59; see also Johnson, *Rambler*, 114 (1751), 245. Letters to the *London Magazine* on this subject, including the one quoted here, were later republished as an anonymous pamphlet, *Thoughts on Capital Punishment* (1770).
38. It was, of course, also possible to draw the conclusion that if the death penalty was not working as a deterrent, what was required was not to find *alternative* punishments but rather to increase the deterrent effect of execution by adding to it further humiliations such as hanging in chains and dissection by surgeons. For arguments to this effect put forward in the 1730s and 1750s, see Beattie, *Crime and the Courts*, 525–30.
39. G. Berkeley, *The Querist* (1735–7), queries 53–4: *Works*, ed. A. A. Luce and T. E. Jessop (9 vols., Edinburgh, 1948–57), VI, 109; see also H. Grove, *A System of Moral Philosophy*, ed. T. Amory (London, 1749), 466–7.

40. *London Magazine*, 35 (February 1766), 59 (quotation); Berkeley, *Querist*, query 53, 109. The same argument was used by the Commons Committee on the Criminal Laws of 1751 in proposing that transportation be replaced by hard labour in the royal dockyards as a punishment for certain lesser offences: Beattie, *Crime and the Courts*, 522-3.

41. P. Delany, *Eighteen Discourses and Dissertations upon Various very Important and Interesting Subjects* (London, 1766), 162-3. The idea of contriving employment for offenders so that they would be reformed and trained in some skill while at the same time being punished was quite frequently canvassed in the 1730s and again in the 1750s and 1760s. Its appeal clearly owed something to the example of Amsterdam's famous houses of correction, which were cited by several writers including Berkeley: *Querist*, query 55, 109; Beattie, *Crime and the Courts*, 549-54.

42. Quoted *London Magazine*, 35 (1766), 307, and *Critical Review*, 23 (April 1767), 254.

43. Quoted *Critical Review*, 23 (April 1767), 255.

44. Quoted with approval by the *Critical Review*, 23 (April 1767), 254-5. Beccaria's remarks on adultery reflected his own experience: his marriage to the commoner Teresa Blanco had been fiercely opposed by his father who used the full weight of his authority as the head of an aristocratic household in seeking to prevent it.

45. See also P. Verri, *Meditazioni sulla felicità* (1763), quoted in *OCAP*, xiv.

46. Goldsmith, *Vicar of Wakefield*, 150-1.

47. Extract from a sermon preached at the Assize of Chester, March 1766, quoted *London Magazine*, 35 (1766), 424-5; see also two other sermons, published as *Artificial Dearth, or the Iniquity and Danger of Withholding Corn* (London, 1756).

48. *Monthly Review*, 32 (1765), 533. Sir William Blackstone's *Commentaries on the Laws of England* had begun to appear in 1765 but the fourth and final volume, which dealt with the criminal law, was not published until 1769.

49. *Critical Review*, 23 (April 1767), 257.

50. Written in 1775, Bentham's *Rationale of Punishment* was not however published until 1811, in Paris, under the title *Théorie des peines et des récompenses*; it finally appeared in English in 1830.

51. A paper by William Turner with exactly the same title, 'An essay on crimes and punishments', appeared three years later in the *Memoirs of the Literary and Philosophical Society of Manchester*, 2 (1785), 293-325.

52. Bentham, *A Fragment on Government* (1776), ed. J. H. Burns and H. L. A. Hart (Cambridge, 1988), 13-14, note g; *An Introduction to the*

Principles of Morals (1789), ed. J. H. Burns and H. L. A. Hart (London, 1970), 298, note a2; H. L. A. Hart, *Essays on Bentham* (London, 1982), 41, 45–6.

53. Blackstone, *Commentaries*, IV, 4.

54. S. Romilly, *Observations on a Late Publication, intituled, Thoughts on Executive Justice* (London, 1786), 2, 105; D. Liebermann, *The Province of Legislation Determined: Legal Theory in Eighteenth-Century Britain* (Cambridge, 1989), 213–14.

55. W. Cobbett, *Parliamentary History* (36 vols., 1806–20), XIX, 240 (italics added).

56. Above p.78.

57. This was the opening sentence of ch.27 as rendered in the first English translation of Beccaria's treatise in 1767. Of all Beccaria's maxims it was the one quoted most frequently by his contemporary British admirers – and even by conservative defenders of the country's penal regime like Martin Madan and William Paley: Madan, *Thoughts on Executive Justice* (London, 1785), 34, 131–2; Paley, *Principles of Moral and Political Philosophy* (2nd edn, London, 1786), 549.

58. See 10 and 11 William III, c. 23 (1699) and 12 Anne, c. 7 (1713); Beattie, *Crime and the Courts*, 173, 178.

59. Smith, *Mild Punishments*, 5, 6–7.

60. 'Debates in the year 1810 upon Sir Samuel Romilly's bills for abolishing the punishment of death', in *Cobbett's Parliamentary Debates* (41 vols., London, 1803–20), XIX (appendix), vii, lxxxv (quotation); Blackstone, *Commentaries*, IV, 19. Cf. Adam Smith, *Lectures on Jurisprudence*, 105.

61. *Gentleman's Magazine*, 54 (1784), 514–15.

62. Cobbett, *Parliamentary History*, XIX, 235. In a similar way Romilly compared the criminal to a 'deluded gamester', confident in the belief that the penal justice system was a 'lottery' stacked in his favour: *Observations on Executive Justice*, 66; 'Debates in the year 1810', xi–xii; cf. J. A. Sharpe, *Crime in Early Modern England 1550–1750* (London, 1984), 174.

63. Blackstone, *Commentaries*, IV, 16–17.

64. *Gentleman's Magazine*, 46 (1776), 254; 54 (1784), 515; Romilly, *Observations on Executive Justice*, 2, 87. See also H. Dagge, *Considerations on Criminal Law* (London, 1772), xxviii, 168; M. Dawes, *An Essay on Crimes and Punishments* (London, 1782), xii, 54, 254.

65. Blackstone, *Commentaries*, IV, 397; Turner, 'Essay', 311; Romilly, *Observations on Executive Justice*, 108–12; Hart, *Essays on Bentham*, 46–8. Rapid execution of capital punishment had been urged intermittently in Britain since the 1750s: Beattie, *Crime and the Courts*, 529, 583.

66. Bentham, *Rationale of Punishment*, 399. Having made this remark, Bentham himself went on (pp.399–409) to provide a much fuller and more thorough discussion of proportionality and analogy of punishment than anything attempted by Beccaria.
67. Beattie, *Crime and the Courts*, 560–9, 573–82, 592–618. Transportation was reintroduced in 1787 following the government's decision to found a penal colony at Botany Bay in New South Wales.
68. Above, pp.81–2.
69. *Gentleman's Magazine*, 46 (1776), 254–5; 54 (1785), 515. See also Turner, 'Essay', 319–21; Romilly, *Observations on Executive Justice*, 59–61; and, for an opposing view, Godwin, *Enquiry*, 678.
70. Beattie, *Crime and the Courts*, 568–76; M. Ignatieff, *A Just Measure of Pain: The Penitentiary in the Industrial Revolution* (London, 1978), 93–109; S. McConville, *A History of English Prison Administration* (2 vols., London, 1981–94), I: *1750–1877*, 88–104. Because of disagreements over a suitable site, the two new London prisons proposed in the Penitentiary Act were never in fact built: the most immediate practical effect of the act, as noted above (p.87), was to widen the sentencing powers of judges.
71. His death at the age of fifty-six, in November 1794, had passed almost unnoticed in the British press: it was as if the man had been eclipsed by the book.
72. *Quarterly Review*, 24 (1820–1), 234. For a perceptive discussion of Beccaria's legacy to Peel and his contemporaries, see Boyd Hilton, 'The gallows and Mr Peel', in T. C. W. Blanning and D. Cannadine (eds.), *History and Biography: Essays in Honour of Derek Beales* (Cambridge, 1996), 88–112.

PC *Dixon* and Commissaire *Maigret: Some Myths and Realities in the Development of English and Continental Police*

CLIVE EMSLEY

PC George Dixon – Dixon of Dock Green – and *Commissaire* Maigret are both stereotypes. The former, the central character of a television series running from 1955 to 1976, is the model beat policeman – avuncular, courageous and honest; the latter, the central character of seventy-six novels written by Georges Simenon between 1929 and 1972, is the cerebral detective able to outwit and out-think the cleverest offender. While, in contrast to much of continental Europe, policing in England to the mid-twentieth century always put the main emphasis on prevention primarily through beat patrols, Dixon and Maigret are not really national stereotypes. During the nineteenth century, for example, the French were praising their *sergents de ville* and their *gendarmes* in terms similar to those used for the bobby.[1] Dickens was full of praise for the detectives of London's Metropolitan Police,[2] though for a long time after him, in fiction most notably, the English police detective tended to be rather similar to the plain, unimaginative bobby, and was overshadowed by brilliant gentlemen like Holmes and Wimsey, or by subtle foreigners like Poirot.

In England during the 1980s and early 1990s Dixon became a benchmark for policing. Policemen, journalists and academics may have recognized that his kind of policing was in many respects irrelevant to their world, but it remained the model of a golden age when life appeared much less complicated, and when crime and criminals appeared much more manageable. Debates about the future of policing or about police behaviour commonly saw reference made to the 'golden age' of policing as exemplified by Dixon of Dock Green.[3] The explanation of why individuals choose to assert a golden age in the past is a subject in itself, but will not be the focus here.

This essay is a broadly chronological survey of policing developments in England and on continental Europe over the last two centuries. It draws on some archival material, but principally on the work of other scholars. Given the size of the task, it is bound to oversimplify some people's arguments and to do violence to others. The aims are modest: first, to give some indication as to why politicians, historians and others have seen particularly the English experience of policing in the way that they have; and second, of the extent to which the English experience of policing was indeed different.

I

Until fairly recently the history of crime, policing and punishment in England was largely ignored by professional, academic historians. The main business of history was politics, international relations, constitutional change, social reform and the great men who directed affairs. (Sometimes a great woman could be a 'great man'.) Much economic history was focused on industrialization or similar processes contributing to the progressive march to the present. Even Fabian social history was much concerned with the steady progress of labour. The overall view of history was Whiggish; history was about progress. The First World War shattered the beliefs of the Whig historian, G. M. Trevelyan. After it he believed that those who had shared his Victorian liberal beliefs were 'no better than a company of antediluvians, who have survived the fire-deluge, sitting among the ruins of the world we knew'.[4] Yet Trevelyan continued to write popular books in the Whig tradition; and the rulers and apologists for inter-war Britain continued to be men who had been educated during the late Victorian and Edwardian periods when, even if there were concerns about the residuum and anxiety that the British economy was losing out to American and German competition, the industrial revolution and the constitutional structure still appeared models for the rest of the world. Moreover the First World War had been the war to end war, and this view was cemented by the fact that the progressive, constitutional side had won. If men like Trevelyan were having doubts, though scarcely reflecting them in their writing, the media of inter-war Britain focused on consensus, emphasizing the resolution of conflict at home and the upholding of traditional values.[5]

There were concerns about increasing juvenile crime during the late Victorian and Edwardian periods, and there was the occasional complaint about police high-handedness or inefficiency.[6] But overall, crime was seen to be levelling out, even declining; and politicians, journalists and senior police officers were sufficiently proud and confident to speak of the best police force in the world.[7] No one appears to have considered stating, let alone asking, by what criteria this accolade was awarded. But then, in general, there was no inclination critically to examine the structure of England's administration or constitution.

Criminals were a race apart; they were outside society, making war upon it. 'Habitual criminals', according to *The Times* in 1870, were 'more alien from the rest of the community than a hostile army, for they have no idea of joining the ranks of industrious labour either here or elsewhere'.[8] The 'criminal class', to use the term which was much in vogue in the mid-nineteenth century, was an element within the poorer sections of the working class. Offenders from a higher social class were not members of the criminal class but 'black sheep' or 'rotten apples'. Of course this tallied with the reality of the numbers processed by the police, the courts and the penal system. Yet a brief glance through parliamentary investigations of financial crises and company law reform, bankruptcy reports and shareholders' inquiries, rather than criminal court proceedings, would show that the value of goods and money stolen or embezzled by the white-collar offender was generally very much greater than that stolen by a poor man from the 'criminal class'. Moreover, the overall annual total accumulated by an aggregate of the former probably amounted to much more than the annual total appropriated by the latter as a group. When a responsible employee was caught with his fingers in the till, he was often not prosecuted; he could be sacked, but sometimes with a sum of money to pay off any debts and limit suspicion. The firm feared that the adverse publicity would be bad for trade, undermining public confidence in its affairs. Documentation concerning such incidents survives, but again not in the records of the police or the courts; finding it can be a matter of chance or luck.[9]

In the early and mid-nineteenth century, as they began to be regarded as a separate, identifiable group, 'criminals' were perceived collectively as morally inferior individuals. They preferred idleness and extravagance to the twin Victorian gospels of work and thrift. Penal policy was devised accordingly to make the offender reflect on his (and, less commonly, her) wrongdoing in the terrible silence and solitariness of Pentonville. Towards the end of the century, as social scientists and medical men fell under the influence of Darwinian ideas, criminals were perceived more as being mentally inferior, and a corresponding shift was made in penal policy.[10] Either way, they were not subjects for historians, but for moral reformers and, later, medical men, who could treat them. They were also subjects for novelists who could feed off, and into, the reading public's fears and desires for vicarious excitement: Dickens's Bill Sikes became a popular bogeyman, Harrison Ainsworth's Dick Turpin a romantic rogue, but fraudsters like Dickens's Mr Merdle or Trollope's Augustus Melmotte have never entered the popular consciousness in such a way. Though they were afraid of them, and even thrilled by them, the respectable classes rarely met 'criminals'; between them and the criminal was the new police. As the thin red line protected the nation's interests overseas, so the thin blue line at home fought the war against crime.

The police were perceived as part of the march of progress. L. O. Pike, in his *A History of Crime in England* published in 1876, could write:

> The comparative security of life and limb and property in recent years is no doubt caused, to a very great extent, by our modern organisation of police – an organisation, however, which would be possible only in a highly civilised country. The development of the Metropolitan Police, and of the borough and county constabulary, out of the primitive system which at its best was of little use to our forefathers, is a very remarkable illustration of our national progress.[11]

Trevelyan's brief references to police development settle the police four-square in nineteenth-century improvement. 'Their social value in dealing with common crime was equalled by their political value in dealing with Radical mobs.' They were 'endearingly' called 'bobby' or 'peeler' by the populace. They were the perfect substitute 'for the fumbling old watchmen, who preserved unimpaired the traditions of Dogberry and Verges'.[12] They had been established by the vision of great men – Henry and Sir John Fielding, Patrick Colquhoun, Sir Robert Peel and the first two commissioners of the Metropolitan Police, Colonel Charles Rowan and Sir Richard Mayne. In the Whig interpretation the example of the Metropolitan Police, created in 1829, had led inexorably to the requirement that corporate boroughs establish forces under the Municipal Corporations Act of 1835. This, in turn, had led to the enabling legislation for the creation of county forces in 1839 and 1840, and ultimately to the obligatory legislation of 1856. European liberals, and not just liberals, flattered the Metropolitan Police by requests for information on how it was organized, and by incorporating some of its attributes into their own forces.[13] But the European governments also maintained their political police sections and their armed gendarmeries. Herein appears to have been the difference between English and continental police so favoured by the English commentators. For English politicians and senior policemen, and subsequently historians of the police, the English forces were different, and by implication superior, precisely because they were non-political and non-military. For Charles Reith, who wrote the classic Whig histories of the English police between 1938 and 1952, they were 'the living germ of true democracy. So long as their means of securing law observance by the people and for the people exists and functions effectively, true democracy and the cherishable liberties which it enshrines shall not perish from the earth.' The English police were 'kin police' whose authority and legitimacy emanated from the people; hence they were quite different from totalitarian gendarmeries which were imposed on the people.[14]

In some respects the differences were only a matter of degree and visibility. They were also a matter of the peculiarities, stemming from the historical development, of particular states. Thus in the United States the traditions of democracy and of distributing political spoils meant that in many towns and cities policemen, like other functionaries, were tied to urban political machines. On occasions this also meant that the police could be tied directly to industrial and business interests. Whatever the structure of local watch committees, English policemen were never used as blatantly in the interest of capitalism as some were in the United States, yet it would be quite wrong to suppose that

English urban policemen during the nineteenth century were quite independent of local politics. The borough watch committees considered their head constables as their servants. Often the head constable was allowed to get on with the day-to-day administrative and operational matters of policing; equally it was possible for watch committees to give direct operational orders and require that they be carried out. In particular, during the nineteenth century English borough policemen found themselves used by political factions in temperance struggles.[15]

Borough policemen in Victorian England were responsible to the watch committees selected by the elected town councils. Though little detailed work has been done on the municipal police of nineteenth-century continental Europe, similar relationships appear to have existed elsewhere. There was a long tradition of municipal pride in Italy, and after unification urban policing became extremely complex involving local police (*guardie municipali*) recruited from the community and controlled by municipal government, the police of the interior ministry (*guardie di città* or *guardie di pubblica sicurezza*) and the military police, the Carabinieri. The *guardie municipali* concerned themselves principally with traffic and enforcing local ordinances; but there was often open hostility between them and the two national police forces.[16] In France municipalities had control over the selection of their police, but the situation could be complicated by the central government's appointment of a *commissaire* for every town with a population over 5,000; larger towns had more such centrally appointed officers. Problems occurred when the *commissaire* and the mayor failed to see eye to eye; and even though the *commissaire* might have the backing of Paris, the local municipality had discretion in the amount it paid him.[17] In Prussia policing was regarded as a prerogative of central government throughout the nineteenth century, though the urban élites were given certain responsibilities, notably with reference to providing the funds. During the revolutions of 1848 liberals sought to secure a role for elected representatives in this as well as in other areas, and the government in Berlin was sufficiently alarmed to authorize the minister of the interior to impose a state police director on any municipality if he saw fit. This caused considerable friction in those municipalities where such officials were appointed, particularly over the issue of finance. The municipalities insisted that, if the government in Berlin was going to appoint a police director, then it had taken responsibility for the whole of the police and, accordingly, should meet the whole bill; the government insisted that it was only responsible for the director's salary. The municipalities went to court over the issue and won a judicial ruling in their favour; at the same time, with a slight liberalization in the policies of the central government at the close of the 1850s, a degree of municipal control was restored.[18]

Policemen in capital cities were different. They were generally responsible directly to central government rather than to any committee of local citizens. In this the Metropolitan Police of London was little different from its European counterparts and central government resisted all calls for the devolution of its authority in this respect. Initially the English county police forces were responsible to committees of magistrates and then, after the Local Government Act of 1888, to standing joint committees of magistrates and elected county councillors. Rural police in Europe were generally of two kinds: rural guards and gendarmes. The former were usually appointed by local worthies and had a poor reputation for efficiency. The latter were soldiers. But one element which was developed in England, in direct contrast to the other European states, was a system of inspectors whose task it was annually to review each independent local force and assess its efficiency. The certificate of efficiency ensured a government payment of one quarter, later one half, of the cost of the police force. From its creation in 1856 this system began to develop a degree of uniformity in the English police which was unique outside the gendarmeries.

For all that Europe industrialized in the nineteenth century, vast tracts of land remained populated by peasants who often had little conception of the new nation state in which they lived, little grasp of its laws and, in many instances, little knowledge of its language. The gendarmeries of continental Europe originated in the forces which followed in the wake of the revolutionary and Napoleonic armies as part of the administrative structure of the French Empire. They were maintained or reconstituted after the fall of Napoleon, at least in part, as instruments of internal colonization for the new nation states.[19] England had no such peasantry in the nineteenth century, while a common language and ideas of Englishness and even Britishness[20] appear to have been long present in the population. On some of the Celtic fringes of the kingdom, however, there were such problems. The Rebecca disorders in Wales in the 1830s and 1840s saw armed Metropolitan policemen patrolling alongside armed soldiers, a fusion of police and soldiery reminiscent of the gendarmeries. John Bull's other island saw the development of an armed, paramilitary force, in the Royal Irish Constabulary. Perhaps this was the least military of the European gendarmeries – its men were never soldiers responsible to a minister of war, and as the century progressed the force lost much of its military capability – yet in its deployment, its armament and system of patrolling, it appears a gendarmerie in all but name.

If Victorian England did not need a gendarmerie, similarly its rulers believed for many years that neither did it need a political police. Historians may differ about the reasons for the relative equipoise of the second half of the nineteenth century, but there is no gainsaying the fact that England was less violently disturbed than other nations and that the country's rulers felt themselves secure in a way that their continental counterparts did not. Moreover, most British radicals from the late eighteenth century onwards maintained a belief in Britain as the freest nation in the world, and if Parliament needed reform it remained, nevertheless, a model institution.[21] Every regime in nineteenth-century France – Napoleonic, Bourbon, Orleanist, Republican – originated in violent political upheaval. The states of nineteenth-century Germany were forged in the violence of the Napoleonic bloodletting; they experienced tremors in 1830 and revolution in 1848. The German Empire was created in war; and by the end of the century it was home to the SPD, the largest socialist party of the period, avowedly Marxist and revolutionary. Before unification the Italian states witnessed one revolutionary upheaval after another – 1820–1, 1830–1, 1848–9. Unification came through armed struggle, and even after unification the leaders of the state did not feel secure. The Habsburg monarchy began the post-Napoleonic period determined to maintain the balance of power and the status quo, and to check any form of liberal or nationalist aspirations across the whole of Europe. It ended the century determined to maintain the ramshackle empire against nationalist aspirations from Czechs, Poles, Romanians, Serbs, Ukrainians and others. Russia had similar problems, but its autocracy and administrative system also provoked a savage form of political terrorism which achieved its greatest success in 1881 with the assassination of Tsar Alexander II. Throughout continental Europe these problems were considered as necessitating the employment of political policemen. Special squads were created to sit in bars and listen to conversations and songs.[22] But these political policemen also had roots in the older concept of police employed by old-regime monarchs when *police, polizey, polizei* meant the general administration and supervision of territory; it was in the mid-eighteenth century that Antoine Gabriel de Sartine, as *lieutenant général de police de Paris*, could boast that when three individuals met together in the street for a conversation, one would be his man.[23]

This concept of a supervisory police, involving the use of spies, ran counter to the eighteenth-century Englishman's perception of his liberties. Developments in French policing in the wake of the events of 1789 only served to confirm English prejudices. Lord Dudley voiced the beliefs of many when, following the brutal hammering-to-death of two families in the East End of London in 1812, he declared that he would rather half a dozen people had their throats cut every few years than that the country be subjected to the police system of Napoleonic France; a system which he construed as essentially political and intrusive.[24] Fearing a fifth column in league with revolutionary France, and then concerned about the unrest which accompanied the economic disruption following Napoleon's final defeat, the British government did employ some notorious political agents. But the activities of these agents served to convince Englishmen of the unsavoury nature of political police, and determined efforts were made to ensure that the new police could never be construed as political spies. The behaviour of Sergeant William Popay in the early 1830s briefly compromised and seriously embarrassed the Metropolitan Police, but for most of the nineteenth century the English police survived without the kind of political sections to be found in their European counterparts, and the relative passivity of the country, and of its radicals, facilitated this. When, following the ruthless suppression of the Paris Commune in 1871, the Home Office decided that it ought to collect information on communists and the International Workingmen's Association, it wrote to Karl Marx for details. The Special Irish Branch was established at Scotland Yard during the Fenian bombings of the early 1880s. The 'Irish' part of its name was soon dropped and its remit was widened as the governments of continental Europe increasingly insisted that Britain keep an eye on the political exiles who sought refuge on her shores, and as British governments themselves gradually began to share worries about these exiles and then about the spies of a potential enemy.[25] Yet as late as 1914 the Home Secretary could respond angrily to parliamentary questions about a political police in Britain, protesting that such a thing simply did not exist.[26]

II

To date, the serious academic study of the English police has concentrated overwhelmingly on the nineteenth century and on the origins of the service; perhaps there is some significance, too, in that fact that the original, critical assessments which appeared in the 1970s were the work of American students of English history.[27] Several monographs have appeared subsequently on the police and maintenance of public order during the twentieth century, and particularly on the problem of policing strikes; but much remains to be explored.[28]

By the beginning of the twentieth century a much greater convergence between English and European police was emerging than has generally been acknowledged, and the First World War gave a further boost to this. The spy scares before 1914 saw chief constables beginning to forge links with the embryonic secret service. When war came these links became stronger initially as the police watched for spies and saboteurs funded by German gold, then, after 1917 as fear of the German threat began to be superseded by fear of the Bolsheviks. The search for subversives and the links with the secret service continued after the war. Vernon Kell, the head of MI5, was a regular guest at the annual conference dinner of the borough chief constables during the inter-war period.

The strike waves in the years before the war had also witnessed an increase in the central direction of the English police. During the 1890s the Home Office had begun urging chief constables to enter into mutual aid agreements with their neighbours to provide assistance in emergencies. The strike wave of 1910 to 1912 in coal mines, and on the railways and docks, led to Winston Churchill, the young, interventionist Home Secretary, ordering police around the country with disregard for the constitutional niceties. Civil servants in the Home Office began bypassing watch committees and standing joint committees to liaise directly with chief constables. In many respects such moves were logical: national strikes required some form of national response, while highly educated civil servants, responsible for the supervision of law and order across the whole country, doubtless considered it more sensible to deal directly with the experts in the field – the police – rather than the amateurs on local police committees. During the war itself chief constables had more experience of bypassing their police committees, having instead to make reference to the Authorised Competent Military Authority of their district. The fears of civil unrest which followed the war brought legislation in the shape of the Emergency Powers Act 1920 which permitted the Home Secretary to give direct orders to local police forces without reference to their local police committees, and to move large numbers of them as he thought fit to deal with internal disorder. Chief constables who had confrontations with left-wing police committees were invariably backed by the Home Office; and they maintained, and appear to have believed, that their actions were non-political since they were simply preserving the British way of life from alien creeds.[29]

Indirectly the First World War accentuated the moves towards greater uniformity in the different police forces. Low pay and poor conditions had fostered a trade union in the Metropolitan Police shortly before the war. The union spread into the provinces. The demands of war increased policing duties but, at the same time, thinned police ranks. Wartime inflation eroded police pay. All of this helped boost support for the union. In 1918 and again in 1919 there were police strikes. The first strike led to the appointment of the Desborough Committee with its recommendations for greater uniformity in pay, training, uniforms and administration, and the prohibition of police trade unions.

The Desborough Committee has earned a mention in those Whig histories which have pushed their surveys into the twentieth century. It was another example of progress, adding to the steady improvement of the system. The increasing centralization and the bypassing of the local police committees was not acknowledged. However, both these historians and contemporaries in the inter-war years recognized that there were new problems in police–public relations.[30]

During the nineteenth century the police had mainly been called upon to confront members of the poorer sections of the working class. These people were generally inarticulate and lacking in political power and influence. When the police were created the working class, and especially the poorer sections, had taken a considerable amount of its leisure in the street. But changes in leisure meant a decline in the amount of working-class activity for the beat constable to supervise. Increasingly during the inter-war years the working class disappeared into its own homes to listen to new gramophones and radios, or found its pleasure in cinemas, dance halls and sports stadiums. At the same time groups from higher up the social scale were beginning to find themselves the objects of police supervision and action for the first time, primarily because of the motor car. By the 1930s highway offences were clogging the courts. The number of persons prosecuted for both indictable and non-indictable offences declined slightly, but the percentage charged with traffic offences increased from just over 6 per cent in the first decade of the century to 43 per cent in the early thirties. As the little girl put it to her mother in a *Punch* cartoon of 31 August 1927: 'Mother, what *did* policemen do when there weren't any motors?'[31]

Few traffic offenders then, as now, regarded themselves as criminals; and, of course, the problems created for the police by the motor vehicle and by motor vehicle legislation were not unique to England. On the spot fines were introduced for traffic offences in Vienna and France during the 1920s; similar legislation was contemplated for England, but the journal *Justice of the Peace* preferred that the motorist be offered the choice of a fine or a court appearance so as to avoid the possibility of charges of bribery and corruption against the police.[32] A few years later the journal waxed lyrical over the courtesy of the German police in traffic matters, making an implicit contrast with the English constable's behaviour.

> Does the motorist enter a one-way street at the wrong end? Instead of a peremptory challenge, or perhaps even worse, the threat of a

summons and the production of a notebook, there is an apology for having to interfere, followed by a request to be allowed the pleasure of indicating an even better alternative route.³³

This was a far cry from the *Schutzpolizist* of imperial Germany who set off on his beat 'armed as if for war' with pistol, sabre and brass knuckles.³⁴ But the politeness, though possibly accentuated for the English visitor, was in keeping with the ideas of Dr Wilhelm Abegg who was responsible for the police in the Prussian Interior Ministry in the early 1920s, and who probably did more than anyone to shape the Prussian police in the Weimar Republic. '[I]n today's world', he urged in 1926, 'all means must be employed to overcome public hostility towards the police and to bring about general recognition that the modern police is not only the authorised defender of the existing state structure, but also the ever-ready helper and protector of the public.' Abegg's police took the development of police–public relations seriously; press bureaux were opened and a police exhibition was held in Berlin in 1926.³⁵

While the Whig historians of the English police rarely ventured into serious comparative history,³⁶ it would probably be fair to say that they would have construed Abegg's intentions of moving the Prussian police towards the English model. Yet, as noted above, the English police experience was such that constables had very rarely confronted members of the middle class before the early twentieth century, while there was no formal press bureau at Scotland Yard until 1927 – some twenty years after it was first proposed, and rejected by the then commissioner on the grounds that it was no part of police duty to give information to the press.³⁷ Partly because of the devolved structure of policing, the reluctance of some police committees to spend money, and the conservatism of some chief constables, scientific and technological advances – not to mention social advance in the sense of the employment of women police officers – were slow to be introduced to many forces in the inter-war period. Home Office committees, and the occasional enlightened senior policemen, accepted that there were things that could be learned from overseas.³⁸

When it came to so-called 'gang busting' in towns like Sheffield and Glasgow, or dealing with crowds on the streets, especially those which senior officers regarded as espousing 'un-English creeds', the police could be rough.[39] In Liverpool in 1921 a meeting of the unemployed was savagely handled by the police. Eleven years later a minor disorder during a demonstration over the means test in Birkenhead was followed by what amounted to a police riot. In neither instance was there an inquiry. The argument was that any such could only play into the hands of extremists; the implication again was that, while there might be the occasional 'black sheep' or 'rotten apple' there was nothing wrong with the police institution. When criticism did appear in the press, it was generally in the left-wing press, and in the case of the *Worker's Weekly* in 1927, it resulted in the proprietor and the editor being prosecuted for libelling a whole force when, the court agreed, just one individual may have been to blame.[40]

This was not a deliberate conspiracy; and a strong legal reason could be advanced as to why the Home Secretary could not authorize inquiries into the behaviour of local police – he was not the police authority. But the reluctance to investigate these issues also resulted from a firm belief in the superiority of most things English, which, as suggested earlier stemmed from the education and formative years of the nation's rulers in the inter-war period. There was a Royal Commission on Police Powers and Procedures in 1929 following disquiet over the behaviour of Metropolitan Police Officers, who were the Home Secretary's charge, but this was not before the Home Secretary, Sir William Joynson-Hicks, had suggested that the public abstain from criticism of the police for twelve months. 'It is an indisputable fact', he stressed to his audience in support of this request, 'that the British police force is one of the finest if not the finest in the world.'[41]

In France during the Third Republic, in contrast, the police were continually at the centre of political and press debate. Ministers, even ministries, fell as a result.[42] The violence of the police in the affair of 6 February 1934 – thirty-four civilians dead – and the *affaire de Clichy* three years later – five civilians dead – was the subject of inquiry by the National Assembly on each occasion. In the former instance the inquiry found that, while the police had been attacked, they were also guilty of 'pointless brutalities'. The Clichy affair led to the prefect of police seeking to professionalize the way that his men handled disorder in future, and to develop new technology to this end. Riot-control squads were established, while experiments were made with tear gas, plastic bullets and coloured dyes to be squirted from fire hoses. There were never similar casualties when the English police confronted crowds, and there were no suggestions about professionalizing English police tactics. English policemen used unauthorized weapons in dealing with crowds, but these weapons never included firearms. Perhaps the key difference which led to the French casualties was the fact that the French *flic* always carried a gun, and frightened men in frightening situations will use any means to defend themselves. English bobbies did carry guns, but not as a rule; the tradition of the unarmed policeman was generally maintained, unlike some other traditions, and there was, probably, a positive result.[43]

Professional training in dealing with street disorders had tragic results in Abegg's Prussian police. Abegg's men were increasingly non-military in their origins, yet they too were armed. The unrest in Weimar Germany prompted fears of some sort of coup or revolution. In consequence, in October and November 1927, the police journal *Die Polizei* outlined the kind of tactics which were expected to be necessary for the police; these were ominously entitled *Strassen und Häuserkampf* (street and house fighting), and were largely military in nature. The proletariat of the Wedding and Neukölln districts of Berlin sympathized with the Communist Party, and were regarded by the police as their potential 'enemy'. In 1928, as part of their professional riot training, the police sealed off Wedding. In May the following year, working-class unrest and political demonstrations led the police to move into the suspect areas and deploy their professional tactics of house and street fighting against the long-suspected 'enemy'. Thirty-three people were shot dead, six in their own flats, and 198 were wounded.[44]

An obvious, easy response would be to assume that the Prussian police were Nazi sympathizers. Probably there were some sympathizers, though there is the danger of hindsight here – the Nazi Party was still small in 1928, winning only twelve seats in the Reichstag that year, and before the summer of 1932 any sympathizers in the police would have had to be circumspect about how they behaved and voiced their opinions. Moreover, the evidence reveals the Prussian police to have been fully prepared to act against the SA and other Nazi activists during the late 1920s and early 1930s; it was the lack of support which they felt they received from the government and administration, and particularly the courts, which led them to start to give up the struggle. The subsequent Nazi regime became particularly attractive to some policemen. It allowed them to get on with their jobs as professionals unfettered by democratic busybodies and controls, and with enhanced budgets. More importantly, the way in which *Polizeijustiz* (police justice) developed during the Third Reich gave the criminal police (*Kripo*) and the Gestapo the authority to hold people under preventive detention, and to overrule or simply ignore court decisions.[45] The Nazi regime also promised order and a respect for authority, something which struck a chord with many Germans, and not just the police, whose professional duty was to maintain order and who, in many respects, represented authority on the streets. It is increasingly clear that the Gestapo, an institution whose very name has become a byword for police terror, depended significantly on denunciation and probably could not have functioned as well as it did without the active co-operation of at least a part of the German population.[46] But to return to the police proper, there is probably a much more prosaic reason why they, as individuals, accepted Nazi authority. The Weimar police were created with the Weimar Republic; they signed contracts for twelve years. Many of those contracts were coming up for renewal in 1932 as the Nazis came to power. It would have taken a brave man to throw up his job and pension given the state of the German economy at the beginning of the 1930s.[47]

The police of European countries occupied by the Germans faced similar problems. They had to carry on their usual policing duties, but taking cognizance of directives from the occupying military. One Parisian *inspecteur*, a veteran of Verdun, recalled in his memoirs:

> It was important to avoid incidents, not only in our own interest as policemen, but also in the interest of the Parisians. We would only forget that we were in the hands of the enemy, not to be agreeable to him, but because the population needed us. After having seen the Germans at work, I ask myself what would have happened if Paris had only had *boche* police (*des policiers boches*).[48]

This is not to excuse the actions of the senior officers of the Vichy police – René Bousquet, Maurice Papon and Paul Touvier – and many of their men, still the subject of furious debate in France, but to draw attention to the ordinary *flic* in the occupied zone who, like many of his fellow countrymen in the second half of 1940, must have believed the war to be over. There were similar problems for the police in Vichy.[49]

In 1940 Penguin Books published a book by François Lafitte describing the internment of aliens. While he believed that most police officers 'behaved with courtesy and kindliness', many of the police chiefs who gave the orders

> appear almost to have imagined that they were swooping on criminals. Was it necessary ... to proceed with such secrecy that even the police officers were not told until they came on duty, paying visits *at all hours of the night*, in some cases with lorry-loads of soldiers accompanying the police vans? Was it so often necessary to give such short notice that in many cases the individuals concerned had no time to put their affairs in order or even to communicate with relatives?

Lafitte went on to comment particularly on 'the stupid and callous behaviour of the police in East London', for the policemen in the book were English bobbies; and the internment described was that of enemy aliens in May 1940.[50] Harry Daley, a sergeant in the Metropolitan Police based at Vine Street in central London, recalled in his memoirs a few young constables at the time of Munich wearing black shirts off duty and distributing anti-Jewish literature in the West End. These constables were patriotic when war came; but, during the Blitz, other officers complained to the local inspector about Daley's behaviour. Daley's fault was inviting the local publican and his wife from across the street to share the air-raid shelter beneath the police station; the publican and his wife were Jews.[51] Who can be sure of the response of the English police, or other institutions, to occupation?

III

Len Deighton's *SS-GB* is a novel set in Nazi-occupied England in 1941. Its central character is Detective Superintendent Douglas

Archer: 'as long as the Germans let him get on with the job of catching murderers, he'd do his work as he'd always done it.'[52] That, of course, is a story, originating in the imagination of the novelist. The stories of historians require some sort of archival basis, and if they also require imagination and a literary turn, there are limits to how far that imagination can wander; England was never occupied by the Nazis.

It is one of the peculiarities of English history that its constitutional structure, administrative and governmental system has evolved peacefully over the last three centuries. The traditional Whig interpretation concluded that this stemmed largely from the relatively bloodless Glorious Revolution of 1688 which produced a model constitution capable of gradual evolution. A more prosaic explanation might be that, in the last three centuries Britain has only lost one major war – against her own colonists in America; and then it was her principal international rival who had allied with the colonists, and was left bankrupt. Since 1688 no British government has fallen through insurrection or catastrophic military defeat; the constitution has not had to be redrawn in the aftermath of revolution or military defeat. In contrast a Belgian, a Dutchman, a Frenchman, a German, an Italian, a Russian, approaching his fiftieth birthday in 1950 or 1960, would have lived under a variety of different regimes precisely because of war, coup and/or revolution. Nineteenth- and twentieth-century Englishmen have never had to rethink their government system from the ground up and have never had questions of police and policing thrown into the centre of political debate. The Whig history, which still infuses much of the official thinking on policing, was written in a period far more stable, far less critical and challenging – perhaps, too, far less cynical – than our own.

Notes

1. Compare, for example, the much quoted: 'Amid the bustle of Piccadilly or the roar of Oxford Street, P.C.X 59 stalks along, an institution rather than a man' ([Andrew Wynter], 'The police and thieves', *Quarterly Review*, 99 (1856), 160–200, at 171).

Le sergent de ville à Paris . . . c'est la providence du citoyen paisible, la terreur des criminels. Sans lui vos femmes, vos mères, vos soeurs seraient à chaque instant exposées aux grossièretés du premier manant. A qui s'adressent-elles dans la rue, en votre absence, pour faire cesser ces lâches insultes? Au sergent de ville seul, car cet homme, c'est la loi en costume officiel.

A ses agents, les travaux, les ennuis, les dégoûts; à nous les plaisirs et la joie. (A. Durantin, *Les Français peints par eux-mêmes*, quoted in Alfred Rey and Louis Féron, *Histoire du Corps des gardiens de la paix* (Paris, 1894), 116)

Le gendarme est l'expression la plus complète, la plus éloquente, la plus vraie du dévouement, du sacrifice tels qu'ils sont définis par la religion. Le gendarme est l'héritier direct des ordres de chevalerie nés au XIIe siècle. Les chevaliers disaient: 'Mourir pour la foi et défendre les faibles.' Le gendarme dit: 'Mourir pour la loi et défendre la justice ...' Leurs casernes sont de petits monastères où se conserve pure la religion du devoir ... Au milieu de notre civilisation moderne, l'homme le plus digne de respect est le gendarme, parce qu'il est la sentinelle de la loi. (Baron Ambert, quoted in the article 'Gendarmerie' in *Grand dictionnaire universelle du XIXe siècle*, Paris, 1865).

2. See, for example, Charles Dickens, 'A detective police party', *Household Words*, 1 (1850), 409–14 and 457–60.
3. See, *inter alia*, 'We can't leave it to old George [Dixon] any more', *Financial Times*, 28 July 1981; Robert Reiner's comment that 'the style of policing public order has been transformed from the image of Dixon to Darth Vader', *Times*, 10 November 1986; 'Double injustice from the wrong arm of the law', accompanied by a photograph of Jack Warner (the actor who played Dixon) with the caption 'Dixon of Dock Green was honesty personified', *Sunday Times*, 19 November 1988. The first substantive chapter of P. A. J. Waddington, *The Strong Arm of the Law: Armed and Public Order Policing* (Oxford, 1991) is called 'The eclipse of "Dixon of Dock Green"'.
4. Quoted in David Cannadine, *G. M. Trevelyan: A Life in History* (London, 1992), 86.
5. Ken Ward, *Mass Communications and the Modern World* (London, 1989), 120–4.
6. John R. Gillis, 'The evolution of juvenile delinquency in England, 1890–1914', *Past and Present*, 67 (1975), 96–126.
7. V. A. C. Gatrell, 'The decline of theft and violence in Victorian and Edwardian England', in V. A. C. Gatrell, Bruce Lenman and Geoffrey Parker (eds.), *Crime and the Law: The Social History of Crime in Western Europe since 1500* (London, 1980); Clive Emsley, 'The English

bobby: an indulgent tradition', in Roy Porter (ed.), *Myths of the English* (Oxford, 1992), 114–35.

8. *The Times*, 29 March 1870.

9. George Robb, *White-Collar Crime in Modern England: Financial Fraud and Business Morality 1845–1929* (Cambridge, 1992); Clive Emsley, *Crime and Society in England 1750–1900* (2nd edn, London, 1996), 140–2.

10. Martin J. Wiener, *Reconstructing the Criminal: Culture, Law and Policy in England, 1830–1914* (Cambridge, 1990).

11. L. O. Pike, *A History of Crime in England* (2 vols., London, 1876), II, 457.

12. G. M. Trevelyan, *Illustrated History of England* (London, 1956), 626. (The first, unillustrated, edition appeared in 1926.) G. M. Trevelyan, *British History in the Nineteenth Century (1782–1901)* (London, 1923), 199.

13. Rey and Féron, *Histoire de Corps des gardiens de la paix*, 175–80; Steven C. Hughes, 'Gendarmes and bobbies: Italy's search for the appropriate police force', paper presented to the Southern Historical Association, New Orleans, 1987. Professor Hughes has also discovered a large number of papers relating to the London Metropolitan Police in 1860 in the Biblioteca Comunale di Bologna, Collezione di Marco Minghetti. Personal communication, 25 May 1991.

14. Charles Reith, *The Blind Eye of History* (London, 1952), 173 and 20.

15. Clive Emsley, 'Police and industrial disputes in Britain and the United States', in David Englander (ed.), *Britain and America: Studies in Comparative History 1760–1970* (New Haven, 1997), 112–31; idem, *The English Police: A Political and Social History* (2nd edn, Harlow, 1996), 89–91 and 108–10. See also Carolyn Steedman, *Policing the Victorian Community: The Formation of English Provincial Police Forces 1856–1880* (London, 1982).

16. Richard Bach Jensen, 'Police reform and social reform: Italy from the crisis of the 1890s to the Giolittian era', *Criminal Justice History*, 10 (1989), 179–200; Jonathan Dunnage, 'Law and order in Giolittian Italy: a case study of the Province of Bologna', *European History Quarterly*, 25 (1995), 381–408.

17. Marie-Thérèse Vogel, 'Les polices des villes entre local et national: l'administration des polices urbaines sous la IIIe république', Doctorat de science politique, Université Pierre Mendès France, Grenoble II, 3 vols. (1993), provides an excellent introduction, though its principal focus is on the situation in Grenoble.

18. Elaine Glovka Spencer, *Police and the Social Order in German Cities: The Düsseldorf District, 1848–1914* (DeKalb, 1992), 141–3.

19. Clive Emsley, *Gendarmes and the State in Nineteenth-Century Europe* (Oxford, 1999).
20. Linda Colley, *Britons: Forging the Nation 1707–1837* (New Haven, 1992).
21. Ibid., 336–7.
22. Richard J. Evans, *Kneipungsgespräche im Kaiserreich: Stimmungsberichte der Hamburger Politischen Polizei, 1892–1914* (Reinbeck bei Hamburg, 1989); Edgar L. Newman, 'Quand les mouchards ne riaient pas: les ouvriers chansonniers, la justice et la liberté pendant la monarchie de juillet', in Philippe Vigier, Alain Faure et al., *Répression et prison politiques en France et en Europe au XIXe siècle* (Paris, 1990).
23. Philip John Stead, *The Police of Paris* (London, 1957), 49; for a rational assessment of the number of spies and informers in eighteenth-century Paris, see Alan Williams, *The Police of Paris 1718–1789* (Baton Rouge, 1979), 104–11.
24. David Philips, '"A new engine of power and authority": the institutionalization of law-enforcement in England 1780–1830', in Gatrell, Lenman and Parker, *Crime and the Law*, 174.
25. Bernard Porter, *The Origins of the Vigilant State: The London Metropolitan Police Special Branch before the First World War* (London, 1987).
26. *Hansard's Parliamentary Debates*, LXI, 30 April 1914, col. 1874, and LXII, 5 May 1914, col. 121.
27. Robert D. Storch, '"The plague of blue locusts": police reform and popular resistance in northern England 1840–57', *International Review of Social History*, 20 (1975), 61–90; idem, 'The policeman as domestic missionary', *Journal of Social History*, 9 (1976), 481–509; Wilbur R. Miller, *Cops and Bobbies: Police Authority in New York and London, 1830–1870* (Chicago, 1977); Philip Thurmond Smith, *Policing Victorian London: Political Policing, Public Order, and the London Metropolitan Police* (Westport, 1985) (originally a Ph.D. thesis, Columbia University, 1976).
28. Roger Geary, *Policing Industrial Disputes 1893 to 1985* (Cambridge, 1985); Jane Morgan, *Conflict and Order: The Police and Labour Disputes in England and Wales 1900–1939* (Oxford, 1987); Barbara Weinberger, *Keeping the Peace? Policing Strikes in Britain 1906–1926* (Oxford, 1991). More general, and significantly opening up the area, are David J. V. Jones, *Crime and Policing in the Twentieth Century: The South Wales Experience* (Cardiff, 1996), and Barbara Weinberger, *The Best Police in the World: An Oral History of English Policing from the 1930s to the 1960s* (Aldershot, 1995).
29. See, *inter alia*, Emsley, *The English Police*, 139–40.
30. See, for example, David Ascoli, *The Queen's Peace: The Origins*

and Development of the Metropolitan Police 1829–1979 (London, 1979), ch.8; T. A. Critchley, *A History of Police in England and Wales* (revised edn, London, 1978), 184–98.

31. Clive Emsley, '"Mother, what did policemen do when there weren't any motors?" The law, the police and the regulation of motor traffic in England, 1900–1939', *Historical Journal*, 36 (1993), 357–81.

32. *Justice of the Peace*, 90 (1926), 27 February, 135, and 16 October, 574.

33. Ibid., 94 (1930), 6 December, 754.

34. R. B. Fosdick, *European Police Systems* (reprint Monclair, NJ, 1969), 231.

35. Richard Bessel, 'Policing, professionalisation and politics in Weimar Germany', in Clive Emsley and Barbara Weinberger (eds.), *Policing Western Europe; Politics, Professionalism, and Public Order, 1850–1940* (Westport, 1991), 187–8.

36. Reith, with his conceptualization of 'kin police' and 'despotic totalitarian police' in *The Blind Eye of History*, is the exception. The problem for many European countries, in Reith's analysis, was that in overthrowing their old regimes and creating new systems for making laws, they had failed to create the right sort of police – the 'democratic means for securing law enforcement' – but had kept the old gendarmeries. 'It is unnecessary to look far beyond this fact to account for the comparative failure of democracy elsewhere than in Britain and the United States' (p. 244).

37. See, for example, Metropolitan Police Archive 554.85, 'Report by H. Alker Tripp on visit to America, October 1934' (an investigation of the police traffic role).

38. *Justice of the Peace*, 91 (1927), 30 April, 332. In 1909 William McAdoo, a former Commissioner of the New York City Police, had expressed astonishment that the press were not allowed into Scotland Yard and only received information formally, in writing. William McAdoo, 'The London police from a New York point of view', *Century Magazine*, 18 (September 1909), 649–70, at 657.

39. For 'gang-busting' in Sheffield and Glasgow see Sir Percy Sillitoe, *Cloak without Dagger* (London, 1955).

40. *Justice of the Peace*, 91 (1927), 12 March, 184.

41. Ibid., 92 (1928), 28 July, 501.

42. Jean-Marc Berlière, 'La professionalisation: revendication des policiers et objectif des pouvoirs au début de la IIIe République', *Revue d'Histoire Moderne et Contemporaine*, 36 (1990), 398–427, at 406–11.

43. Clive Emsley, 'Police forces and public order in England and France during the inter-war years', in Emsley and Weinberger, *Policing Western Europe*, 167–9 and 171.

44. Bessel, 'Policing, professionalisation', 201–2.
45. Peter Lessmann-Faust, '"Au poste perdu": La police en Prusse 1930–1933', and Robert Gellately, 'L'émergence de la "Polizeijustiz" dans l'Allemagne nazie', both in Jean-Marc Berlière and Denis Peschanski (eds.), *Pouvoirs et polices au XXe siècle: Europe, États-Unis, Japon* (Brussels, 1997).
46. Robert Gellately, *The Gestapo and German Society: Enforcing Racial Policy 1933–1945* (Oxford, 1990).
47. Bessel, 'Policing, professionalisation', 203.
48. 'Jean de Cordestieux' [Jean Delbousquet], 'La vie secrète des commissariats', fol. 320, MS volume in the library of the Institut des Hautes Études de la Sécurité Intérieure, Paris.
49. H. R. Kedward, *In Search of the Marquis* (Oxford, 1993), and Simon Kitson, 'The Marseille Police in their Context, from Popular Front to Liberation', unpub. Ph.D. thesis, University of Sussex (1995). Both note the problems for the French police in Vichy, and the ambivalence shown towards policies inspired or directed by the Germans. The hostility was often most apparent when the Germans interfered with the French police's own way of doing things or encroached upon their independence and discretion.
50. François Lafitte, *The Internment of Aliens* (London, 1940), 75 and 90.
51. Harry Daley, *This Small Cloud: A Personal Memoir* (London, 1986), 172–4.
52. Len Deighton, *SS-GB* (London, 1978), 12.

W. E. Adams, Chartist and Republican in Victorian England

OWEN R. ASHTON

In his pioneering work, *Chartism and the Chartists* (1975), Professor David Jones was one of the earliest of a group of modern historians to appreciate the standing of William Edwin Adams (1832–1906) in the first great working-class movement in the world.[1] Jones also paid tribute in his extensive and annotated bibliography to the merits of Adams's *Memoirs of a Social Atom* (1903), judging it to be 'one of the most interesting and substantial' within the genre of radical working-class autobiography.[2] Adams, of course, as the *Memoirs* underline, was not, and never pretended to be, a national Chartist leader; rather, he was classically representative of a distinct coterie of middle-rank or second-line leaders, whose contribution to radical politics, both in and after Chartism, is beginning to be appreciated.[3] By nature, quiet, unassuming and self-effacing, Adams nevertheless could wield a pen with such effectiveness and determination that he was even able to leave his mark on Victorian political history in a number of ways. In 1858, as the author of a pamphlet entitled *Tyrannicide*, Adams justified both Orsini's plot and any future assassination attempt on the life of Napoleon III; its publication helped bring down a Whig government headed by Lord Palmerston over his mishandling of a Conspiracy to Murder Bill, a measure which, it was widely believed, had been introduced at the dictates of the French government to prosecute the likes of Adams.[4] Secondly, from 1864 until the turn of the century, a period regarded as the influential heyday of provincial journalism, Adams was employed by Joseph Cowen Jr as editor-in-chief of the *Newcastle Weekly Chronicle*. Through his efforts it became one of the greatest provincial newspapers with a reputation beyond Tyneside for both the quality of its journalism and, as 'the pitmen's bible', for its advanced radicalism.[5] In turn, Liberal leaders like Gladstone were sensitive to such opinion when formulating domestic reforms. Thirdly, he played a key role both professionally and personally in the political campaigning for the extension of the suffrage to the Northumberland miners: it led directly to the election of Thomas Burt, who, as the MP for Morpeth, was one of the first working men to enter the House of Commons.[6] Lastly, as the author of *Our American Cousins* (1883), he pushed for greater transatlantic alignments based on a continued faith in the republican form of government as the only blueprint for a real democracy. In this endeavour, he found common ground with such prominent Americans as the liberal-republican and fellow journalist, Henry Demarest Lloyd, who was trying to defend the maturing republic against its exposure to political and corporate corruption.[7]

W. E. Adams was born in humble circumstances on 11 February 1832 in Cheltenham Spa, the son of a tramping plasterer. He was raised by his widowed maternal grandmother, Anne Wells, and her three unmarried daughters, all of a radical persuasion. From their little home in the lower end of the High Street, they worked as washerwomen to the Spa's wealthy and fashion-conscious residents. After an intermittent education at a dame and then a Wesleyan day school, Adams started work as a bookseller's errand boy, but in 1846 was apprenticed for seven years as a journeyman printer to the proprietor of the Tory newspaper, the *Cheltenham Journal*.

His experience in the workplace and as a member of a radical household, made Adams conscious of the profound inequalities in the world around him. The 1832 Reform Act had been a great disappointment to his and other working-class families who lived in the old market and trading area of the Spa. Under the terms of the Act, Cheltenham had become a Whig pocket borough in the control of the Berkeley family, who were leading Gloucestershire aristocrats.[8] Cheltenham was still a thriving tourist centre where class differences and social snobbery flourished. Whilst remaining politically invisible after 1832, the Adams family, like their neighbours, were resentful of the ways in which they were both exploited and looked down upon by the wealthy, whose needs they had to provide for or service in order to survive. The final pressure came from the Anglican Church. The *Cheltenham Journal* on which Adams worked was very much the eyes and ears of a modernizing Evangelical cleric, the Revd Francis Close, the incumbent of the parish church of St Mary's (1826–56). His zeal and conservative-inspired clericalism, led Tennyson, a local resident, to suggest that Close was trying to make the Spa 'a polka, parson-worshipping place' with himself as 'pope'.[9]

The extended family within which Adams grew up remained remarkably uninfluenced by the respectable strait-jacket provided under Close's spiritual autocracy.[10] Adams's aunts were not antireligious, but they were anticlerical and viewed Close as a symbol of a Church establishment, which stood as an ideological prop for the corrupt political system on their doorstep. Both his grandmother and the aunts were, of course, politically aware. In the 1830s they read such radical newspapers as the *Weekly Dispatch* and Cobbett's *Political Register*; they warmed to the writings of Thomas Paine, not least because their poverty and Cheltenham's decadence illustrated his critique of government by 'Old Corruption'. Not surprisingly, Adams was inspired to join the National Charter Association by that Paineite thinking which stressed the importance of popular sovereignty, self-reliance and individual freedom. Writing on the stirring events of the French Revolution in 1848, he recalled: 'I had previously read the "Rights of Man" and other political works of Thomas Paine, which seduced me from bed at five o'clock for many mornings in succession. And now I was fairly in the maelstrom.'[11] Adams was born only six years before the Chartist movement officially started in 1838, and his exposure to the movement began relatively late. Before completing his indentures, however, he was chairing branch meetings of the National Charter Association, the internationally-orientated Fraternal Democrats and the Cheltenham People's Institute, a radical literary and debating society which he himself had founded. Still in his teens, he became an active local campaigner, collecting signatures for the third great National Petition and involved in organizing an election for a delegate to represent them at the Chartist Convention of 1848. He was not willing to resort to physical force, but subscribed to the view reported by their delegate, J. P. Glenister, that 'they desired agitation, and a long pull and a strong pull for the obtainment of their rights'.[12]

Having all the 'effrontery of youth' Adams emerged by 1850 as an acknowledged local leader presiding over a whole constellation of political and cultural activities. Moreover, by his exceptional efforts he involved his Chartist community in the national plans and brought it to the attention of leaders like Feargus O'Connor, Ernest Jones and, later, Thomas Cooper and Robert Gammage.[13] Like J. B. Leno in Uxbridge and Thomas Frost in Croydon,[14] Adams had a number of personal talents and attributes which set him apart and helped define his role as the archetypal middle-ranking Chartist leader, who acted as an important conduit between policy-makers at the centre and activists in the provinces.[15] He was able to read and write well. As a young compositor in a literacy-based occupation, Adams became acutely conscious of his unique identity at the interface between a traditionally oral and a modern, print-based society and culture. Chartism, in fact, occurred at the time of a battle to control the developing technologies of cheap publishing. In his own working-class district of the Spa, where the main forms of discourse for transmitting political ideas were still the spoken word from platform speeches, personal canvassing, songs and day-to-day conversations, Adams noted the social significance of the transition to the world of print: 'To be able to read and write was a distinction then. Anybody who could do more was almost accounted a phenomenon.'[16]

He used his abilities in various ways. At one moment, he was corresponding with members of Parliament concerning the treatment of Chartist prisoners.[17] At another, in the homes of fellow Chartists or, in defiance of Close, at ritual Sunday morning gatherings – usually the first opportunity to meet after the arrival of Saturday's mail – Adams would read aloud to colleagues from the *Northern Star* and then comment on its reports of activities across the country.[18] Significantly, studying the varied reactions of his audience made him even more aware of the transforming power of the printed word. It was this experience that led to his becoming a professional journalist in later life.

Secondly, Adams was a labour aristocrat in a trade which gave him an aura that transcended his own workplace authority. It also gave him the opportunity to develop personal friendships and trade-based networks with other printers in the Spa. This position was a key factor in persuading the proprietor of the radical Liberal *Cheltenham Free Press* to allow him to publish his first article, an emotional appeal in May 1851 on behalf of the 250-strong Polish-Hungarian Legion that had fled tsarist tyranny.[19] Few local

Chartists anywhere could boast such a reputation for exploiting the propaganda value of the contemporary provincial press.

Finally, Adams had considerable powers and confidence as an orator on the Chartist platform in the Spa. In his *Memoirs*, for example, he recalled how his ability to articulate political ideas and hold the crowd's attention at open-air meetings even shocked his Chartist aunt: 'Great was her astonishment to observe her precocious nephew on the platform proclaiming at the top of his voice the inalienable right of every man to the suffrage!'[20]

By 1851 Adams and his colleagues had become crusading republicans. Initially, they had identified with the leadership of the socialist Chartist Julian Harney, but the great sea-change in their political thinking was supplied by W. J. Linton, the talented poet, wood-engraver and journalist, and a new member of the Chartist National Executive. Linton, who wanted to adapt Chartism to the new conditions consequent upon the failure of the popular risings in 1848, was inspired by the lofty idealism of the Italian patriot Giuseppe Mazzini. In a series of articles he expounded upon Mazzini's proclamation to the peoples of the world concerning the organization of democracy. The central themes of Mazzini's anti-socialist republicanism, as interpreted by Linton, stressed the consciousness of duty as well as the rights of man – the latter being valuable only as the means of discharging the former; it also emphasized the holiness of work, the importance of education and the need for harmony between properly constituted nation states.[21] The concept of 'a duteous and exalted people' in pursuit of the goal of a common humanity was, of course, incompatible in Linton's mind with the ideas and privileges of a monarchical system.[22] But Adams was attracted to republicanism by a more definite notion of what the word implied than a mere rejection of the evils of monarchy, the end of which in Britain he believed would come to pass by common consent on the death of Queen Victoria. The pure republicanism which he and his Cheltenham colleagues believed would come was not simply a democratic form of government, but 'a system of morals, a law of life, a creed, a faith, a new and benign gospel'.[23] In essence, Adams viewed Mazzinian republicanism as a passive rather than an activist creed: 'Bear in mind we were Republicans, not Revolutionists. It was no part of our business to disturb, or attempt to disturb, the established order of things. We wanted to make Republicans, not a Republic.'[24]

For the rest of his life Adams remained a devoted propagandist of Mazzinian ideals for the regeneration of humanity. He did so in a number of ways and in circumstances partly dictated by his type of work and surroundings. Firstly, in Cheltenham in 1851 on Linton's suggestion he helped found and became the first president at the age of eighteen of a small band of ardent campaigners, who called themselves the Cheltenham Republican Association. Their aim was to challenge by peaceful means the formidable clerical and aristocratic prejudices that were so ingrained around them. Adams recalled in his *Memoirs* how, at their meetings, they combined for instruction and propagandism:

> The works of the revolutionary leaders were read and discussed; candidates for membership were examined; the prospects of the cause abroad and at home were pondered; plans were devised for making our ideas known by personal canvassing and the circulation of tracts; and occasionally essays by the members themselves on some point of doctrine or practice were produced for consideration and debate.[25]

Ultimately, of course, as Adams himself admitted, with less than a score of members and 'poor in purse', they were 'never strong enough to impede anything'[26] or able to sustain an independent movement.[27] Such weaknesses however, should not distract us from appreciating the remarkable and largely nonsectarian nature of the challenge the Cheltenham Chartists still posed at this time. Adams, for once, exaggerates when he states that their little group, or tendency, were ostracized,[28] for the evidence tells a different story: republican and social-democratic Chartists in the Spa worked together over a range of concerns of both local and national importance.

Common cause was made, for example, over a successful anti-privilege issue – the campaign to save a number of footpaths in the vicinity of Cheltenham and Prestbury from being swallowed up by residential housing, the drive for which was being led by local unscrupulous estate agents.[29] Prompted by a sense of duty to defend for others the freedom to roam, Adams at this time was already revealing some of those traits of character which, by the end of the nineteenth century, were to earn him a reputation as a leading conservationist on Tyneside.[30]

Undoubtedly, the most important aspect in the radical political culture after 1851 was the concern with foreign affairs and the receptiveness of men like Adams to the plight of European political refugees, who faced retribution from continental despots restored to power after the revolutionary failures of 1848. As Adams recalled: 'The idea of Fraternity was as sacred to us as any ideas expressed in our republican formula. And Fraternity if it meant anything meant the offer of such help as we could give to the struggling peoples of the Continent.'[31]

Accordingly, they issued resolutions and addresses of moral support for the republican cause in newspapers and at protest meetings; printed tracts and leaflets reminding people to be on their guard in England lest their own aristocratic government cave in to the demands of European reactionaries to refuse asylum to refugees; made general financial contributions to Mazzini's appeal for a 'Shilling Fund' in aid of European freedom; and, on their own initiative, channelled funds in the direction of fleeing Poles and Magyars. Adams was to be found in the thick of all this activity, and was also instrumental in supporting the local branch of the Friends of Italy, an influential pressure group established by Mazzini and his English allies in May 1851. Its aim was to unite middle- and working-class radical patriots in a common cause for the civil and religious freedom of that country. As Margot Finn has pointed out, Chartists largely avoided the Society,[32] but in the Spa, perhaps more so than in other urban areas, conditions were propitious for such a cross-class alliance. Cheltenham had a small but important radical middle class drawn from its resident literati, the professions and Dissenting chapels. Led by Henry Solly, the Unitarian minister,[33] and Sydney Dobell, a minor poetic figure, the group were very interested in the cause of freedom for oppressed nationalities. It is clear from Adams's writings that whilst his 'friends of freedom' campaigns were part of a wider, working-class international struggle, sufficient common ground existed to allow co-operation between its supporters and the Spa's bourgeois radicals. In Adams's view men like Solly and Dobell could be trusted because they had stood aloof from the Cheltenham balls and parties, rejected the patronage of the Berkeleys and opposed the clerical autocracy of Francis Close. Encouraged, too, by Linton, who increasingly favoured cooperation with bourgeois elements over foreign affairs, Adams's group therefore entered into an alliance with the Spa's radical middle class in order to collect funds, publish tracts and hold meetings on behalf of a free Italy.[34]

In the spring of 1854 on the completion of his apprenticeship, Adams began to widen his horizons and enjoy new if not exhilarating experiences. In the company of two other Spa republicans he left home and tramped to W. J. Linton's republican household at Brantwood, a mansion estate on the eastern side of Lake Coniston. In this beautiful but isolated spot – deliberately chosen to avoid surveillance by their enemies both at home and from abroad – Adams worked as a compositor on the production not only of his mentor's monthly magazine, the *English Republic*, but also on Joseph Cowen's *Northern Tribune*, a republican paper circulating among members of the flourishing Newcastle Republican Brotherhood. Adams's role however was not simply that of the back-room boy. The camaraderie of the experiment to produce a new educational literature threw up moments for reading, discussion and, as Adams recalled, 'dreaming together the establishment of an English Republic'.[35] In Linton's company, Adams became intimately associated with his master's life-long projects for the regeneration of humanity. Indeed, for the rest of his life they remained close friends.[36]

When the short-lived venture came to an end in April 1855 Adams tramped back to Cheltenham, but as the prospects for work were gloomy there he decided to try his luck in London. Life in the capital was to prove more stimulating and certainly more exciting than anything he had ever known before. He managed to find work as a compositor on the *Illustrated Times*, quickly joined a small republican club which had links with European revolutionaries and studied in what time he could spare at Frederic D. Maurice's Working Men's College.[37] It was in London that Adams firmly established his mid-century reputation as 'a fierce Republican'.[38] A number of factors contributed to this new and rapid rise to prominence in and beyond radical circles. As a foot soldier attempting to proselytize for the republican cause in London's public places, he was prepared on Sundays to defy both the Sabbatarians and the overzealous Metropolitan Police Force.[39] He was one of the few and faithful among the Chartists who still had the courage to defend in public the action of the Sepoys, native Indian soldiers from Bengal, whose massacre of Europeans had triggered off the 'so-called' Indian rising of 1857 and then a ferocious imperial backlash. He became extremely active in the social, ceremonial and political life of a network of radical clubs, coffee houses and debating halls. At one of these – the John Street Institute – Adams remembered how 'The platform was perfectly free. Chartism, Republicanism, Freethought, Socialism – all sorts and conditions of thought could be expounded ... if capable exponents desired to expound them.'[40]

It was in the heady and charged atmosphere of another of these debating clubs – the Temple Forum in Fleet Street – that Adams found the inspiration to write in February 1858 his diatribe against Louis Napoleon entitled *Tyrannicide: Is It Justifiable?* – a question to which, in defence of Orsini's actions, he gave a 'clear affirmative'.[41] The pamphlet was widely publicized and the Palmerston-led government decided to prosecute, but it was Adams's friend, the well-known radical bookseller and publisher of his pamphlet, Edward Truelove, and not he who was indicted. Radicals of all persuasions came together to resist this attack on the rights of public discussion. A defence committee was appointed with Charles Bradlaugh as secretary and John Stuart Mill, Harriet Martineau and Joseph Cowen Jr amongst its members. The prosecution, however, was brought to an abrupt end, much to Adams's and Truelove's disgust, by a secret agreement between defence counsel and the Crown prosecution in June of the same year.

The dust had hardly settled on this controversial affair when Adams again found himself out of work. He moved to Manchester, cotton capital and shock city of industrial Britain, where he secured employment once more in a printer's office; he also took advantage, as in London, of the city's new opportunities for self-improvement.[42] His talents however as a ready and effective working-class writer had impressed the Republican and secularist leader, Charles Bradlaugh, who now invited him to contribute a political column to his new free-thought and radical newspaper, the *National Reformer*, launched in 1860. Simultaneously, Adams kept himself in the radical limelight by writing under his own name for the *Investigator: A Journal of Secularism*, which was also under Bradlaugh's editorial control.[43] In Manchester, too, whenever chances presented themselves and against the grain of the new trend in collaborationist politics in the city,[44] he 'pestered' the editors of Manchester papers 'with letters in defence of Mazzini or in explanation of revolutionary enterprises'.[45] In the *National Reformer*, which circulated widely, Adams's writings were suffused with his radical republican thoughts upon key issues of the day. Whilst Bradlaugh and his co-editor, the mercurial Joseph Barker, devoted their time to debunking the Scriptures, Adams defiantly censured the 'criminal' policies of Napoleon III, exposed Palmerston's connivances with the French leader, championed the cause of Garibaldi and rallied behind the North when the American Civil War broke out in 1861.[46] In respect of reviving interest at home for securing democratic reforms, Adams railed against the privileges of and anachronistic powers exercised by the House of Lords.[47] The policy of demystifying the powers of the monarchy, already begun by him in the *Investigator* in December 1858 with an article on one of his Cromwellian heroes, Sir John Elliot, who had challenged the tyrannical rule of Charles I, was now continued with vigour.[48] Referring to the French invasion scare of 1859, Adams wrote an open letter in the *Reformer* to Prince Albert reminding him that when the country prepared for war, the working classes for their part did so on the understanding that 'The Throne is not applauded; when we volunteer it is for the defence of the Country, not the Crown.'[49] According to Bradlaugh's daughter, Hypatia Bonner, 'Such was the eloquence of his articles impeaching the oppressor, or pleading the cause of the oppressed that it quickened the blood in the veins of his readers.'[50]

In 1862 Adams, by now a family man, was again unemployed and living in considerable hardship back in London. A temporary respite from poverty was offered in the form of a post as paid secretary of the Central Committee of the Friends of Poland at its offices in Southampton Street, Strand.[51] By the end of May 1863, however, he was in the fortunate position of being able to resign on the understanding of becoming a political journalist in Newcastle upon Tyne. The reason for leaving this radical pressure group, like the explanation for joining, was largely owing to Bradlaugh. Joseph Cowen Jr, the leading radical republican in the north of England, successful Tyneside industrialist and proprietor of the *Newcastle Weekly Chronicle*, had been making enquiries about Adams's journalistic work. Ideologically they were already close: both were members of the Friends of Italy and part of the radical fraternity which embraced Mazzini and the Orsini group. On Bradlaugh's recommendation, Cowen invited Adams to write a weekly political article over the signature of 'Ironside', with the prospect of obtaining a permanent position. Within eighteen months Adams was editor-in-chief, a position he kept until virtually the turn of the twentieth century. During this long editorial reign he earned a reputation both as a first-rate political columnist and as a hard-working, independently minded innovator and propagandist of a quality radical newspaper.[52] He turned the *Weekly*, stablemate of Cowen's highly successful *Daily Chronicle*, from a dull provincial sheet into one of the finest news magazines in England. By the mid-1870s, the *Daily* could claim sales in excess of 40,000 per day, the largest in the north-east, and the *Weekly*, in excess of 31,000, the largest of its kind in the north of England. They also had news and press agencies as far apart as London, New York, Paris and Antwerp.[53] For its instructing qualities, as well as its advanced radicalism, Adams's *Weekly* came to attract international praise. One competent American critic, Paul Carus, the Positivist-inspired editor of the *Open Court*, a Chicago journal with a high intellectual standard, described the *Weekly* as 'the best in the world'.[54] Even Cowen, himself, who always liked to exercise complete proprietorial control, yielded in the face of the paper's enormous political and business success. From the early 1870s Adams was given virtually a free editorial hand when his employer publicly acknowledged the fact that the *Weekly* was 'Adams's paper'.[55]

A key reason for Adams's sustained success stemmed from the composition of over 500 letters written under the pseudonym of 'Ironside', into which work he put, according to one close observer, 'not only the whole of his thought but many fine qualities of style'.[56] The choice of 'Ironside' as a title was a brilliant move. For the general readers, it was a constant reminder of the region's identity as a centre of heavy industry, one made world-famous by their labours in shipbuilding and repair, armaments manufacture and coal mining. For the politically aware, it was welcomed as a Cromwellian icon[57] around which to rekindle that indigenous republican spirit and reverence for the Commonwealth past, which had so inspired the Newcastle Chartist Republican Brotherhood of the mid-1850s.[58]

Between them during the 1860s Adams and Cowen created a vibrant radical political culture from the offices of the two *Chronicles* in central Newcastle.[59] Its focal points were an awareness of and demand for universal suffrage, moral republicanism, trade union rights, co-operatives and liberty of the subject. By 1867, in conjunction with the role played by the advanced platform politics of the Northern Reform League, Adams's work as a political propagandist had helped place Cowen where he wanted to be – at the head of an aggressive radicalism or 'militant democracy'.[60] Not surprisingly, Cowen's immense popularity as an ultra-radical made him an obvious successor to his more moderate father as radical-Liberal MP for Newcastle, when the latter died in 1873.

To Adams, author of a pamphlet on manhood suffrage,[61] the 1867 Reform Act represented only a partial victory. Joseph Cowen Sr was again returned at the top of the poll in Newcastle in the general election of November 1868.[62] However, in such boroughs as Morpeth in the nearby coalfield, it became apparent that the pitmen were still excluded from the vote on account of the peculiar tenure on which they held their houses. Adams considered this anomaly to be a gross injustice and, with advice from his friend Thomas Burt, the Northumberland miners' leader, committed the *Weekly* to a franchise crusade on their behalf in 1869.[63]

Against a background on the 'coaly Tyne', where political progress and disappointment had become juxtaposed, the year 1871 was full of drama, not least for two important events: the long industrial strike known as the Nine Hours Movement and the famous speech in early November by the ambitious politician, Sir Charles Dilke, who openly speculated about abolishing the monarchy. Both affairs briefly elevated Newcastle into the national consciousness and public mind. The Nine Hours Movement has been extensively researched,[64] but biographers of Dilke have paid little attention to the grass-roots context which promoted his notorious speech.[65] Some work has been done by Margot Finn[66] and Nigel Todd[67] regarding Cowen's groundwork in the affair. However, a clearer view of the propitious circumstances in which Dilke found himself being carried away in his speech can be more firmly established by exploring the nature of the republican publicity and impetus offered by Adams himself in the *Weekly Chronicle* during that year.

The early months of 1871 witnessed the build-up of a strong labour organization for a nine-hour working day. Against a background of economic depression, the strike movement started on 25 May and ended on 9 October when the employers conceded. Not surprisingly, the engineers' victory generated considerable and sustained excitement; it also raised the hopes of other groups of workers who wanted to follow in their footsteps. Whilst this industrial conflict was going on, republican clubs, some of whose members were also out on strike, reconstituted themselves in Newcastle and Gateshead, and new ones sprang up in the nearby pit villages. Inspired by the establishment of the Third French Republic in September 1870, then incensed by news at home during 1871 of the Prince of Wales's disreputable behaviour and of the Queen's persistent absence from public life but continued demands for bigger allowances, the movement went from strength to strength.

The organizational side of the Newcastle Republican Club's activities was in the hands of a number of talented working men including T. J. Bayfield, a candidate for the Gateshead and Newcastle School Boards, Thomas Gregson, an ex-Chartist, and James Birkett and James Mckendrick, both of whom were involved in the Nine Hours Strike.[68] The membership – in excess of a hundred and never less than fifty over the next three years – was predominantly male, although at least three women appear to have taken an active part in social activities.[69] The club met regularly at the Mechanics' Institute on New Bridge Street or, as was the case when Dilke addressed them, in the larger Lecture Rooms in Nelson Street. In order to co-ordinate their activities more effectively, closer links were forged with other branches nearby through the establishment in April 1872 of a union known as the Northern Republican League.[70]

W. E. Adams wholeheartedly welcomed the setting-up of the Newcastle Republican Club because, like the Cheltenham Association he belonged to in 1851, it offered 'the best possible school in which to train honest, bold, pure and practical politicians'.[71] What needs to be stressed here is how actively Adams now tried from his influential position at the *Weekly* to promote an interest in and an understanding of Mazzinian republicanism. Under his 'Ironside' leader letters and elsewhere as 'Robin Goodfellow', the impish author of the sardonic 'Gossip's bowl' column, he made a broad-based attack on those structures of privilege which stood in the way of the cause of democracy. The first object for bitter invective was Napoleon III, whose fall from power in August 1870 was enthusiastically welcomed as a fundamental prerequisite for initiating a transformed society in Europe.[72] Recalling the French emperor's treachery and tyranny of many years, Adams pronounced on the eve of his decisive defeat at the hands of the Prussians, that 'Republics are the only natural guardians of liberty. They never fail.'[73]

Napoleon's demise – 'nothing more than a bloody panorama' – was then used as a basis for attacking 'the evils and superstitions of monarchy' worldwide.[74] Here he systematically stripped away the centuries of mystique surrounding the reverence for and worship of kings and queens, showing clearly that without them the throne was nothing. There followed a number of blistering attacks on what he referred to as the 'high-born lounging classes', the practice of governmental jobbery and the powers of the unreformed House of Lords.[75] It was in this context that Adams expressed a set of anti-monarchical sentiments concerning court scandal and financial extravagance. They were of a kind which Antony Taylor's recent research has shown were both prevalent elsewhere and long-standing within the radical tradition.[76] The Prince of Wales, for example, by his involvement in the Mordaunt Divorce Case, was held up as an unedifying representative of the 'lounging class';[77] while the Queen, by her long seclusion and demands for dowries or pensions, had allowed the Crown to become 'little more than a gilded and pretentious sham'.[78]

Adams, however, was not just concerned with expense-based critiques of the monarchy. Two other issues surrounding the activities of the Crown also drew invective at this time. Firstly, he criticized the fact that members of the royal family were paying visits to the deposed Napoleon III at Chislehurst and inviting him and his family to meet them at Marlborough House. Such associations were particularly worrying for republicans because they lent credence to reports already circulating that English aristocrats, like Lord Granville, were trying to aid Napoleon's political manoeuvrings towards a restoration of the French Empire.[79] Secondly, he tried to draw parallels between a local issue over the preservation of common land and the Crown's attempts elsewhere to restore such lands to the monarch. In Newcastle, a long-standing dispute over access to public land came to a head in 1870 with a successful defence of preserving the Town Moor, the city's 'green lungs', against further encroachment by enclosure.[80] By contrast, Adams was alarmed at the ways in which the centralizing impulses of the state were removing the people's freedom to roam through common land at Hainault and Epping, and in the New Forest; in all three it was the case that access to open spaces was being filched from the public and returned to the Crown.[81] From all these concerns he reasoned by early August 1871: 'The members of the House of Brunswick must not be surprised if respect for royalty should not gradually decline in England.'[82]

Interestingly, a week later he was engaged in responding to this statement in a way which also served as yet another dimension to his politicizing campaign, namely the review of republican books in the *Weekly*'s 'Literary notices' column. Since working people all over Newcastle were now openly debating the future of the monarchy, his inclusion of a review of *What would be Legal Steps towards a Republic?* was both apt and well timed. The pamphlet, written anonymously by 'J.W.' and published in London by Edward Truelove, the Radical bookseller, proposed five legal steps towards establishing a republic, in response to the question posed by the title. Adams agreed with four of them – more political teaching, the removal of ecclesiastical legislators, abolition of the House of Lords and the repeal of the Act of Settlement – but he thought that an unrestricted suffrage would be infinitely preferable to the author's fifth suggestion of an educational qualification.[83] For Adams, republicanism and democracy were inseparable, a position he made plain again, much to the delight of the unenfranchized pitmen, with articles through August on the need for more rational and radical parliamentary reforms.[84]

Sir Charles Dilke's speech in Newcastle upon Tyne on Monday 6 November should therefore be viewed against a background in which a dynamic set of circumstances – Adams's republicanism, working-class anti-monarchism, euphoria over the Nine Hours Day victory and the pitmen's tenacity in pursuit of the vote – enjoyed a coterminous if not overlapping relationship.[85] By 1871, Dilke, the MP for Chelsea, was a rising star in the Liberal firmament. He had a shrewd awareness of the importance and potential of organized labour, and a vision of how it might be harnessed in order to push the party along the road to radical reforms.[86] In Parliament he enjoyed a reputation as an advanced radical, not least for his anti-monarchical rhetoric and action in voting against the Queen's request for royal grants when they came before the House in February 1871.[87]

In the autumn of 1871 Dilke, in order to enhance his standing country-wide, arranged to deliver at great industrial centres a series of platform speeches advocating a redistribution of seats so as to make parliamentary representation more equitable.[88] The first lecture was delivered in Manchester where 'he stuck firmly to his brief'.[89] The second lecture was scheduled for Newcastle upon Tyne on Monday evening, 6 November. Prior to the event Adams duly advertised the details. Readers were assured of the prospect of 'a great treat' since Dilke was going to 'deliver an address on general politics' in the popular meeting place afforded by the Lecture Rooms in Nelson Street.[90] Intriguingly, at some point between the Manchester speech and Dilke's address in Newcastle, the subject of 'general politics', or even the original brief on the redistribution of seats, metamorphosed into the more appealing but topical and ultimately controversial subject of 'The state of representation and the cost of royalty'.

Several reasons can be suggested for this change of subject for the Newcastle speech. Firstly, Dilke's visit was not an isolated event. Already, Charles Bradlaugh, the leading republican journalist and politician, had made three visits and was known to be preparing for a fourth in November.[91] At one of these, held on 20 February 1871, he had addressed the Newcastle Republican Club on the subject of *The Impeachment of the House of Brunswick*, subsequently published in 1872.[92] According to the historian, Feargus D'Arcy, this lecture 'constituted one of the most searching exposés of the extravagance, incompetence and corruption of the Hanoverian dynasty to appear in print'.[93] Another visitor was George Odger, the prominent London trade unionist and a vigorous republican orator between 1871 and 1873.[94] He was invited at the end of June 1871 to address the public inauguration of the Newcastle and Gateshead Republican Club at the Lecture Room; the large audience was, it is clear, suitably inspired by his stirring lecture on 'The government of the people, by the people, and for the people'.[95] Secondly, Dilke's host in Newcastle was not, as some historians have suggested,[96] his fellow radical Liberal MP Joseph Cowen Sr, but the latter's son of the same name, whose politics were far more advanced than his father's. In respect of the rise of republicanism, as Nigel Todd points out, 'Joseph Cowen Jr stoked the flames in November 1871'.[97] We might safely assume, therefore, from this turbulent state of affairs, that Cowen Jr had informed Dilke of how Bradlaugh's and Odger's speeches had already warmed up the platform atmosphere at the Republican Club. This would fit in with the opening remarks made by Dilke in his speech on the eventful night of 6 November. Before a 'very crowded and enthusiastic audience' and following a rapturous introduction by Joseph Cowen Jr, who took the chair and was seated alongside Bayfield of the Nine Hours League, Dilke rose and responded with these revealing remarks:

> I am announced, I see, to speak to-night on Representation and Royalty, and although you may have read my remarks on the former subject made a few days ago in Manchester, I will make one or two further observations. On the other hand, I understand that some of you are exercised in your minds about Royalty, and I desire to compare notes with you on the subject. (Loud applause)[98]

Cowen's influence also extended to persuading Dilke to stay another day – Tuesday 7 November – in order for him to speak at the inaugural soirée of the Ouseburn Engine Works, a co-operative workshop established in Newcastle to employ those workers who had been sacked by their employers for supporting the Nine Hours League during the strike.[99]

The public outcry provoked by Dilke's speech, his more restrained language at subsequent venues in the face of a boisterous loyalism fanned by the announcement of the Prince of Wales's near-fatal illness on 23 November, and his steady retreat thereafter from financial criticisms of the monarchy, have, like his motives, been well documented.[100] The immediate reaction on Tyneside however has been overlooked, save for noting the general outlines of a continued expansion of republican activity, on the one hand, amongst the working classes and, on the other, a 'loyalty fever' generated both by the local Conservative press[101] and an embarrassed Newcastle City Council.[102]

For Adams and Cowen, there was nothing extraordinary about the criticisms Dilke made in his 'Cost of the Crown' speech. He had uttered nothing stronger than was delivered by Bradlaugh either earlier in the year or on the following Sunday, 12

November, when, at the same venue, the latter spoke on 'The coming Republic'.[103] Adams however, took full advantage of the anti-monarchical ferment in order to poke fun at the authorities, who were alarmed by their city's tarnished image. In the devilish Robin Goodfellow mode, he began the 'Gossip's bowl' thus:

> Newcastle loyalty is under a cloud. The warm reception accorded to such able and outspoken orators as Sir Charles Dilke and Mr. Bradlaugh appears to have compromised the ancient repute of the town for enthusiastic adherence to the Altar and the Throne. What a pestilent hotbed of revolution that lecture room in Nelson Street must be! Would it not be well to raze it to its foundations, if it has any? Nothing short of this will get rid of the plague.[104]

Elsewhere, his comments were more measured and perceptive: 'It is idle to pretend that Royalty, even among the ignorant and dissipated, can maintain its place in public favour. The Republican movement however, as I have before endeavoured to show, is based on a higher principle than that of mere economy.'[105]

Years later, by which time radicals were bitterly attacking Dilke for his close friendship with the Prince of Wales,[106] Adams roundly condemned, as Dorothy Thompson puts it, 'both the message and the messenger':[107]

> What would be the value of a revolution which had for its roots the accidental unpopularity of a prince of the blood? What again, was the worth of that paltry cry about the Cost of the Crown, raised by Sir Charles Dilke before his own tremendous lapse?[108]

Ironically, it was Joseph Cowen Jr, by a symbolic gesture late in November 1871, who reminded friend and foe alike that 'the republican question is certainly not a personal question'.[109] At a banquet held in honour of the MP and leading nonconformist, Edward Miall, from the chair Cowen opened the after-dinner proceedings by proposing a toast 'to drink to the health of the Queen'.[110]

Between 1872 and 1876 Adams remained active in publicizing arguments for a republic as a more rational, coherent and democratic form of government. Until it came about he stressed, 'the spirit of flunkeyism would prevail'.[111] In respect of these goals, two issues of national importance particularly absorbed his energies: the campaign by the north-east's pitmen to secure their right to the vote; and the outright opposition of many radicals to Disraeli's plans to emphasize the Crown's role as the symbol of the new age of Empire.

By the early part of 1873 the Newcastle and Gateshead Republican Club, like many others in the Northern Republican League, appears to have run out of energy. A faithful group of activists however, including Bayfield and Mckendrick, moved without difficulty into supporting the 'neo-Chartist programme of the revived Northern Reform League'.[112] Numerous meetings of the League were held across the north-east in the summer and autumn of 1873, particularly in support of the pitmen's franchise campaign. In his leader column, Adams was arguably the campaign's best image-builder. He gave full coverage to their meetings and rallies, publicized their grievances and way of life, and encouraged them, in the wake of the agricultural labourers' strike of 1872, to see themselves as 'pioneers of political progress'.[113] Such popular pressure did prove effective when, backed by an economic boycott of the Morpeth shopkeepers, the Northumberland miners' applications to be admitted to the franchise were recognized by the Revision Court in the borough of Morpeth in September 1873. Six months later, Adams and his wife were among the honoured guests invited to a temperance banquet to celebrate Thomas Burt's historic parliamentary election victory as the first miners' MP.[114]

In 1876 Benjamin Disraeli's Royal Titles Bill, which elevated Victoria's title from 'Queen' to 'Empress of India', revived anti-monarchical sentiments among radicals. They interpreted it as a challenge to popular and inherited constitutional liberties.[115] For Adams, the title was both 'tawdry' and a slide into 'a new form of Caesarism'.[116] Posters, too, went up on the walls of buildings in Newcastle reflecting this concern. Two lines of one stated:

> Disraeli's feet have digged Britannia's grave;
> He made an Emperor, as he made a slave.[117]

Pointedly, Adams warned later that 'Monarchy itself is not so sacred an institution that the English people will always be inclined to witness the subordination of popular liberties'.[118] Queen Victoria may well have been troubled by this kind of political discontent from amongst her Newcastle subjects. According to Nigel Todd, 'For "some years" during the 1870s she reputedly had a disdain for Newcastle upon Tyne, ordering "the blinds of her railway carriage" to be "drawn down whenever she passed through Newcastle on her way to and from Scotland".'[119]

Adams continued from time to time to argue the case for republicanism – as in admiring articles on the frame of government in the USA,[120] or sounding a discordant note over the 'mania' surrounding the Queen's Golden Jubilee celebrations in June 1887.[121] Increasingly, however, from 1875 his moral republicanism found expression in support of a number of locally based campaigns, namely over improving access to knowledge, upholding children's rights, animal welfare and protection of the environment.

Between 1874 and 1880 Adams was an active member of the committee which, in the face of much local opposition, successfully campaigned to open a free public library service for the city.[122] He firmly believed that a republican government would not work until every citizen was educated and able to reason out and perform his or her duties to society. To hasten that process was, in Adams's view, one of the functions of libraries. He also did much to build up the public library's stock on the subject of republicanism. In 1876, for example, in conjunction with Julian Harney, who was living in Boston, USA, he facilitated the acceptance of a transatlantic gift of a large collection of books on the workings of republican government in the Commonwealth of Massachusetts.[123] Later, in 1902, he presented a large number of radical books (about 200) from his own library to the flourishing institution. Among these were works by Bradlaugh, Harney, Linton, George J. Holyoake and Thomas Cooper.[124]

Adams also believed that republicanism as a system of morals should be taught from an early age. This was the thinking behind his initiative of encouraging children not only to play, but also to develop feelings of kindness which would act as a basis for establishing a 'duteous people' in adult life. To this end he personally took the lead by forming a 'Children's corner' in the *Weekly* in 1876. Here, as the genial 'Uncle Toby' and centred on the 'Dicky Bird Society', he stressed kindness and compassion to animals as an important method of moral and mental training: by 1890 the society had a membership worldwide of 300,000.[125]

This children's initiative, of course, enjoyed a symbiotic relationship with his campaigns to protect animals from cruelty. Through the columns of the *Weekly*, for example, he would reproach all who were guilty of succumbing to those fashion trends that either involved the killing of birds for their plumage in order to decorate ladies' bonnets, or the culling of seals to make expensive garments. In both instances the targets for his criticism were the monied ranks – a fact that did not appear to inhibit the RSPCA from awarding him in 1879 a diploma for his sterling work against the cruelty of fashion.[126]

A variety of motives inspired Adams's involvement in protecting or conserving the environment. He had long enjoyed using open spaces either to relax or for attending political meetings when living in both London and Manchester.[127] He also appreciated the fact that such places provided an important habitat for wildlife. His particular contributions to the growing conservation debate in Newcastle during the late 1870s and 1880s took various forms: he supported civic attempts to conserve two large open spaces – the Town Moor and the Leazes – for the people, free from further urban encroachment; undertook the planting of trees on both as well as along the city's major thoroughfares; and helped develop Portland Park, Jesmond, for such rational recreational activity as the game of bowls.[128]

On the face of it these small pieces of homely reform appear unconnected. They were, however, all inspired by Mazzinian notions about what constituted public duty and citizenship.[129] Both were essential virtues for the successful introduction of a republic. His concern for free libraries, kindness towards animals and parks for the people were all part of a pattern of thought, which derived from lofty ideals about service to and respect for all living things in the ethical community. On these issues, of course, if Adams was not working outside the sphere of contemporary, advanced Liberal politics, then, guided by his idealism, he was certainly at its cutting edge.

Adams's republican activities are important in a number of ways. His eventful career suggests that republican sentiments were not an episodic phenomenon; rather, they were an integral part of the radical mainstream both in Cheltenham and across the north-east. Secondly, by his expense-based critiques of the Crown in 1871, Adams showed that he was sufficiently pragmatic to adapt his idealism to the specific issue of the day: anti-monarchical outbursts and classical republican arguments were not therefore incompatible and could be complementary. Lastly,

Adams by his attraction to the idealist and abstract moral republicanism of Mazzini, underlines the point made recently regarding a new research agenda for the whole subject.[130] There is a need to move beyond the monarchy–anti-monarchy dichotomy, pay more attention to the arguments for the alternative forms of government and assess how effective republican thinking was in promoting the end of what its adherents saw as both anachronistic and a bar to political modernization. For Adams, the starting-point was always to be the destruction of the roots of privilege and oppression, but not to substitute new restrictions and tyrannies in place of the old. Drawing on the well-known lines of Byron, he noted in his *Memoirs*:

> I wish men to be free,
> As much from mobs as Kings, from you as me.[131]

As the twentieth century approached, Linton, his old friend and mentor, wrote to him encouragingly about the cause: 'we are indeed though still far from the Republic. Yet the Future is sure.'[132]

Notes

I would like to thank the following for their help in the preparation of this essay: Dorothy Thompson, Joan Hugman, Stephen Roberts, Antony Taylor and David Nash.

    1. David Jones, *Chartism and the Chartists* (London, 1975). There are at least nine direct references to Adams's involvement listed in the index.
    2. Ibid., 212.
    3. See, for example, Stephen Roberts, *Radical Politicians and Poets in Early Victorian Britain* (Lampeter and New York, 1993); Owen R. Ashton, *W. E. Adams: Chartist, Radical and Journalist (1832–1960)* (Whitley Bay, 1991).
    4. Margot Finn, *After Chartism: Class and Nation in English Radical Politics, 1848–1874* (Cambridge, 1993), 180–7.
    5. Maurice Milne, 'William Edwin Adams', in J. O. Baylen and N. J. Gossman (eds.), *Biographical Dictionary of Modern British Radicals*, III: *1870–1914* (Brighton, 1988), 14–18. See also Ashton, *W. E. Adams*, 112.
    6. Thomas Burt, *An Autobiography* (London, 1924), 219–20. Alexander McDonald was also elected at the same time as the miners' MP for Stafford. For Burt, see Lowell J. Satre, *Thomas Burt, Miners' MP, 1837–1922* (London, 1999).

7. Alun Munslow and Owen R. Ashton (eds.), *Henry Demarest Lloyd's Critiques of American Capitalism, 1881–1903* (Lampeter and New York, 1995).
8. Adrian Courtenay, 'Cheltenham Spa and the Berkeleys, 1832–1848: pocket borough and patron?' *Midland History*, 18 (1992), *passim*.
9. W. E. Adams, *Memoirs of a Social Atom* (2 vols. in 1, London, 1903; repr. New York, 1968, with an Introduction by John Saville), 23.
10. For an assessment of the effectiveness of Close's clerical rule, see Owen R. Ashton, 'Clerical control and radical responses in Cheltenham Spa, 1838–1848', *Midland History*, 8 (1983) and A. F. Munden, 'Radicalism versus Evangelicalism in Victorian Cheltenham', *Southern History*, 5 (1983).
11. Adams, *Memoirs*, 119.
12. *Northern Star*, 8 April 1848; see also R. G. Gammage, *History of the Chartist Movement* (facsimile of the 1894, second edn, repr. London, 1969), 306–7.
13. Adams, *Memoirs*, 170–2; see also R. G. Gammage, *Reminiscences of a Chartist* (repr. by the Society for the Study of Labour History, 1983, with an Introduction by W. H. Maehl), particularly 31–3.
14. For an appreciation of the role of J. B. Leno and Thomas Frost, see Dorothy Thompson, *The Chartists* (London, 1984).
15. Christopher Godfrey, *Chartist Lives: The Anatomy of a Working-Class Movement* (London and New York, 1987), particularly 457–8.
16. Adams, *Memoirs*, 71.
17. Ibid., 151.
18. Ashton, *W. E. Adams*, 135.
19. Ibid.; see also *Cheltenham Free Press*, 17 May 1851.
20. Adams, *Memoirs*, 173.
21. For an appreciation of Mazzinian thought and contribution to English radical politics, see Gregory Claeys, 'Mazzini, Kossuth, and British radicalism, 1848–1854', *Journal of British Studies*, 28, 3 (July 1989), 225–61. See also Adams's tribute to Mazzini when he died, in his 'Ironside' column, *Newcastle Weekly Chronicle*, 16 March 1872.
22. For Linton's understanding of republicanism, see the eponymous title and exposition by him in the *National Reformer*, 16 June 1867.
23. Adams, *Memoirs*, 266.
24. Ibid., 320. These comments were, of course, written in the 1890s. They are more measured and reflective than those appearing in the *Weekly Chronicle* in the early 1870s. Compare, for example, with those cited below, n. 73.
25. Ibid., 267.
26. Ibid., 268.
27. Dorothy Thompson, *Queen Victoria: Gender and Power*

(London, 1990), 92–3.

28. Adams, *Memoirs*, 268.
29. *Cheltenham Free Press*, 8 June 1850; see also Ashton, *W. E. Adams*, 51 and 140–1.
30. Report of proceedings and presentation address to W. E. Adams, with list of subscribers, 6 June 1898. Copy in Newcastle Central Library.
31. Adams, *Memoirs*, 270.
32. Finn, *After Chartism*, 166–7.
33. C. S. Nicholl (ed.), *The Dictionary of National Biography: Missing Persons* (Oxford, 1993), 622–3.
34. Finn, *After Chartism*, 166. The society's branches in Britain contributed over £12,000 to Mazzini's and Garibaldi's activities.
35. *Newcastle Weekly Chronicle*, 8 January 1898: 'Gossip's bowl'.
36. See, for example, MS Eng. 180, letters to W. E. Adams from W. J. Linton, 1855–97, Houghton Library, Harvard University Library. Microfilm copy available in Newcastle Central Library.
37. Adams, *Memoirs*, 376–7.
38. Aaron Watson, *A Newspaper Man's Memories* (London, 1925), 52.
39. Adams, *Memoirs*, 314.
40. Ibid., 314.
41. John Saville, 'William Edwin Adams, Chartist and Radical', in John Saville and Joyce Bellamy (eds.), *Dictionary of Labour Biography* (London, 1984), VII, 1–4 particularly 2.
42. Adams, *Memoirs*, 383–95 for Adams's life in Manchester and an appreciation of its Free Library, Working Men's College and Hallé concerts, which led him to write (p.387): 'So Manchester was not such a bad place after all.' For its intellectual influences on undermining the radical challenges during this period, see Martin Hewitt, *The Emergence of Stability in the Industrial City: Manchester, 1832–67* (Aldershot, 1996), in particular 262–93.
43. Hypatia Bradlaugh Bonner, *Charles Bradlaugh: A Record of his Life and Work* (2 vols. in 1, London, 1908), I, 71.
44. Hewitt, *Emergence of Stability*, 283.
45. Adams, *Memoirs*, 392.
46. See, for example, *National Reformer*, 16 June, 21 July, 18 August, 22 September, 17 November, 8, 15 December 1860; 12 January, 27 July 1861; 23 August 1862.
47. Ibid., 14 April, 9 June 1860.
48. *The Investigator*, 15 December 1858: 'Sketches of Commonwealth men'.
49. *National Reformer*, 7 July 1860.
50. Bonner, *Charles Bradlaugh*, I, 123.

51. Finn, *After Chartism*, 214–15.
52. For a discussion of the public visibility of the nineteenth-century newspaper editor, see J. H. Weiner (ed.), *Innovators and Preachers: The Role of the Editor in Victorian England* (Westport, 1985), particularly the Introduction.
53. Maurice Milne, *Newspapers of Northumberland and Durham* (Newcastle, 1971), 65–8 and 69; *Newcastle Weekly Chronicle*, 25 December 1875.
54. A. R. Schoyen, *The Chartist Challenge: A Portrait of George Julian Harney* (London, 1958), 275.
55. Milne, *William Edwin Adams*, 65.
56. Watson, *Memories*, 55.
57. Roger Howell Jr, 'Cromwell and the imagery of nineteenth century radicalism: the example of Joseph Cowen', *Archaeologia Aeliana*, 5th series, 10 (1982), 193–7, particularly 194; J. P. D. Dunbabin, 'Oliver Cromwell's popular image in nineteenth century England', in J. S. Bromley and E. H. Kossmann (eds.), *Britain and the Netherlands* (The Hague, 1975), V, 141–63; See also Eugenio F. Biagini, *Liberty, Retrenchment and Reform: Popular Liberalism in the Age of Gladstone, 1860–1880* (Cambridge, 1992), 41–50, for an assessment of Oliver Cromwell as a source of inspiration for radical republicans like Adams and Cowen.
58. Susan Scott, 'The *Northern Tribune*: a north east radical magazine', *Bulletin of the North East Labour History Society*, 19 (1985), 9–17. Scott explores the nature and vitality of republicanism in Newcastle led by Joseph Cowen Jr with the help of the veteran Chartist, George J. Harney.
59. William Duncan, *The Life of Joseph Cowen MP* (London and Newcastle, 1904), 24–5.
60. Nigel Todd, *The Militant Democracy: Joseph Cowen and Victorian Radicalism* (Tyne and Wear, 1991), *passim*; see also Joan Hugman, 'Joseph Cowen of Newcastle and radical liberalism', unpublished Ph.D. thesis, University of Northumbria at Newcastle (1993), *passim*.
61. W. E. Adams, *An Argument for Complete Suffrage* (London, Manchester and Newcastle, 1860).
62. T. J. Nossiter, *Influence, Opinion and Political Idioms in Reformed England 1832–74* (Brighton, 1975), 160.
63. Adams, *Memoirs*, 537–47.
64. E. Allen, J. F. Clarke, N. McCord and D. J. Rowe, *The North East Engineers' Strike of 1871* (Newcastle, 1971).
65. See, for example, Stephen Gwynn and Gertrude M. Tuckwell, *The Life of the Rt. Hon. Sir Charles Dilke* (2 vols., London, 1917), I; Roy Jenkins, *Sir Charles Dilke: A Victorian Tragedy* (London, 1965); David

Nicholls, *The Lost Prime Minister: A Life of Sir Charles Dilke* (London, 1995).
66. Finn, *After Chartism*, 283–4 and 293–4.
67. Todd, *Militant Democracy*, 93–5.
68. For Newcastle Republican Club activities, see, for example, *Newcastle Weekly Chronicle*, 25 February, 4 March, 27 May, 1 July, 18 November 1871.
69. Ibid., 26 October and 7 December 1877. The three women were a Miss Gallon, Miss Clark and Miss Atkinson.
70. Ibid., 6 April 1872.
71. Ibid., 4 and 25 March 1871: 'Gossip's bowl'.
72. Ibid., 20 and 27 August, 10 September, 15 October 1870: Ironside's letters.
73. Ibid., 2 April 1870: 'The new coup d'état'. After the declaration of the Republic, Adams supported France against Prussia; see Ironside's letter 'The conduct of the war', *Newcastle Weekly Chronicle*, 15 October 1870. After the establishment of the Paris Commune in March 1871, Adams remained undeterred by its 'wild proceedings'; see Ironside's letter 'The republican movement', *Newcastle Weekly Chronicle*, 15 April 1871.
74. Ibid., 22 October 1870, Ironside's letter.
75. Ibid., 26 February 1870: 'The lounging class' by Ironside; 18 February 1871: 'The cost of the royal family', by Ironside; 22 July 1871: 'The defeat of the Army Bill' by the House of Lords, by Ironside.
76. Antony Taylor, '*Reynolds's Newspaper*, Opposition to monarchy and the radical anti-jubilee: Britain's anti-monarchist tradition reconsidered', *Historical Research: Bulletin of the Institute of Historical Research*, 68, 167 (October 1995), 318–37; and also his 'Republicanism reappraised: anti-monarchism and the English radical tradition, 1850–1872', in James Vernon (ed.), *Re-reading the Constitution: New Narratives in the Political History of England's Long Nineteenth Century* (Cambridge, 1996), 154–78.
77. *Newcastle Weekly Chronicle*, 5 March 1870: 'The Mordaunt scandal', by Ironside.
78. Ibid., 29 July 1871: 'The new royal pension', by Ironside.
79. Ibid., 22 October 1870, 24 June and 5 August 1871.
80. Antony Taylor, '"Commons-stealers", "Land-grabbers" and "Jerry-builders": space, popular radicalism and the politics of public access in London, 1848–80', *International Review of Social History*, 40, 3 (December 1995), 383–407, particularly 386 and 405.
81. *Newcastle Weekly Chronicle*, 17 June and 29 July 1871: Ironside's letters.
82. Ibid., 5 August 1871: 'Royalty and loyalty', Ironside's letter.
83. Ibid.: 'Literary notices'.

84. Ibid., 19 August 1871.
85. Todd, *Militant Democracy*, 92.
86. For the view that Dilke was a Liberal modernizer, see Dorothy Thompson, 'The fallen mighty', review article on Nicholls's, *The Lost Prime Minister: A Life of Sir Charles Dilke*, *Times Higher Educational Supplement*, 18 August 1995, 2; and John Belchem, *Popular Radicalism in Nineteenth Century Britain* (London, 1996), 122.
87. Feargus A. D'Arcy, 'Charles Bradlaugh and the English republican movement 1867–1878', *Historical Journal*, 25, 2 (June 1982), 374.
88. Gwynn and Tuckwell, *Dilke*, I, 138.
89. Ibid.; and Jenkins, *Dilke*, 69.
90. *Newcastle Weekly Chronicle*, 4 November 1871: 'Gossip's bowl'.
91. Ibid., 19 November 1871, front-page advertisements. Bradlaugh also came to Newcastle in July and September 1870 and February 1871.
92. Ibid., 25 February 1871.
93. D'Arcy, 'Charles Bradlaugh', 373.
94. John Breuilly, Gottfried Niedhart and Antony Taylor (eds.), *The Era of the Reform League: English Labour and Radical Politics 1857–1872* (Mannheim, 1995), 346–7.
95. *Newcastle Weekly Chronicle*, 1 July 1871.
96. Finn, *After Chartism*, 294, where no distinction is drawn between Joseph Cowen Sr, the more moderate Radical and an MP, and his son Joseph Cowen Jr, the ultra-radical, who only became an MP in 1874 after his father's death.
97. Todd, *Militant Democracy*, 93.
98. *Newcastle Daily Chronicle*, 7 November 1871, and *Newcastle Weekly Chronicle*, 11 November 1871. Both papers carried verbatim reports of the speech.
99. Finn, *After Chartism*, 294.
100. See, for example, Nicholls, *The Lost Prime Minister*, and n. 65 above.
101. See, for example, *Newcastle Courant*, 10 November 1871: Editorial; *North of England Farmer*, 11, 18, 25 November and 2, 9, 16 December 1871.
102. Todd, *Militant Democracy*, 95. In their Loyalty Address, the Newcastle councillors referred, in relation to Dilke, to 'the scum that has appeared'.
103. *Newcastle Weekly Chronicle*, 18 November 1871: 'Mr. Bradlaugh in the north'.
104. Ibid.: 'Gossip's bowl'. Adams went on to satirize the feverish loyalist preparations by the 'middle classes' in Newcastle in support of the Crown.

105. Ibid., 25 November 1871: Ironside's letter 'What does she do with it?'
106. Taylor, 'Reynolds's Newspaper', 328. This was certainly the case by 1883.
107. Thompson, *Queen Victoria*, 107.
108. Adams, *Memoirs*, 330.
109. *Newcastle Weekly Chronicle*, 16 December 1871: extract from a commentary on the republican movement in Birmingham.
110. Ibid., 25 November 1871: banquet to Mr Miall, MP.
111. Ibid., 30 March 1872: Ironside's letter 'The House of Commons'.
112. Todd, *Militant Democracy*, 116.
113. *Newcastle Weekly Chronicle*, 21 June 1873: Ironside's letter on 'The miners' demonstration'.
114. Todd, *Militant Democracy*, 113–14; *Newcastle Weekly Chronicle*, 7 March 1874.
115. Taylor, 'Reynolds's Newspaper', 321–2.
116. *Newcastle Weekly Chronicle*, 18 March 1876: Ironside's letter on 'The Queen's title' and 1 April 1876: Ironside on 'Caesarism in England'; 11 May 1878: Ironside on 'Imperialism'.
117. Ibid., 1 April 1876: 'Gossip's bowl'.
118. Ibid., 17 May 1879: Ironside on 'The prerogative of the Crown'.
119. Todd, *Militant Democracy*, 80.
120. *Newcastle Weekly Chronicle*, 26 December 1874: Ironside's letter on 'The centenary of the American Republic'.
121. Ibid., 18 June 1887: 'Gossip's bowl'. Adams was relieved that 'luckily' the Jubilee treats 'cannot fall more than once in a lifetime'. He was to be proved wrong, but did not comment on the Diamond Jubilee in 1889.
122. Joan Knott, *The First Hundred Years, Newcastle upon Tyne City Libraries* (Newcastle Polytechnic School of Librarianship, Occasional Papers, no. 3, 1980), particularly 7–13.
123. Owen R. Ashton and Joan Hugman, 'George Julian Harney, Boston, U.S.A. and Newcastle upon Tyne, England, 1863–1888', *Proceedings of the Massachusetts Historical Society*, 107 (1995), *passim*.
124. *Newcastle Daily Chronicle*, 16 May 1996: tribute to Adams by Basil Anderton, City librarian.
125. Norman McCord, *British History 1815–1906* (Oxford, 1991), 455.
126. Ashton, *W. E. Adams*, 136–8.
127. Adams, *Memoirs*, 230 and 386.
128. Ashton, *Memoirs*, 140–1.
129. Interestingly, Adams's crusades were, in many ways, being

replicated at this time by the Secularist and Positivist, F. J. Gould, in the city of Leicester. See David Nash, *Secularism, Art and Freedom* (Leicester, 1992), 154–66.

130. David S. Nash, 'Re-assessing Victorian Republicanism', paper delivered at Leeds Centre of Victorian Studies Conference, 'Age of Equipoise? Re-assessing Mid-Victorian Britain', Trinity and All Saints, Leeds, July 1996.

131. Adams, *Memoirs*, 227.

132. MS Eng. 180, Houghton Library: Letter, 21 November 1892, Linton to Adams.

'A Reckless Spirit of Enterprise': Game-Preserving and Poaching in Nineteenth-Century Lancashire

JOHN E. ARCHER

Poaching is the epitome of both rural and social crime. It was generally committed by impoverished farm labourers who sought to feed their families and as such this activity was condoned by the bulk of the rural community, both farmers and labourers. This is how historians, myself included, have viewed this relatively uncomplicated crime.[1] On a subjective level it is difficult not to respond with admiration and an enthusiasm born out of hindsight for these men. Moreover this subjectivity appears all the more valid when it is supported by the more objective conclusion that the game laws were class-bound and totally iniquitous even in an age, such as the nineteenth century, not given to such sensibilities of thought.[2] It is therefore not surprising that historians of crime and rural society, such as David Jones, have found the subject an attractive one, particularly when research centred on the arable, eastern and southern counties where the capitalist market-led agrarian economy was most highly developed. This largely completed picture of poaching perhaps requires a few finishing touches, not least an examination of the decline of poaching in the last two decades of the century, before it can be mounted and framed in an exhibition of the nation's past legislative scandals.

However is poaching as a crime, both social and rural, really as straightforward? Have certain subtleties, nuances and complexities been overlooked or underplayed by historians? By concentrating on largely rural and arable counties in the southern half of the country they have consigned to oblivion great tracts of land which were neither so rural, so village-bound and agrarian nor necessarily predominantly arable. Counties such as Derbyshire, Cheshire, Lancashire and Yorkshire bear some kind of examination in order to determine whether game-preserving and poaching were universal in their similarities and impact. This essay is concerned with just one county, Lancashire, which does not immediately spring to the mind as a bastion of rural social crime and coverted landscapes. In examining this region one has to pose and answer fundamental questions concerning the amount and whereabouts of game preserves, the volume of poaching and the types of people involved. What emerges is a story of increasing complexity and variegation and one which, no doubt, could be replicated in other northern industrializing counties. An understanding of northern poaching can lead us far from the quiet of the game covers, since the paths stretch back to the towns and there branch out into the very heart, and a dark one at that, of Victorian fears: violence, gangs and the criminal classes. In effect this is a study of a rural crime but in an urbanizing environment.

To what extent does Lancashire repay historical attention either as a game-preserving county or as a region peopled by poachers? Barry Hines in his sensitive novel *The Gamekeeper* hints at an answer to the first of these questions when he noted that the world record for 12 August is held by a Lancashire shoot. On that day in 1915 eight guns dispatched 2,900 grouse at Abbeystead, north-east of Preston.[3] The most significant point about Lancashire in the early twentieth century, according to the great local shooting enthusiast Major Willoughby-Osborne, was that it was 'a county of great contrasts' offering the most varied shooting in Britain. Sixty years earlier the county had already gained this reputation. Superintendent William Storey of St Helens police force confirmed to the 1846 Select Committee: 'I am in a county which abounds with game . . .'[4] To the south of Preston (see map 1) along the plain and to the north on the Fylde, the agriculture and topography were and are reminiscent of some of the classic game regions in eastern England. However Lancashire's additional attractions lay to the eastern side and northern end of the county where the largely uncultivated moors and hills rise. Abbeystead, Bleasdale and Angelzarke, to name but three, offered an ideal environment for grouse.

Moving further south three estates dominated, partly because of their sheer size but also for the large head of game that was usually shot on them. The 18,000-acre Clifton estate at Lytham stretched extensively across the Fylde region where record seasons yielded 1,652 partridges in 1859–60 and 2,756 pheasants in 1893–4. Ground game, hares and rabbits, frequently went into five figures over a season.[5] Close to Liverpool were the

Estate (and family):
 1. Holker (Cavendish)
 2. Quernmore (Garnett)
 3. Over Wyresdale (Molyneux)
 4. Clifton (Clifton)
 5. Claughton (Brockholes)
 6. Cuerden (Parker)
 7. Hoghton (de Hoghton)
 8. Witton (Fielden)
 9. Billington (Petre)
10. Euxton (Parker)
11. Rufford (Hesketh)
12. Lathom (Bootle Wilbraham)
13. Bickerstaffe (Derby)
14. Altcar (Molyneux)
15. Crosby (Blundell)
16. Croxteth (Molyneux)
17. Knowsley (Derby)
18. Speke (Derby)
19. Bold (Bold-Hoghton)
20. Worsley (Bradshaw)

Map 1: Important game preserves in Lancashire

neighbouring landowners and keen sportsmen, the earls of Derby and Sefton with 47,000 and 18,500 acres respectively. But if we concentrated on just these three magnates we would be overlooking one important feature of Lancashire landowing because over 50 per cent of resident Lancashire landowners with estates exceeding 3,000 acres were located on the fertile plains between the Fylde and Liverpool.[6] The small market town of Ormskirk, for example, was surrounded by the estates of the Heskeths at Rufford, Lord Skelmersdale and the Scarisbricks, all of which were intensively preserved.

Intensive preservation was not a historical constant – weather conditions during the breeding season ensured that. However it is the desire and motivation of the preserver that requires further elaboration since that too could fluctuate; furthermore their ambitions could be restricted to a limited number of species. Some landowners were, by the standards of the day, remarkably liberal and generous towards their tenants. Colonel Charles Townley had, for example, allowed his tenants to shoot over their farms for forty years, and Parker of Cuerden Hall gave permission to all his tenants to kill rabbits on their farms, but 'they had availed themselves of the permission to such purpose that not only the rabbits have been extirpated, but also the hares, pheasants, and partridges . . .' As a result he began proceedings against the sons of one of his respectable tenants.[7]

During the early 1840s some landowners subsided under political pressure from the Anti-Corn Law League (A-CLL) who had begun a populist attack on the game laws. Some gave up preserving altogether whilst many sacrificed the rabbit and were thus able to turn the situation to their advantage in terms of increasing their personal popularity and more importantly by drawing in their tenant farmers to the pro-game lobby. Henry Bold Hoghton of the Bold estate near Liverpool allowed his tenants to kill or preserve ground game 'as they please'.[8] The advantages or pay-off for this liberal approach were considerable, not least the stemming of complaints from angry tenants about crop damage, and improved his paternalistic position within the community through the dispensing of a privilege. As a *quid pro quo* Hoghton demanded of his tenants that they had in future to act as informal gamekeepers by keeping a strict eye on the winged game and trespassers.

Lancashire farmers were not necessarily ill-disposed towards the game laws because the very nature of these laws, which provided protection for private property, enabled landholders to criminalize all uninvited visitors to the countryside. One point emerged again and again in the 1846 Select Committee from northern witnesses and one which failed to find an echo in East Anglia; intensive game preservation was welcomed and encouraged by farmers: 'The preservation of game is a protection to the land, ... many of the farmers are very favourable to the protection of game.' Jones, the superintendent of police, claimed farmers actually begged local landowners to preserve game, 'for the purpose of preventing trespassers and other persons prowling over their lands.' William Storey of the nearby St Helens police force likewise emphasized that 'encouragement to poaching and excess of crime exists on lands that have either no gamekeeper at all, or are neglected by an insufficient watch of bad servants.'[9] That farmers requested to have game preserved on their lands is not inconceivable in the north. Garnett of Quernmore Park near Lancaster, stopped having keepers when he discovered that one of them had 'threatened to smash the head of a poacher'. Local farmers, however, soon complained of poachers breaking down their fences, and so Garnett was forced to rescind his decision on the understanding that the new keepers were not to go out at night. One wonders whether such an injunction would have solved the farmers' problems. Farmers were also, it was claimed, too frightened to complain when gangs of ten or more simply took the liberty of sleeping in their barns.[10] The pro-game lobby was keen to emphasize that crime already existed in the countryside, with or without game preserves, and that, in other words, the game laws were not the cause of criminality but the consequence of a wider criminality.

In order to counter the argument put forward by the increasingly successful and essentially urban A-CLL, the police and landowners claimed poaching was no different from other property crimes; moreover poachers were neither selective nor particular over what they brought home with them after a night's wandering. To reinforce this view it was claimed that poachers were no respecters of private property in general and would leave field gates open and damage fences in pursuit of whatever quarry they happened to chance upon. In order to make the above accusations stick, Lancastrian and north Cheshire authorities had to argue that the poachers were somehow qualitatively and quantitatively different from poachers from other parts of the country. In the north, poachers belonged to gangs, sometimes extremely large ones, which allowed them to act as they pleased and openly terrorize property-holders. Such gangs slotted early into the Victorian stereotypes of the criminal classes since these people came not from the countryside but the towns, locations which by definition made them migratory outsiders who had few or no links with the countryside and, furthermore, were totally immune to the ties of deference that were thought to create stability in organically structured village societies. These arguments have a resonance for no other reason than the plain facts of geography. In Lancashire, and in many areas of Yorkshire too, landowners were often perverse enough to pursue their sport in close proximity to large and expanding conurbations. Their covers and preserves, with each passing year, were slowly being located within the suburbs. The rights of the few became the temptation of the many. Thus around Liverpool, from the Ince Blundell's estate on the coast through the Sefton and Derby estates at Croxteth and Knowsley, down to Hale and Bold on the Mersey estuary, there was a semicircular barrier of privilege marking the boundary between town and country. This determination to preserve was an act of optimistic folly and one which gave rise to what Hopkins has called the poaching war's 'second front'.[11] Landowners had to fight to keep one of the few attractions left to them in an otherwise increasingly unattractive landscape.

Attempting to identify who and quantify how many poached in Lancashire or anywhere else for that matter are nigh on impossible tasks. However, tabulated evidence, with all its shortcomings, need not be dismissed altogether as it can be suggestive and, more importantly, be deployed when used for comparative purposes. In this context the *British Parliamentary Annual Criminal Returns* on serious crimes between 1834 and 1851 make a significant insight. If a league table is constructed of the English counties for armed night poaching, Lancashire comes top or second, with the most convictions in four of the eighteen years. Using similar parliamentary evidence, Lancashire came out worst for the number of gamekeepers murdered between 1835 and 1843. Although the figure is only four deaths, it is significant that the more traditional game counties such as Norfolk and Suffolk recorded fewer homicides. Moving forward to a twelve-month period from 1860 to 1861, eighteen Lancashire keepers came close to death in poaching affrays, again significantly higher than in most other counties.[12] These admittedly impressionistic figures suggest a high level of violence connected with the game laws, a facet of Lancashire which appears to have been of long standing. As early as 1826 the Lancaster Grand Jury were petitioning Parliament with complaints about the vicious affrays then occurring on the Lancashire Plain between Preston and Liverpool, within or adjacent to the region John Walton has called the 'industrial triangle' of Wigan, Prescot and Warrington.[13]

Such evidence brings to light the first distinctive feature of Lancashire poaching; the violence which Lord Skelmersdale termed 'a reckless spirit of enterprise'.[14] Although only a sample number of years has been examined through the pages of the local press the violence is evidently on a scale which is not only greater than in the traditional game counties further south, but also brings to mind the conclusions arising out of that rather ill-tempered debate between Stone and Sharpe on the long-term decline of violence in England and Wales. Although the protagonists disagreed on many issues relating to English violence they both accepted Gurr's original finding that homicides fell and remained at a low and constant level throughout the nineteenth century.[15] This admittedly limited study of poaching forces me to wonder if serious violence declined in the clear and unambiguous manner that is unanimously agreed upon. With the exception of Cockburn's sensible intervention in the debate, one felt that the level of analysis could have been taken a stage further.[16] National figures might well mask many regional variations and it could be argued that by examining the locations of violence a rather different picture may emerge. Any historian with only a passing familiarity with the works of Munsche, Hopkins and David Jones will be struck by the frequent references to violent poaching affrays. 'The poaching war' and 'the long affray' are just two phrases frequently used to describe the events taking place between 1800 and 1870. It certainly is the case that overall violence declined on a national scale, but this decline may have been brought about by a disproportionately large decrease in urban-located violence. In such circumstances possible increases in rurally located violence would be masked by the overall figures. One possible supposition is that rural violence did rise after 1815 and remained at a relatively high level until the 1860s. If such a hypothesis is correct it may well explain, in part, why the collective attentions of the political public, press and Parliament were increasingly turned towards what were increasingly perceived to be the focal points of violent behaviour in Britain, namely the poaching affrays which were the very epitome of rural violence. Whilst the newly established borough police forces, by restoring order to the urban streets, claimed credit for the decline, unjustly in my opinion as the decline in violence appears to have pre-dated their formation, such a claim could not be made for the countryside on two counts. First, rural areas even after 1839 and 1856 remained thinly policed; and second, even had they existed in greater numbers their impact on poaching affrays would not have been decisive. Until 1862 and the passing of the Night Poaching Prevention Act many county constabularies did not involve themselves in game law offences, either officially or unofficially.[17] This would partly explain why a majority of county chief constables put their signature to a petition to the Home Secretary early in 1862 which pleaded: '... this is the only law of the land [game laws] openly set at defiance by gangs of armed men at night ...'[18] On the passing of the new Act shortly afterwards the police gained the right to enter the poaching war.

Returning to the earlier supposition that poaching affrays were frequent and violent, map 2 identifies the location of major bloody affrays involving gangs of poachers over a limited sample of years between 1824 and 1862. Certain pockets or flash-point areas readily display themselves, not least the Lune Valley to the east and north-east of Lancaster, the area around Blackburn and Clitheroe and the plain lying between Prescot and Ormskirk. In the Lune area one of the main attractions for poachers was the Pudsey Dawson estate straddling the villages of Burrow and Hornby where, in 1850, nightly attacks were reported. In one such affray all three keepers were rendered unconscious by an armed gang supposedly from Lancaster. That city was home to one notorious family who repeatedly figure in press reports and court records, the Woodhouse family. They appeared to have operated over a fairly wide area. Brothers Thomas and William

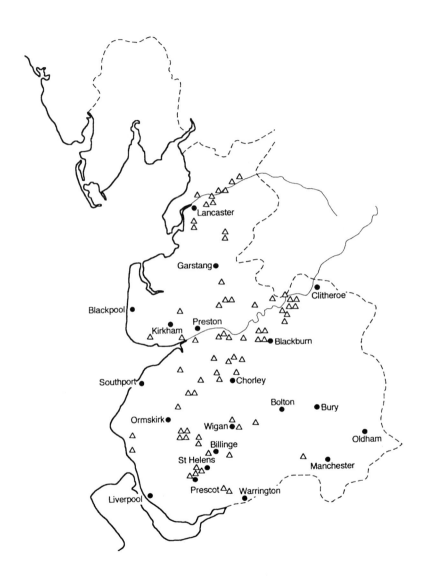

Map 2: Major poaching affrays in Lancashire 1824–1862

had been imprisoned for poaching at Over Wyresdale in January 1861, but by the October of the same year they were both re-arrested on a more serious charge of wounding with intent to murder Matthew Goth, keeper to Garnett of Quernmore. It would appear that Goth had disobeyed Garnett's 'strict injunction' not to go out at night. Only Thomas was found guilty and was sentenced to fifteen months with hard labour.[19]

Every region of the county not only boasted a brace or two of professional or notorious poachers but also violent and 'desperate' men, none more so than in the Clitheroe area, where two keepers were murdered, in 1843 and 1858. One incident contained many of the ingredients associated with the 'Frontier West'. It is fitting that the narrative begins in the beerhouse of Peter Hitchen where John Briggs and James Dickinson were drinking quietly until interrupted by the arrival of three police constables who had come to arrest them for assault and poaching. In the ensuing confusion a knife and loaded pistol were drawn but the police successfully handcuffed the men, whereupon they refused to move. During the intervening wait for a post chaise the beershop was attacked by fifty to sixty 'ruffians', six of them armed, who broke down the locked door and released the prisoners. The place was shot up, the windows smashed and money stolen from the more law-abiding drinkers. This episode would have sat well in Bob Storch's thesis contained in 'A plague of blue locusts' since the Lancashire constabulary was barely a year old at this time and clearly very unpopular, given both the speed with which a gang was mustered and the fact that six of them were armed. Briggs and Dickinson, themselves now armed with guns, made their escape and headed in true outlaw fashion for the hills, with their passage marked by various violent episodes along the way. Between Chatburn and Downham they met with a keeper whom they laid out and left in the road, and two months later came reports of the two 'prowling the hills' and committing a number of robberies and 'outrages of the most atrocious kind'. From Bolton by Bowland to Bacup and finally into the Yorkshire Dales near Hawes came news of highway robbery, pot-shots at travellers and bungled police attempts to arrest them. By the summer Briggs was finally arrested and charged with burglary and attempted murder, for which he was transported for life. Dickinson, on the other hand, remained at large.[20]

One facet, and also a contrast with the situation in East Anglia, became evident when the Lancastrian poachers were examined. At present data on 800 poachers convicted between 1815 and 1880 have been collected. Although their occupational status was not always recorded very few of them were listed as farm labourers. Three possible explanations can be posited for this. First, where no occupation is stated the convicted were in fact farm workers. This was almost certainly the case in East Anglia where the variety of occupations was considerably less than in Lancashire. Second, the farm worker who turned to poaching was considerably more skilful than his urban counterpart and was therefore able to escape detection more often. Some contemporary evidence supports this contention, for, as William Storey of St Helens police argued, poaching 'requires a more clever fellow to poach than to steal'.[21] A third possibility may be that northern farm labourers, especially those living on estates, poached less than their southern counterparts. Again Storey maintained (rather ambiguously) that the 'lower orders were more careful the nearer they live to any gentleman's preserve or mansion'.[22] Moreover a Lancastrian farm worker on relatively high agricultural wages was less likely to poach out of economic necessity. All three explanations may well contribute to the relative absence of farm labourers from the courts, but they do not account for the many urban and/or industrially occupied poachers who figured so frequently in the courts. The list of occupations was as diverse as the county's economy: glassblowers with their four-day week from the St Helens region, weavers, miners, mechanics, pavement layers and canalmen all figure prominently. Moreover many hailed from the towns and fast-expanding industrial villages, and travelled considerable distances in some cases for their nightly escapades. At Tarleton, eight miles from Preston, a gang of twelve met up with and fought a keeper with fourteen tenant farmers as helpers before escaping across country to the Ribble estuary and thence to Preston by boat.[23]

Three miles further south at Rufford on the Hesketh estate a gang of eight were confronted by fourteen keepers and watchers, including the butler, the grooms, footmen and the estate bricklayer. After threatening that 'we will kill every damn one of them', all but the head keeper ran away. It transpired later after their arrest that the group had met up in Ormskirk; Horrocks had come from Chorley, Montgomerie from Standish, Paddy Shea (one of the few Irish), 'Big Bob' Wright and Draper from Liverpool, and Bickerstaffe from Ormskirk itself. All had travelled considerable distances not only to rendezvous but also to poach. Even the surviving folk-songs in the county suggest the poachers were mainly urban-based.[24]

Whilst it is difficult to estimate how many were first-generation urban dwellers who were simply continuing their rural criminal pursuits from a new address, it is undoubtedly the case that some defendants, charged with larceny offences, had returned to their previous haunts. In one case of a violent robbery of a farmhouse ten miles north of Preston, one member of the gang had formerly been a farm servant of the victim. Such evidence can blur the dividing line between urban and rural crime, a point repeatedly made by contemporaries. The mobile urban criminal who sought the relative security of the under- or unpoliced rural hinterlands was a figure of almost mythic stature in the 1830s, particularly in the 1839 report.[25] But as with that other Victorian 'invention', the criminal class, we should do well to recognize and treat seriously the perceptions and concerns of the period.

One remarkable contrast that emerges out of a comparison between the Lancashire and East Anglian poachers concerns the age differential and profile of the gangs. In the latter region violent poaching was a young, single man's game. This finding was not altogether unexpected, given the restricted employment opportunities and low wages which this group experienced after the decline of live-in farm service from the beginning of the nineteenth century. An examination of eighty convicted armed night-poaching gang members from Lancashire revealed that only 5 per cent were under twenty years of age and 50 per cent were thirty years old and above. Moreover additional evidence suggests that the great majority were married with families. This latter fact was sometimes raised in court by defendants in the hope that it would provide some mitigating circumstances. On one such occasion this kind of defence backfired. Forty-year-old Liverpudlian Thomas Draper, when given the opportunity to put in a plea for his own defence, moved the court with the story of his wife's recent death. No doubt sensing rising sympathy, he elaborated further on his destitution by claiming that he had 'sold the very sheets she had died in for food'. At this point the judge clearly experienced a sense of *deja vu* and retaliated by saying that he now recalled meeting Draper at the Liverpool assizes a year previously when he had used exactly the same story.[26]

The rather different age profile of the Lancastrians may suggest that their poverty cycle followed a rather different course in so far as they would have been more often than not the heads of young families without access to either philanthropic or poor-law doles, which were more plentiful in rural areas. However, many young northern agricultural servants lived with their employers up to the time of their marriage. This not only provided them with constant work, food and a regular income of £18 to £20 a year, but also ensured that they were under far greater constraints with regard to their work and leisure activities. In such circumstances young single farm workers had far fewer opportunities to poach than the older industrially occupied men, nor was the need to do so quite as pressing if the economic motive is the sole consideration.

The Lancashire poacher would appear therefore to have been married, urban or industrially located, with a tendency to work in gangs of between six and twenty, and to be violent when challenged. This raises the question: why the propensity to violence? A combination of possible explanations come to mind, the first being that because these men were to all intents and purposes urban dwellers, they were as a result untouched by the paternalistic ethos that often pervaded small village communities. They doffed their caps to no one, and the normal forces of social control experienced by farm workers close to large estates did not touch their lives. Second, as the gangs were operating outside their normal environment they sought safety in numbers, a feature which was reinforced by the commercial nature of their undertaking. Nets a hundred feet in length required an element of teamwork, as did sacks loaded with dead game. They were, after all, in the words of one poacher 'skinning the manor'. The collective character of much of Lancashire poaching consequently increased the odds of violent confrontation if challenged by the head keeper and his team of watchers. Finally, contemporaries noted on a number of occasions that urban poachers tended to be less skilful than rural ones. As a result they were less subtle in their approach to their work. It was not unusual for them to fire off their guns close to the hall. This kind of brazenness was in effect a challenge to the keepers, but again strength in numbers was meant to intimidate.[27]

The location of the violence and the laws governing such behaviour are salient points which need to be borne in mind in this context. Street violence in the towns was covered by a host of fairly minor summary charges which could bring either a short prison sentence or a small fine from the magistrates. However, violence at night in a game-preserving area was prosecuted under a tranche of different and tougher game laws which carried harsher penalties ranging from transportation to imprisonment with hard labour. The stakes were, in other words, much higher, and this increased the poacher's determination to evade arrest.

It would be erroneous to assume that all the violence was poacher-initiated. They did not necessarily go looking for trouble, though many no doubt welcomed the excitement of a scrap. Violence worked two ways in so far as the Lancashire keepers could be unusually brutal and appear to have warmed to their task far more than in some other counties. Although it is difficult to separate cause from effect when assessing keeper behaviour, many of them, it would appear, were dressed for war, donning leather breast plates and cutlasses as a matter of course. This was in addition to any firearms which they might have been carrying. Chaplain John Clay went so far as to claim that they used angular rather than round shot pellets, which were designed to exacerbate wounds.[28] To use modern parlance, we are looking at a 'dirty war' in which men such as Thomas Gidgeon, keeper to Joseph Fielden, MP for Blackburn, shot 'notorious poacher' Thomas Ainsworth in the back and was acquitted of attempted murder but found guilty on the lesser charge of assault. In a similar case on the same estate general dissatisfaction was caused when charges were dropped against George Lane, the head keeper, when he shot Peter Lister. Local magistrates, colleagues of Fielden, were happy to accept his explanation that he tripped as he was shooting Lister's dog. Summary executions of hunting dogs were commonplace and even 'recreational poachers' out with their ferrets at the weekend had to experience the provocation of watching their animals' brains dashed out.[29] Uniquely one case shows the depths to which the poaching war had sunk in the Blackburn area. A gang of four men, power-loom weavers and mechanics, met up with and fought keepers at Dunkenhalgh Park.

All but one of them escaped after the affray, the remaining wounded poacher, John Pickup, was taken by the keepers and, with the connivance of the estate owner Henry Petre, chained in a pub bedroom for three days until he disclosed the names of his friends. The trial, not surprisingly, attracting a crowded court with a further 1,000 outside, became as much a political battle as a legal one thanks to the powerful oratory of the defence solicitor, the radical W. P. Roberts. Wild applause greeted the conclusion of his speech in which he said, 'the (game) laws ... were fast hurrying to that limbo of tyrannous monopoly which was the righteous doom of all such iniquitous enactments.' For all his rhetoric and the seemingly illegal imprisonment of the defence witness, who had been offered money and immunity from prosecution, Roberts failed to secure acquittals for his clients.[30]

Many of these gangs were not poaching for their own immediate needs – they were not 'poaching for the pot' – they were in it for the money. Game represented to them a valuable commodity which could easily be transported by cart or canal to the large conurbations and sold there for 2s. 6d. a brace to legitimate game dealers. This raises an important question which has frequently been addressed by historians of poaching: was the poacher a social criminal or simply a common criminal? The evidence from Lancashire would suggest a divergence from the East Anglian situation in some respects. It has been possible to trace the criminal careers of a number of poachers which suggests that in a minority of cases the concept of social criminality may well be inappropriate. The following cases, it is hoped, will illustrate this conclusion. The first concerns William McCune, alias Kew or Lankey, who originally emanated from Flookborough in the far north of the county, where he was a brickmaker. Over the space of eight years he migrated south to Blackburn, during which time he collected convictions for night poaching (once), poaching (twice), keeping a disorderly house and vagrancy, before being transported for seven years for stealing a chain guard. In addition he had been tried and acquitted of theft, burglary and night poaching.[31] In another case William Riley had, by 1871, at least seventeen previous convictions to his name, including theft, assault, criminal damage and drunkenness, but only two for poaching. Many other poachers like James Brown, Robert Britchcliffe and James Spencer had convictions for burglary.

William Turner, a Chorley weaver, had at least fifteen court appearances, mainly for illegal fishing and poaching, but he had also been found guilty of rape, assault and theft. And finally Thomas Gilby, 'a notorious bad character' convicted of night poaching in 1862, had since 1841 been convicted of manslaughter, burglary (twice), assault (seven times) and for being 'hidden in a cellar for an illegal purpose'.[32]

There were of course people who repeatedly came up before the magistrates solely on poaching charges, men like 'Tearing Tom' Whiteside of Kirkham on the Fylde, of whom it was said that, 'he had his Christmas dinner at the House of Correction for twenty-one years in succession', which either speaks ill of his skills as a poacher or suggests that he sought out the heat and comfort of gaol on a regular basis. Another confirmed poacher was 'Lurkum' James Harrison, a Preston brickmaker, who poached and dealt in live game.[33] Each region of the county had its professional poachers, but the number of people like Turner, Spencer and McCune who had previous convictions for non-poaching offences is striking. Such cases lend weight to John Clay's reported conversation with a poacher in Preston gaol who said, 'no man should go home empty handed – anything before nothing'. 'There were no poachers', another told Clay, 'who would not take on thing if they could not get another, unless it was too hot or too heavy.'[34]

Such attitudes and brief case histories display considerable differences from the East Anglian poachers whom I have studied in the past. Moreover they contrast strongly with Howkins's findings in Oxfordshire, where poachers were mainly local agricultural labourers who rarely travelled above two miles for their quarry.[35] Lancashire poachers frequently travelled long distances, fifteen miles or more, and utilized the ferries, canal barges and the railways to reach their destinations. One can well understand how and why the Victorians came to fear the existence of a criminal class of mobile, urban-based recidivists. Such examples may well undermine the prevailing notion that poaching was invariably a social crime.

This is especially true of the Lancashire gangs which came to serve a useful function for the policing authorities. The Lancashire Constabulary, which had been established in late 1839 with a strength of 502, making it the largest county constabulary in the country, was severely reduced in manpower in

April 1842 to 355. Ratepayer anger at the expense of policing and magisterial antipathy especially in the northern and predominantly rural half of the county had combined to make the 'new' police extremely unpopular. In fact Lancashire came very close to making what nowadays would be the unthinkable decision of disbanding their force altogether.[36] The police therefore found themselves in the very difficult position of having a reduced force and very little support from the very people whom they were meant to be protecting. In order both to improve their strength and justify their existence the police had to amplify both criminal behaviour and the dangers to society which these criminals presented. Rather fortuitously for Woodford, the chief constable, and his men the timely arrival of the Plug Plot riots of August 1842 brought an expansion of numbers. In addition, however, it is also possible to discern two interrelated themes which contributed to the police's reinstatement as a necessary and welcome reform, namely the lawlessness of poaching gangs and the supposed export of crime from Liverpool into the surrounding countryside. The latter issue has, in the depression years of the 1980s and 1990s, taken on the appearance of a recognized fact or popular truth in the county. It is therefore all the more fascinating to trace how this contemporary prejudice burst into life in the nineteenth century.

Turning to the first of these interrelated themes, Woodford had specifically ordered his force not to become involved in the game laws because, 'there was a great outcry about the police being established for the purpose of protecting game'.[37] Such an order was reluctantly carried out by William Storey of the Prescot division who complained to the 1846 Select Committee that he had searched people at night, and 'I have found game in their possession which I knew they had no right to touch, and I have had to let them go about their business and they have laughed at me.'[38] The police felt powerless to act although it soon became apparent that their attitude and hence behaviour towards poaching gangs began to harden. Poachers were, in their eyes, also highway robbers, burglars and common thieves. Once such labels could be attached to these gangs, it would be possible for the police to target them. This process began to occur around January 1843. Whatever Woodford was claiming in public about his men not being used to uphold the game laws, it was clear that they were actively involved in the poaching war. The steward to Lord Sefton of the Molyneux estate just north of Liverpool informed his employer that a policeman, in a recent affray, 'behaved well – he was engaged with four [of them] until he could not resist any longer', having been 'deserted' by all but one keeper. He went on to say that he had 'authorized' the local divisional inspector to employ 'probably half a dozen extra policemen for ten days or a fortnight', a plan which had been put to him by Liverpool's head constable, Whitty.[39]

Although not mentioned by name, the gang which the police and the Molyneux estate were attempting to detect and arrest was the 'Long Company'. It was just one of a number of gangs operating in south Lancashire and north Cheshire in the 1840s; the others being the Warrington gang, the 'notorious' Pepper Street gang, the Appleton gang, the Hollins Green gang, the Haydock gang and the St Helens gang.[40] How far these groups can be properly construed as being gangs, possessing their own internal structures, bound together by kinship or neighbourhood links and working together is open to conjecture. The Long Company, which was claimed to have forty men within its ranks, does appear to have possessed some of the attributes one would normally associate with such confederacies. The first published reference to them came in December 1841 when a Rainford farmer was murdered two miles from St Helens. Five 'desperate characters', all members of the Long Company which had been 'the plague in the neighbourhood for years', were arrested, of whom three were charged and found not guilty at the assizes. One week after the murder a further three members were arrested and charged with an assault and robbery which took place at nearby Knowsley.[41]

By 1843 the press were reporting that the Long Company's

> conduct had been of so ferocious a character that the farmers and others injured by them, although aware of the parties who had, on many occasions robbed and plundered them, have been so far intimidated as to refuse to give up the names of the offenders to the police authorities.

William Storey, the man in charge of breaking up the gang, later recalled that the farmers 'durst not do anything ... because the next night after they gave information, one of their horse's tails or cow's tails would be cut off'.[42] The farmers took particular exception to the gang's habit of sleeping uninvited in their barns during their three-day-long hunting trips. In an effort to break up the gang Storey brought in two constables from Manchester and dressed and equipped them as 'travelling Scotchmen' or hawkers. This ploy led to the arrest and conviction of fourteen of them for poaching, the illegal sale of game and trespass offences in Billinge, Knowsley and Whiston. This success was, however, short-lived for in November 1843 ten of the gang went to the Knowsley estate where they became involved in an affray with five of Lord Derby's keepers in which Richard Kenyon, the head keeper, was shot in the stomach and died three days later.[43] Eventually five were arrested as a result of one of the gang giving Queen's evidence, in part to claim the £100 reward but also to clear his father of the murder charge. Only 27-year-old John Roberts was charged with murder and subsequently found guilty and sentenced to death. The others were tried and found guilty on the lesser charge of aiding and abetting, but they too were capitally convicted. The death sentences set up an outcry in Liverpool and, as a consequence, two petitions were sent into Sir James Graham, the Home Secretary, who commuted all but Roberts to transportation for life. Roberts for his part was executed at Kirkdale gaol before a crowd of 30,000, many of whom were young men and boys who set up 'a tempest of execration' when the executioner presented Roberts's face to them after the drop. It was reported that the forty policemen drafted in had trouble protecting the hangman from the stones and violence as he cut down the body.[44]

This trial and subsequent interest it generated allow us a glimpse into the lives of one of the most notorious gangs in the south of the county. The group appears to have had at its core a number of men bound together by blood or marriage: there were the Shaws, father and son, two Seddons, one of whom lodged with the former family in the heart of Liverpool's backstreets at Eldon Court. The Jacques were related to Fillingham and the gang had the brothers Woods, Lucas and Webster. Unlike other Lancastrian gangs, their age profile was much younger, around twenty-six years old. Although the core of the group lived in the Liverpool slum area, others resided in nearby villages close to the game reserves at Prescot, Billinge and Eccleston. How they came to meet and work together is never made clear but one possible supposition may be Holt's beerhouse at Ecclestone, a popular drinking haunt where they met up on the night of the murder. One noteworthy feature of the Long Company was their occupational diversity which gave them an assortment of necessary skills. John Shaw had previously been a gamekeeper on the Derby estate at Knowsley and the Hoghton estate at Bold; his son was an unemployed butcher; Thomas Jacques was a carter and John Williams a beershop keeper close to Liverpool cattle market, but more importantly he was a licensed game dealer who sold the game on to St John's Market in the town. Only James Hunt and the gang captain, William Cheetham, were described as full-time poachers, although the latter owned a clogger's shop. It was from here that Cheetham bred and sold live pheasants and dealt in eggs which presumably went to local keepers.[45]

Despite all the hyperbole surrounding the gang, it has been possible to trace some of their activities through the court records. As a result it would be best to conclude that they were primarily a poaching outfit because the authorities achieved a 95 per cent successful conviction rate against them for offences connected with poaching, ranging from trespass and night poaching to murder. However, when we examine the non-poaching charges laid against them the conviction rate drops to only 40 per cent, and even then the offences are of a fairly minor nature: stealing from a garden, theft of stockings and assaulting the police. Some of them were acquitted of more serious offences such as murder and highway robbery. This disparity in the conviction rates suggests the Lancashire constabulary were 'leaning' on them in the two years leading up to the Knowsley murder, but they had had trouble in making charges stick; hence the use of undercover policemen in 1843. The gang however appears to have disbanded as a result of the murder, with four of them remaining at large and on the run.[46]

The existence of the Long Company and other similar gangs gave rise to a contentious issue, namely the poor relations and lack of co-operation between the Liverpool and Lancashire police forces which amounted, in the words of a contemporary, to 'a system of jealousy' between the two. Around the mid-century south Lancashire experienced not only a number of poaching affrays but also a number of violent armed robberies. At

Knowsley four masked men armed with pistols broke into a farmhouse where they pistolwhipped the occupants and tied them up before making off with money and a gun. A month later another farmer suffered a similar robbery at the hands of six 'rough fellows' who shortly afterwards tried to shoot a policeman as they made their way 'across the fields to Liverpool'. In the same week four men from Liverpool were transported for life for armed robbery, burglary and shooting at a farmer at Simonswood.[47] Such events gave rise to a scare among farmers close to the town who felt vulnerable to attack from armed robbers. Moreover the police, both town and country, appeared ineffectual. The county constabulary for their part accused the Liverpool force of non-co-operation in their mutual fight against serious crime, but more seriously they accused them of exporting their criminals into the countryside – an accusation admitted to by a former chief superintendent of the borough police who claimed that there was 'seldom committed a serious robbery' in the town and 'in Liverpool we found it to be the fact burglaries were rarely committed; they were committed in the outskirts, at a distance of two or three or four miles'. The boroughs, claimed Woodford, 'are the nurseries of crime, and we have to keep a larger force in the immediate neighbourhoods of these boroughs, in order to protect ourselves from their thieves'.[48] This unco-operative attitude brought an angry response from Lord Sefton, whose Molyneux estate was close to the town: in correspondence to his steward he called for

> a direct interference and enquiry into the state of the Borough Police and its connexion with that of the County, as it appears ... there is no unity of action betwixt them, a most important matter considering that the burglars herd within the Borough and commit the depredations without. There can be no doubt that the majority of them are Poachers ...[49]

The Liverpool force had been from its inception in 1836 the largest in the country outside the Metropolitan district, with a complement of 390, but more importantly it possessed a ratio of one policeman to 631 of the population. Given the geographically compact size of the borough it clearly made sense for the town's criminals to cross the boundary into the relatively unpoliced county, especially as the latter's force had received instructions not to intervene in game law cases. Here they could act with relative impunity, further aided by poor inter-police relations. It would seem that the localized nature of policing contributed in some measure to the perceptions of increased criminality in one area whilst simultaneously contributing to the perception of a lack of serious crime in another. As yet there appears to have been little conception of a united fight against all crime shared by the different forces up and down the country. This may have arisen from the fact that each force was responsible to its own particular watch committee or quarter sessions who demanded police effectiveness in their own respective areas of jurisdiction only. In such an operational environment the notion of a 'policeman state' put forward by Gatrell would surely require some kind of qualification. National policing or, more properly in the context of England, a nationally conscious and united effort in combating crime was clearly some way off. It also suggests that crime as yet was not perceived to be a national problem, only a localized issue, a point verified by the fact that nearly half the counties of England and Wales had failed to establish forces in 1839–40.

Whilst the Liverpool poacher aided the rise of the modern-day myth that crime in Lancashire is committed by Liverpudlians, the urban poacher in general remained a feature of the Lancashire poaching war into the last third of the nineteenth century. At times he offered a serious threat to wider concerns on law and order, not least during the 'cotton famine' of the 1860s. And his presence and activities may well have contributed in large measure to the most important law relating to poaching in the second half of the century, the as yet unresearched Night Poaching Prevention Act of 1862. In Lancashire's case the coincidence of this new law and high unemployment resulting from the cotton depression gave rise to a series of major confrontations between the authorities and poachers.[50]

Lancashire was, in the nineteenth century, a game county marked out as different from more southerly arable counties by the proximity of major conurbations to the game preserves. As a result, the poaching war which developed proved to be of a more violent character which the authorities chose to view as a wider law-and-order issue. In this process the poachers were branded as common criminals who threatened the social fabric of the community, and for this reason the police chose to act against them, even though they had specific instructions not to become involved in game law offences. And whilst Lancashire possessed its fair share of 'traditional' type rural poachers who 'poached for the pot' or for a living, the presence of the gangs leads the historian into investigating wider questions, some of which concerned contemporaries: policing methods, the criminal classes, the town–country divide and the concept of social criminality. This short essay cannot hope to do justice to such an expanded agenda.

Notes

1. J. G. Rule, 'Social crime in the rural south in the eighteenth and early nineteenth centuries', *Southern History*, 1 (1979), 135–53; J. E. Archer, *'By a Flash and a Scare': Arson, Animal Maiming and Poaching in East Anglia 1815–1870* (Oxford, 1990), 222–49; H. Hopkins, *The Long Affray: The Poaching Wars 1760–1914* (London, 1985); D. J. V. Jones, 'The poacher: a study in Victorian crime and protest', *Historical Journal*, 22 (1979), 825–60.
2. J. Hawker, *A Victorian Poacher: James Hawker's Journal* (Oxford, 1978).
3. B. Hines, *The Gamekeeper* (Harmondsworth, 1979), 148, cited in A. Mutch, *Rural Life in S.W. Lancashire 1840–1914* (Lancaster, 1988), 25.
4. *The Victoria History of the County of Lancashire*, II (1908, repr. 1966), ed. W. Farrer and J. Brownbill, 482; PP, 1846, IX, *Select Committee on the Game Laws*, pt. 2, p. 411, qus. 6857–8.
5. Ibid., 484.
6. J. Walton, *Lancashire: A Social History 1558–1939* (Manchester, 1987), 127.
7. For Townley, see *Preston Chronicle*, 1 October 1857; for Parker see *Preston Chronicle*, 9 February 1850.
8. *Preston Chronicle*, 25 May 1844. C. Kirby, 'The attack on the English game laws in the forties', *Journal of Modern History*, 4 (1932), 18–37, still remains one of the best accounts of the A-CLL attack on the game laws. The number of game licences issued in the county declined by 900 between September 1842 and 1843.
9. PP, 1846, IX, pt. 2, evidence of Jones, pp. 352–3, 361–2; Storey, pp. 413 and 420.
10. *Preston Chronicle*, 30 October 1861.
11. Hopkins, *The Long Affray*, 203.
12. The four years are 1838, 1848, 1849 and 1850. Thirty-seven keepers were reportedly murdered between 1835 and 1843; see PP, 1849,

XLIV, *Return of Number of Persons for Offences against the Game Laws and Number of Keepers Killed since 1832*; PP, 1862, XLVII, *Number of Murders or Murderous Assaults on Servants Legally Appointed to Prevent Violation of Game Laws.*

13. PP, 1828, VIII, *Report from Select Committee on Laws Relating to Game*, 101. See also the evidence of Lord Skelmersdale who places the petition in the context of the locality and the period, pp. 82–4; Walton, *Lancashire*, 119.

14. PP, 1828, VII, 84. Presumably the word 'enterprise' had none of the modern connotations of business undertaking attached to it. Rather the meaning Skelmersdale probably had in mind was of a difficult or audacious undertaking.

15. T. R. Gurr, 'Historical trends in violent crime: a review of the evidence', *Crime and Justice* (1981), 299–353; L. Stone, 'Interpersonal violence in English society 1300–1800', *Past and Present*, 101 (1983), 22–33, and 'A Rejoinder', ibid., 108 (1985), 216–24; J. A. Sharpe, 'The history of violence in England: some observations', *Past and Present*, 108 (1985), 206–15. All these articles are primarily concerned with homicide as opposed to crimes of violence in general.

16. J. S. Cockburn, 'Patterns of violence in English society: homicide in Kent 1560–1985', *Past and Present*, 130 (1991), 70–106. Cockburn's claim to be acting as 'a powder monkey' is rather too modest as he appears, on occasions, to be more like a pair of cannons issuing broadsides in both directions.

17. The issue of police involvement in game law offences is problematical because it varied from county to county. Moreover, even where chief constables claimed police non-involvement in the game war they clearly were deeply implicated. See Archer, *'By a Flash'*, 240–2.

18. *Preston Chronicle*, 30 November 1861; PP, 1862, XLV, *Memorial in 1861 by Chief Constables of Twenty-Eight Counties in England and Wales on Game Laws*. I am presently undertaking a more detailed study of the origins and impact of the 1862 Night Poaching Prevention Act.

19. For Hornby see *Preston Chronicle*, 12 January 1850; for the Woodhouse family, see *Preston Chronicle*, 2 February, 26 and 30 October, 2 November 1861. One of the Woodhouse brothers was suspected of murdering a keeper in 1858 but there was insufficient evidence to convict him. Thomas was also charged with shooting into a gamekeeper's bedroom at 4 a.m. (see *Preston Chronicle*, 10 November 1860), and William was arrested in Preston after absconding for a poaching charge (ibid., 2 December 1861). The family appears to be well known to local historians who have described them as having been 'tinkers' and 'potters'.

20. *Preston Chronicle*, 23 January, 1 May and 14 August 1841. Briggs

was transported for life for attempted murder. R. D. Storch, 'Plague of blue locusts: police reform and popular resistance in northern England 1840–57', *International Review of Social History*, 20 (1975), 61–90.
21. PP, 1846, IX, pt. 2, see answers to qus. 7184–6, p. 429.
22. Ibid., answer to qu. 6907, p. 413.
23. *Preston Chronicle*, 5 February and 4 March 1848.
24. Ibid., 26 February 1848. One of the most famous songs related to the murder of a keeper on the outskirts of Blackburn in 1839. The prime suspect died in poverty and guilt-ridden in New York (see *Blackburn Standard*, 25 December 1839 and 25 November 1840). The words to the song can be found at W290, Blackburn Library.
25. *Preston Chronicle*, 11 December 1842; PP, 1839, XIX.
26. The sample of gang members was taken from the period 1809–58. *Preston Chronicle*, 26 February 1848.
27. On the general violence of poaching gangs see PP, 1828, VIII, 83. Lord Skelmersdale argued that the size of the gangs acted as a deterrent against arrest. Former poacher A.B. claimed gangs could shoot right up to Lord Derby's hall without hindrance from the keepers, PP, 1846, IX, pt. 2, p. 390.
28. Revd A. L. Clay, *The Prison Chaplain: A Memoir of the Rev. John Clay B.D. Late Chaplain of Preston Gaol* (1861), 567, n. 2. The Cuerden keeper wore a leather helmet and breastplate (*Preston Chronicle*, 4 October 1851).
29. For the Gidgeon case see *Preston Chronicle*, 11 September 1841 and 19 March 1842. Ainsworth received just two weeks in gaol. For Lane see R. D. S. Wilson, *The Feildens of Witton Park* (Blackburn, 1979), 58; *Preston Chronicle*, 7 August 1858. A ferret was killed at Little Harwood (*Preston Chronicle*, 27 November 1858). See also ibid., 21 April 1849, for an example of how an incident in which a keeper shot a dog escalated into a tragic affray in which someone was accidentally shot and killed.
30. Roberts, whilst branding Pickup a 'wretch' and 'a traitor' also felt that he had been mentally tortured (see *Preston Chronicle*, 27 November 1858). The three defendants received three months with hard labour.
31. For McCune see LRO, QJC/1 Assize Calendars 1805–37, QJC/6 Sessions Papers, Calendar of Prisoners 1844; *Preston Chronicle*, 18 March, 5 August and 12 August 1837, 16 April 1842.
32. For Riley see LRO, QJC/12 Sessions Calendar January 1871; *Preston Chronicle*, 18 December 1861; for Brown see *Preston Chronicle*, 26 February 1848; for Britchcliffe see LRO QJC/5 1842 Petty Sessions; for Spencer see QJC/5 1842; for Turner see *Preston Chronicle*, 24 September 1859 and 5 June 1861. Turner, whose criminal career appears to have begun in 1842, was eventually sentenced to six years' penal servitude for stealing 30 lb of chloride of lime. This suggests fish poisoning on

a large scale. For Gilby, whose criminal career began in 1841, see *Preston Chronicle*, 27 February 1858 and 23 November 1861.

33. For Whiteside, see *Preston Chronicle*, 18 October 1862. Judging by the number of times his name appears in the press and Quarter Session records this claim appears to be well founded. For Harrison, see *Preston Chronicle*, 29 May 1861. He lived in Preston and often dealt in live game, which he sold to gamekeepers.

34. LRO, QGR 2/42 Preston Chaplain's Reports 1848, pp. 19 and 57.

35. A. Howkins, 'Economic crime and class law: poaching and the game laws 1840–1880', in S. E. Burman and B. H. Bond (eds.), *The Imposition of Law* (New York, 1979), 279–82.

36. *Preston Chronicle*, 2 April 1842. About 36,000 from 241 townships signed the petition calling for 'the abolition or reduction' of the police. Over 50 per cent of Lancashire JPs voted to disband the force, but a simple majority was not sufficient to do this. For the Plug Plot see F. C. Mather, 'The general strike of 1842: a study in leadership, organization and the threat of revolution during the Plug Plot disturbances', in J. Stevenson and R. Quinault (eds.), *Popular Protest and Public Order* (London, 1974), 115–40. The first indication in official records of Liverpool 'exporting' its criminals appears in the questionnaire return from Kirkdale which was adjacent to the town. It stated that crime in the county was 'not generally committed by rural residents but people from Liverpool', PRO HO 73/5, pt. 2, p. 183.

37. PP, 1846, IX, pt. 2, evidence of James Jones, chief constable of Warrington, pp. 396–409. He was, he claimed, only permitted to stop people carrying guns at night.

38. Ibid., evidence of Storey, replies to qus. 7044–9.

39. LRO DDM6/93, Molyneux Correspondence, letter from steward E. Hall to Lord Molyneux 12 January 1843.

40. All these gangs were identified in PP, 1846, IX, by Jones and Storey. It was also claimed that there were more poachers in the St Helens neighbourhood 'than in any district in Lancashire or anywhere else', reply to qu. 6951; 416, PP, 1846, IX.

41. The murder of Rainford farmer, Henry Grayson, is the first documented press record of the Long Company (*Preston Chronicle*, 11 and 18 December 1841). A fuller account of the Long Company has appeared in a special edition, 'Histories of crime and modernity', of the *British Journal of Criminology*, 1999, 'Poaching gangs and violence: the urban–rural divide in nineteenth-century Lancashire', 25–38.

42. *Preston Chronicle*, 1 April 1843, gives a potted history of the gang which had originally appeared in the *Liverpool Times*; PP, 1846, IX, pp. 411–12, qu. 6875.

43. *Preston Chronicle*, 1 April and 18 November 1843; PP, 1846, IX, qu. 6877.

44. For the trial see *Liverpool Mercury*, 29 December 1843 and *Preston Chronicle*, 30 December 1843; for the execution see *Preston Chronicle*, 27 January 1844. Neither Derby nor Stanley signed the petitions, which brings to mind Douglas Hay's point about 'claims of class rather than humanity' saving the condemned, 'Property, authority and the criminal law', in D. Hay et al., *Albion's Fatal Tree* (London, 1974), 44.

45. *Preston Chronicle*, 30 December 1843 and 27 January 1844. At present I have been able to identify twenty-seven members of the gang, which is rather less than the forty claimed by the authorities.

46. Criminal profiles of the gang were constructed by using Liverpool and Lancashire newspapers between 1841 and 1844; PP, 1846, IX, evidence of William Storey; LRO QJC/5 Sessions Papers, Calendars of Prisoners, 1841–3; QGR3/45 Chaplain's Reports, 1841–67.

47. *Preston Chronicle*, 22 February and 29 March 1851; PP, 1852–3, XXXVI, *First Report from the Select Committee on Police*, evidence of T. H. Redin, former chief superintendent of Liverpool Borough Police, p. 86, reply to qu. 1383.

48. Ibid., 97–8, replies from Woodford the chief constable of Lancashire; 89–90, evidence of Redin.

49. LRO DDM6/224, Molyneux Correspondence, letter 6 January 1852.

50. See PRO HO 45 OS 7210, petitions and correspondence relating to night poaching.

'South Wales has been Roused as Never Before': Marching against the Means Test, 1934–1936

NEIL EVANS[1]

One of the most memorable passages in David Jones's finest book is his recreation of Rebecca's attack on Carmarthen workhouse in 1843.[2] Towards the end of his life David was becoming a twentieth-century and contemporary historian. It therefore seems appropriate to honour his memory by considering the largest protest movement in Welsh history, the campaign against Part II of the Unemployment Act of 1934, a series of events which have not received the amount of attention which they deserve from historians, despite some valuable pioneering work and a good deal of fiction.[3] The mainly peaceful marchers of almost a century later paralleled Rebecca's earlier protests. Nor would this comparison have been unthinkable to the protesters of 1935. They lived in a time when references to the Tolpuddle Martyrs, the Chartists and the New Poor Law of 1834 were commonplace and this vantage point helped give them sustenance. Like Rebecca, they found a new system of relief of poverty morally offensive, and both drew on the extensive resources of their communities to combat it. Like Rebecca, in that process, they displayed much of the nature of their community. Had David lived he might well have brought his formidable skills to bear on this issue. The marchers would have been guaranteed his sympathy and empathy. Without him the survivors will have to do the best they can.

Unemployment was a major concern of inter-war governments even if never the prime one. Historians who emphasize the complex pattern of boom and decline in inter-war Britain serve only to stress its importance in south Wales.[4] Even the eminent historian who regards Britain in the 1930s as experiencing a 'mild boom' allows a Welsh nursemaid who served his family to obtrude into the story, and she was surely a displaced casualty of the depression in south Wales.[5] Contemporaries strove to conjure up a graphic image of what it meant. Perhaps the South Wales Council of Social Service did as well as anybody with a simple statistic: 'Every third person you meet in South Wales is either unemployed or dependent upon a home whose breadwinner is unemployed.'[6] The problems were widespread. Early in 1934 Sir Wyndham Portal was appointed by the government to report on 'derelict areas' in south Wales, with the intention of singling out a few unemployment black spots as areas to which special attention could be given by the government. He concluded that the whole of the eastern part of the coalfield qualified, while other observers thought that the whole of it did, and one Welsh Nationalist claimed that the whole of Wales did.[7]

The unemployed were socially visible in south Wales. Though some undoubtedly shunned society because they felt a stigma, many were organized and active. In 1934–5 20,000 were members of clubs for the unemployed. By the next year 27,000 would be members, 20 per cent of the total unemployed in south Wales. Nor was this the full extent of the influence of the clubs. There was some turnover in the composition of the unemployed, and as it was said that club members were more likely to get jobs than non-members, their influence spread beyond the ranks of their current membership. Sir Percy Watkins saw them as 'part of a movement that would make a really valuable contribution towards enabling the victims of unemployment to stand bravely on their own feet'.[8] Clubs and settlements became an established part of the scene in the Valleys and formed part of the area's contemporary image, figuring centrally in a novel set in it.[9] They were significant enough to earn the enmity of the National Unemployed Workers' Movement (NUWM) and other sections of organized labour which viewed them as purveyors of 'dope', an assessment that Watkins was keen to deny.[10]

Their activities were numerous. Many clubs produced plays; the Three Valleys Musical Festival provided musical outlets for the unemployed and raised funds. In 1934 at Mountain Ash twenty-three choirs with around 3,000 members performed under the baton of Sir Henry Wood. Beyond this there was the Unemployed Men's Festival of Song in which 350 members of choirs took part in a broadcast in December 1934.[11] Many clubs provided lectures, social events, adult education classes and radio listening groups. Clubs had an established network of contacts and through it they exchanged experiences and thoughts.[12] Activities were widespread across the coalfield and of a diverse nature. Even that majority of unemployed who were not members of clubs were not isolated from the rest of society. Many attended miners' institutes or chapels, or worked on their allotments.[13]

There was also political activity amongst the unemployed, in which the Communist Party and its satellite organizations specialized. The NUWM never organized more than a minority of those on the dole but it publicized the general issue by its protests and demonstrations. Lewis Jones, its mercurial organizer, was largely responsible for this.[14] It exerted pressure on local authorities in south Wales which were charged with the administration of key aspects of unemployment relief. Prominent in its propaganda exercises were marches of the unemployed, both those which set out from south Wales to bring the attention of London to 'the plight of the minefields', and the now less remembered ones which lobbied the offices of Public Assistance Committees (PACs) within south Wales. National marches started from late in 1927 and there were others in 1930, 1932 and 1934, the last of these having a small women's contingent led by Dora Cox. These marches were opposed by the local and national Labour Party and trade union establishments. The NUWM was more effective in *organizing* the unemployed than was the mainstream labour movement, including the South Wales Miners' Federation (SWMF), though many found the Fed to be an effective means of dealing with their immediate needs in negotiating with the authorities.[15]

Local marches also punctuated the period. In 1928 unemployed men from south Wales marched on the TUC when it met in Swansea. The marches continued through the period and intensified from 1932. Towards the end of that year a march of some hundreds of unemployed workers from Glamorgan arrived in Cardiff to lobby the Glamorgan PAC. Along the way they were greeted by thousands of sympathizers.[16] The achievement of 1935 would be to break this distinction between marchers and sympathizers and mobilize what was in effect the whole community.[17] Over 20,000 people signed petitions in support of the marchers' objectives. The major march of 1933 was across Monmouthshire and culminated in a demonstration in Newport. Again along the way thousands of people turned out to cheer them and offer support.[18] In October 1934 unemployed men from the Ogmore, Garw and Llynfi Valleys marched on Bridgend. At the same time there was a similar march in the Rhondda and another in Monmouthshire, though a projected Glamorgan march did not take place. Also delegations were sent to local government agencies to make the particular needs of the unemployed known. A deputation said to represent 1,500 unemployed in Llanelli demanded that available work be shared around more equitably. Other demonstrations about work schemes also took place in Llanelli. There were deputations to local authorities constantly, and right across south Wales – in Merthyr and the Rhondda, for instance – while at Hirwaun the unemployed met to protest about Fascism and war.[19] The Cardiff and District Unemployed Workers' Association, led by Tom Llewellyn, was also active throughout the decade.[20]

The Communist Party also put the issue of unemployment into the foreground in election campaigns such as the Merthyr by-election of 1934, when its candidate was Wal Hannington of the NUWM.[21] Members were recruited and even political opponents acknowledged the size of the meetings.[22] However, this did not translate into votes for a parliamentary seat. S. O. Davies, the official Labour candidate, won comfortably and Hannington lost his deposit. NUWM activity laboured under the heavy disadvantage of having to attack the local Labour establishment. 'STAND FOR UNITY against LABOUR DICTATORS' proclaimed a leaflet issued by Arthur Horner on Hannington's behalf. South Wales would be prepared to stand for unity against the 'dictators' of the National Government but not those of the Labour Party and the Fed. Horner's comparison of the executive of the SWMF with the government which had transported the Tolpuddle Martyrs must have played rather badly. The sectarianism of the Communist Party's 'third period' or 'class against class' strategy which Stalin had inaugurated in 1928 added to tensions within the labour movement. Social democrats – or 'social Fascists' as they were sometimes dubbed – were enemies of the working class and not to be trusted. NUWM pamphlets of this period constantly depicted Labour councillors as being in league with the police and other agencies of the state.[23] While the NUWM organized such campaigns against Labour councils its support was limited, though onlookers at demonstrations were potential participants.

The NUWM was not the only political force to represent the unemployed. The SWMF provided services to them through scores of unemployed branches which provided legal advice, and this competition was instrumental in creating tension between the Fed and the NUWM. Few people joined both the NUWM and the Fed, for the penny a week required by both was too great a drain on the overstretched pockets of the unemployed. Other bodies such as the Aberdare Trades and Labour Council also represented the interests of the unemployed against officialdom.[24]

All this activity – both the social work and the protest – helped keep the issue of unemployment central to discussion in south Wales. It was not marginalized, as it would be in the 1980s, but was seen as an issue with relevance to the whole community. When a crisis in unemployment relief emerged out of the changing policies of central government having a particular impact on south Wales, this activity was one of the bases upon which a massive structure of resistance was erected.

The issue which disturbed the government was central to the development of democracy and of a social-service state. Historically the acceptance of poor relief had carried with it a loss of political rights. The dismantling of this arrangement began with the extension of the franchise in the 1880s. Accepting poor law medical relief ceased to invoke the loss of civil rights in 1885, and from 1918 no pauper lost the vote. Conservative politicians feared that paupers would use their voting power to improve their economic position, and there is some evidence that this proved to be the case in the 1920s. 'Poplarism' was a thread within socialist politics which advocated the use of local powers to begin the process of social transformation. Governments had singularly failed to control this in the 1920s, even though outside administrators were sent in at Poplar and at Bedwellty.[25] In many ways fears of uncontrolled expenditure were exacerbated by changes in unemployment policy made in the early 1930s. The National Government ended the system of paying unemployment insurance to those who were not covered by contributions. This had been adopted at the end of the war as a temporary expedient but it had persisted. By 1931 the insurance fund was £113 million in debt and the government was keen to restore its actuarial basis.[26] The withdrawal of these payments would create a crisis for the local PACs, successor to the Poor Law Guardians (PLGs), who would become responsible for those formerly covered by the insurance fund. It was resolved by funding the PACs to administer a new system of payments. The PACs had the staff and the experience to assess claims, and a cost-conscious government did not want to replicate this machinery.

This expedient created a situation which Labour-controlled local authorities in south Wales were quick to exploit. What had restrained 'Poplarism' was the fact that the Board of Guardians were spending ratepayers' money which was raised locally. Defiance of central government, in these circumstances, was fairly exceptional. The beauty of the new system for Labour politics was that central government paid the bill while local government assessed it. In effect PACs were given a blank cheque. Central government had foreseen this possibility after the experience of the 1920s but had thought the situation was adequately covered by the fact that single-issue PLG (in which the generosity of relief had been a key election issue) had been replaced by PACs which were drawn from county councils which covered a multiplicity of issues and in which poor relief was unlikely to be a central electoral concern.

In south Wales, Labour-controlled local authorities exploited the situation to give 'generous' relief to the unemployed. Inspectors and auditors for the Ministry of Health complained, but to little avail. In 1932 the Royal Commission on Unemployment Insurance stressed that it was difficult for popularly elected administrators to be 'judicial' and 'resist personal influence' in areas where the electors were beneficiaries of the measures.[27] In Glamorgan the Labour Party offered its administration of Public Assistance in the most generous spirit possible as an inducement to electors.[28] A means test had been applied to this relief, but during the crisis of 1935 councillors in south Wales frequently boasted that this had never been operative in south Wales. S. O. Davies's remarks in Merthyr that 1935 had seen the first introduction of the means test in the town were widely reported, as were similar comments made by Wil Jon Edwards in regard to Glamorgan.[29] On average PACs gave 'full determinations' (that is the maximum amount of relief) to 65 per cent of applicants with 35 per cent getting reduced ones. In Glamorgan the respective figures were 94 per cent and 6 per cent. D. R. Grenfell confirmed that the 'Public Assistance Committee had interpreted their power generously in South Wales', while Councillor D. J. Williams of Gwauncaegurwen paid tribute to the humane administration of Glamorgan and Monmouthshire.[30] For the same situation was observed in Monmouthshire: 'The Council has been fought by the Government, but the scales have stood.'[31]

Labour's political opponents – Tories and ratepayers – made the same charge and it was never denied. The Communist Party also grudgingly admitted that Labour's record in south Wales was better than that of most local authorities on this. The Ministry of Labour wrote to Merthyr Borough Council in November 1934 about its administration of transitional benefit.[32] The *Western Mail* crowned its campaign against Labour councils and against the developing protest movement with the comment that the old system was 'one of the worst chapters in the recent history of Socialist squandermania'. Other newspapers of similar persuasions made related points.[33]

As well as being an economically efficient example of municipal socialism this generous interpretation of the rules was also well adjusted to the desperate problems of south Wales. Transitional payments had been designed as relief for relatively short periods of unemployment and were set at levels which reflected this. Low levels could be endured for short periods, but in areas like south Wales where there was a solid core of long-term unemployment amongst the workless, more generous relief was a necessity. The long-term unemployed faced problems of replacing clothing, household goods and furnishings.[34]

The Unemployment Act of 1934 addressed the issue.[35] It ended the system of parish relief (since 1929 administered by the PACs of the county and borough councils) and amalgamated the relief which they gave with transitional benefit. The Unemployment Assistance Board was designed to remove benefits from both local and parliamentary political pressures. The UAB – a quango – was given the responsibility for setting the rules for the calculation of benefits on a national level. Its officers administered the scales, a system which had been suggested by a Royal Commission of 1932.[36] It was a means to discipline areas like south Wales, and conflict might have been predicted. The local authority poor law scales and the transitional benefit scales would have to be brought in line with each other. The government allocated an extra £3 million to relief and claimed most would be better off. But this was unlikely to be true in an area with strong Labour control such as south Wales.

The Bill was subjected to much scrutiny in Parliament – twenty-seven days in all, the most discussed piece of domestic legislation of the inter-war period.[37] Nye Bevan played a prominent part in opposing it in a series of speeches on both the details and the principles of the Act. In particular he challenged the powers devolved to the appointed UAB which would not be subject to proper scrutiny. He raised many broad political principles regarding freedom and democracy, as well as denouncing the means test and speaking from his immediate experience. Next amongst south Wales MPs as an opponent of the Bill was W. G. Cove of Aberavon who intervened regularly, particularly on matters concerning youth policy and education, as befitted a former teacher. Other south Wales MPs made less frequent contributions. None of this was to any avail, given the huge National Government majority in the House of Commons. Labour voted solidly against, as did some Liberals (including the Welsh Liberal MPs), but the opponents of the bill could never raise more than sixty to seventy votes. The division lists on the Bill and its multitudinous clauses – more than sixty – were highly unequal in length; it passed its final reading by 421 votes to 67. The passage of the Bill illustrates just how shattered the Labour Party had been in 1931 and how prominent south Wales MPs were in the opposition.[38]

Chris Williams argues that we need to think in terms of a broad movement in which Labour and the Communist Party formed a continuum with many shared objectives and policies.[39] Few issues illustrate the salience of this approach better than the events of the winter of 1934–5. Up to December 1934 the opposition manifested itself in two main forms.[40] One was through the channels of the mainstream labour movement, in trade union discussions, trades and labour councils and in public meetings addressed by MPs. MPs played a significant role in this and extended their parliamentary opposition down to grass-roots level. The other was through the continuing activities of the Communist Party and its associated bodies like the NUWM, which focused very largely on the provisions in the Act which could compel long-term unemployed people to enter what were dubbed 'slave camps' where their fitness would be restored through heavy manual labour.

These two strands were not wholly distinct as, for instance, Communists could and did use trade union channels to create discussion and opposition. By December there was some public interest but demonstrations had failed to take off. Christmas provided an inevitable hiatus, but agitation picked up quickly thereafter, especially after the new regulations came into force on 7 January. Meetings and demonstrations were held across the breadth of the coalfield and by the weekend of 26–7 January they were acknowledged to have been the largest events seen in each community. By the next weekend, 2–3 February, they had passed even those totals, with some reaching over 60,000 participants and a total of 300,000 marching on 3 February. But it was not simply the huge demonstrations which were notable. It was the number, the seemingly endless unrolling of protest. Every day there must have been a demonstration somewhere in the coalfield, and frequently multiple actions. People celebrated the inclusiveness of the protests and their peaceful nature. The whole range of community organizations from British Legion to chapels to the NUWM took part. Protests bridged generations and the sexes: young and old, men and women took part. Cases of extreme loss of income caused by the new regulations were publicized widely. The issue dominated public and private conversation. It swept through the coalfield with something of the atmosphere of a religious revival, though with none of the hysteria, and it was an essentially outdoor phenomenon rather than an indoor one.

In January the Fed called an 'all in' conference of labour and community organizations to Cardiff (though with Welsh Nationalists and the CP/NUWM carefully excluded). This was particularly revivalist in tone though its main decisions were to send a deputation to see the minister of labour and to create a Council of Action, which rarely met afterwards. The SWMF found it convenient to pass the insistent calls for a general strike off to this body, which in the event buried them. The deputation impressed the minister of labour with its moderation.[41] At local level there was much co-operation between Communists and Labour people, whatever the injunctions coming from the national Labour Party against such co-operation.

It was the labour movement which articulated this protest. The local press was often supportive of the National Government and more concerned with the worries of ratepayers than those of the unemployed. The crusading *Aberdare Leader* is an honourable exception and it worked hand in hand with its MP, George Hall. The force of public opinion created a turnabout in the attitudes of much of the press. It followed rather than led opinion.

The one significant act of violence – and it was rather minor – was the storming of the UAB offices in Merthyr on 4 February. The next day the government announced a suspension of the new regulations, with claimants being allowed to use whichever relief scale benefited them. This was necessary because in some areas, though largely not in south Wales, the new scales were an improvement. The action was a response to a general political situation in which widespread discontent had been created in many parts of Britain, including from many middle-class supporters of the government. When Parliament reassembled towards the end of January the government found that many MPs were communicating intense anger on behalf of their constituents: south Wales MPs were prominent, confirming their importance in the whole issue. As an election was due within two years the government was concerned. The day after the 'standstill' it still lost the Liverpool Wavertree by-election, a normally safe seat, though the intervention of the rogue Tory, Randolph Churchill, at least partly explains this. The pressure from south Wales was part of the generally hostile atmosphere which faced the government but was far from being its only concern.

Back in south Wales the protests continued, though in a rather less concentrated form than before. Women's sections of the Labour Party had played a part in them from the beginning, but a series of women-only meetings addressed by Rose Davies and Elizabeth Andrews, the leading women in the party in south Wales, began to be held. Here there was a stress on the particular hardships which unemployment imposed on women from the management of straitened budgets. The extensive women's organization in the Labour Party was one of the resources upon which the marches could draw. This was supplemented by growing activity amongst women organized by the Communist Party. Some women had joined the unemployment marches across south Wales in 1934 and at many places Women's Guilds were organized, while the party produced a leaflet on the issue specifically aimed at women. The fact that seven women spoke at the south Wales party congress in Cardiff in November 1934 was seen as evidence of the success of the tactic. More fancifully, women's participation in the demonstrations was read as evidence of a revolutionary mood in south Wales. Again there was stress on the way women suffered through unemployment, and this was probably more appealing than any thoughts of Petrograd. The march of women in Merthyr, which culminated in the sacking of the UAB offices, was the culminating moment in this trend of women's organization. In early March 1935 it was predicted that 5,000 women in south Wales would turn out to march against the means test on International Women's Day. But as this was not subsequently celebrated in the Communist press we must assume that the turnout was disappointing.[42]

Militants aimed at a token general strike across south Wales for late February which would continue the pressure on the government and the UAB. Large marches still took place, but the pattern of constant smaller marches culminating in weekend crescendos which had characterized the two weeks before the withdrawal of the regulations was not repeated. The marches were more isolated and patchy. Many urged their continuance. Communists wanted to repeal the Act rather than have the regulations withdrawn, and beyond that to bring down the National Government. Labour people wanted the end of the Act or to ensure that the pressure was maintained on the government while the UAB considered its new regulations.

By their nature, mass demonstrations are inevitably hard to sustain for long periods, though in 1935 what was remarkable was the energy channelled into them and the length of time they were kept up. But the energy did begin to wane. By March there were some disturbances, often instigated by the police, who seemed to sense that the hour for action had come. Later protest meetings were marked by dissension between Labour and the Communists, with MPs sometimes being shouted down; tensions were apparent and often arose from the call for a one-day general strike. This was an interesting change of tack, a variation in style of action which might well have produced a good response, but it was defeated by those in the Fed (like Jim Griffiths) who insisted that any action had to involve all trade unions in south Wales, or subsequently be called throughout Britain. Despite some evidence of support it was never called, and the protests became lower-key as the memory of January–February faded. The last massive rally was of 60,000 people in the Rhondda on 24 February. But the same day the projected Rhondda strike for the next day was called off.

Why was south Wales able to mobilize such a concerted protest? Some reasons for this have already been provided: the visibility of the unemployed in south Wales, and the long-term preparation of the ground by the NUWM. But these alone would not have produced this kind of response. The degree of unity achieved demands explanation. This is particularly the case as there were variations in the level of unemployment across south Wales in the 1930s and in many communities the bulk of the workforce remained in work. Why then did whole communities make common cause in 1935?

The movement was built on foundations largely laid by the Communist Party but it spread beyond the limits achieved by NUWM protests in south Wales because it was aimed at the National Government rather than at Labour-controlled local authorities, as were the bulk of marches before 1935. Local authorities registered their own protests at the Act with regularity and were happy to assist with the peaceful protests. Frequently Labour control of local authorities manifested itself in the form of buses laid on to take marchers home from demonstrations. Councillors could use the occasion to advertise the virtues of a Labour-controlled local authority after years in which their opponents on the left had accused them of being collaborators in the capitalist system and the state. They had lost a significant degree of local power and influence through the legislation and had their own reasons to welcome the protest movement. So at a political level there was unity imposed by opposition to the government.

Economically, too, there were forces which brought a diverse society together. Unemployment varied in intensity across the coalfield, but all miners had reasons to see the cause of the unemployed as their own in 1935. Low wages, lay-offs and short-time working were a feature of the depression in south Wales. In many areas pits opened and closed fitfully, leaving a very ragged line between the employed and the unemployed. There was little real difference in the living standards of many who were in work and those who were out of it. Some linked the plight of the 'unemployed and underpaid employed'.[43] Unemployment and low wages had created a common experience of poverty: 'In Abertillery, for instance, children of the employed workers receive food in the feeding centres, set up for the children of the unemployed; such are their miserable conditions.'[44] 'It has been admitted on all hands that the wages in the South Wales coalfield are too low, and a few years ago the men had to submit to wages cuts that were not imposed in any other district in the country.'[45]

In the meetings held to protest against the means test it was frequently argued that it was an attempt to drive down wages: if there was any gulf to bridge between employed and unemployed it was done by effective argument. Beyond that there was altruism as expressed by David Bowen, secretary of the Co-op in Aberdare: 'Yes he knew he was "all right", and he wished everyone else was all right ... if those people who were all right would only give a thought to those less fortunately blessed there would not be so much suffering in the world.'[46]

In the rather more prosperous anthracite area of the coalfield, mergers and rationalization in the mining and tinplate industries were causes for concern, and there were many derelict collieries marking the landscape.[47] At the end of 1934 there was much talk of closures and many job losses in the Swansea Valley. Further west there were mergers in the tinplate industry and fears expressed that these would lead to some shift of production out of south Wales.[48] If the western portion of the coalfield was more prosperous in general terms, this was spotty and only relative:

> [Carmarthenshire] has not been scheduled as a Special Area, ... in spite of the fact that unemployment is rife throughout the area. At our own doors is a sorely stricken district ... Burry Port where over a thousand men out of a total employable population of 1450 are on the dole. There are equally distressing conditions in some parts of the anthracite coalfield.[49]

One of these areas of concern in the anthracite area must have been Cwmamman, where in 1936 it was alleged that the area had suffered 75 per cent unemployment for five years.[50]

Concern about mergers and rationalization was not confined to the west. Jim Griffiths noted in his presidential address to the SWMF in 1935:

... the new P.D. Group becomes a dominating force in the coalfield ... – this ... means fewer pits, – more machines – less men. Thus we have to contemplate still further reductions in the number of persons employed, and still more thousands of men thrown on the scrap heap. This policy of closing pits will have calamitous results for whole communities in South Wales.[51]

Protest, however, rarely comes from the totally defeated. There were also limited grounds for optimism. The Bridgeman wage award of 1934 was a small victory for the miners: if it was not a major advance, at least it demonstrated that something could be won from the owners. Jim Griffiths was credited for having 'succeeded in arresting the downward trend in wages, and there was now an upward trend'.

Solidarity went beyond the working class. The middle classes, such as they were in south Wales, were also drawn into the movement. In 1910, as in 1831, workers' protests had used the shopocracy for target practice, resenting their alliance with coal owner and ironmaster.[52] No such conflict was evident in 1935. Shopkeepers recognized, in the depression, the force of the widely acknowledged downward multiplier.[53] They knew that the fate of the unemployed influenced directly their own livelihoods and the well-being of the community. The idea of spending power was well appreciated[54] and underlay much of the local discussion of the regulations, as Dai Grenfell illustrated: 'The new scale would reduce the spending power of the people of South Wales by a tremendous margin and trade and tradespeople would suffer in addition to the unemployed.'[55] Little Dan the Grocer had become aware of Mrs Evans Fach's warning that he and the butter from Carmarthen did after all depend on the miner.[56] One shopkeeper observed: 'Coming into contact with them [the unemployed] daily, I know only too well their troubles and I can sympathise with the people.' Even those newspapers which represented a middle-class and ratepayer mentality were obliged to come into line and support the movement. Political propaganda against the Act emphasized the common interests of the whole community, and the message clearly got through. Jim Griffiths laid out the general principles involved: 'Whole villages in the mining areas were dependent upon the moneys received by the unemployed, the deprivation of which would mean absolute ruin, and traders would be forced into bankruptcy.'[57] Distress was seen as an issue for the whole area, not simply for the unemployed, as Councillor A. J. Chick observed at Pontypridd: 'It was a serious matter for individuals, but ... the cumulative effect of these regulations ... would be a much more serious matter for an area which was already burdened with distress.'[58] The wage bill of the industry in south Wales had been £64 million in 1920 when 250,000 had been employed. Now with 138,000 employed it stood at a mere £15 million: 'The loss in purchasing power was tremendous.'[59] The effects of the means test could be represented in hard cash, and it was widely suggested that the lost income in Glamorgan and Monmouthshire would be £1.5 million a year.[60] The suspension of the regulations was seen as being good for traders as well as for the unemployed. 'It was a good thing for every doctor and cobbler, solicitor and publican, cinema owner and chimney sweep, tinker and tailor ... One cinema dropped an average of £17 a week last week and the week before. One public-house we know dropped in the two weeks £15.'[61]

Middle-class support may also have been influenced by the fact that the Act gave relatively little relief to the rates. It had been trumpeted as a great social charter because it promised to be the saviour of the ratepayer. As poor relief (a local charge) and transitional benefit were amalgamated into one form of relief payable by central government the ratepayers should have been major beneficiaries. In the event the government still levied a proportion of the charge from local government and thus gave only limited benefits to the hard-pressed shopkeepers.[62] There was also a good deal of support from teachers for unemployed and workers' causes, though this is less surprising than for the shopkeepers, given the prominence of teachers (or former teachers) in the leadership of the labour movement and their direct experience of the effects of the dole on children. Rhondda teachers and doubtless many others passed a resolution condemning the regulations.[63]

Part of this deeply rooted community support was the backing of churches and chapels. Labour was by the thirties respectable enough to win chapel support. In the past socialists had routinely been accused of atheism and free love, but a decade or more of Labour rule in the Valleys had not undermined the social foundations.[64] The chapels had long tilted their theology towards socialism, and this eased the process of acceptance.[65] In 1934 the Revd John Phillips published a volume entitled *Jesus the Agitator* which condemned the relief scales of the unemployed.[66] Glamorgan Congregationalists were discussing the issue of unemployment before the Act was operative. The Revd Jenkin Lloyd asked for work or honourable maintenance, an end to the means test, the raising of the school-leaving age and pensions at sixty – an impeccable list of Labour demands in the period.[67] Some chapels like Ebenezer English Baptist Chapel in Senghennydd had socialist ministers.[68] But support from religious institutions and clergy extended far beyond the ranks of those who were closely associated with the labour cause. It also went beyond the bounds of nonconformity into the Anglican and Catholic Churches. But chapels in particular joined enthusiastically in the demonstrations, with some cancelling Sunday services in order to do so. All the churches in Cwmbach supported the protests; and in Mountain Ash, Sunday schools closed to allow the demonstrations to take place.[69] Occasionally there was friction over the employment of the Sabbath for protests, but this was not as frequent as might have been expected.[70]

Christian support for the protests was based on the perceived threat to the family which the regulations offered. The Revd E. Emrys Elias of Mount Carmel, Caerphilly, thought that 'the church could play a big part by protesting against something that tended to lower the standard of morality and sending the ordinary man lower than he was'.[71] The Pontypridd and District League of Christian Churches was of a similar mind. The Act was a penalty on thrift and a premium on prodigality, and 'We view with serious concern the tendency of the act to disrupt family life ... which has been the foundation of our national life and prosperity.'[72] In Merthyr the sisterhoods joined in protests and issued a manifesto which stressed the impact which unemployment had had upon women with the consequent knock-on effect on the family: 'The spirit of discontent and pessimism now prevailing amongst the women is a menace to the well being of the homes and the community.'[73]

Ministers of religion were often prominent in the marches and spoke on political platforms against the regulations. At a large demonstration in Pontypridd three ministers spoke.[74] At Llanelli the Revd W. M. Rees of Pontyberem agreed with the view of a local MP that it was a 'damnable act'.[75] There was little doubt that churches saw an opportunity in the movement to rebuild their credibility in an increasingly secular age. The Revd R. B. Owen of Windsor Road Church, Caerphilly, let the cat out of the bag: 'They as ministers in Caerphilly wanted them [the unemployed] to realise they were interested in this matter . . . They as ministers would like a closer identification with them and to be of some help in their troubles.'[76]

There was not unanimity in the relationship between the churches and the labour movement, however. George Hall raised a local storm when he criticized the churches for not taking part.[77] Some sections of the churches also criticized their involvement in the agitation. The Revd Austin H. Birch, writing from Chepstow, found biblical texts to underwrite the means test, surely a delight to the *Western Mail*, whose editorial line had been similar. The clergy of the rural deanery of Aberdare found a rather more direct answer than a text and suggested that they understood the matter better than someone who lived in 'delightful surroundings' and 'Dr. Birch should be dumped into Abercwmboi . . . for twelve months and be compelled to exist on the pittance doled out to the inhabitants . . .'[78] The Revd W. Bradshaw caused great controversy when he published an article in the *Methodist Recorder* arguing that little poverty was being endured. Ministers were as quick to condemn him as the 'usual suspects' like Nye Bevan.[79]

The demonstrations of 1935 tell us a good deal about society and culture in south Wales in the 1930s. Primarily they reflected the nature of its community. Some observers felt that community had been undermined by the impact of the depression.[80] Others felt that a dense network of community organizations survived the terrible impact of the slump.[81] The experience of 1935 seems to weigh heavily on this latter side. Organizations were dense on the ground, as any reader of the local press of the period is forced to recognize, and the demonstrations proved the ability to mobilize them when the very livelihood of the general community was threatened. Community was laid out on the streets for the world to see.

Urban spaces are arenas around which people flow individually or in groups. No one has understood this as well as L. S. Lowry, whose canvases depict urban contexts and events which pattern groups of people. The narrow streets of the south Wales Valleys which converged on particular central points provided distinctive frames for flows of people. The daily journey to work, the route of the funeral cortège and the walk away from settlements on to the hills were everyday examples of this. Common, but less frequent, were the routes taken by marching gangs which spread strikes, trade union demonstrations aiming at a public hall or an open space, chapel demonstrations, political rallies, carnival routes, the paths taken by gazooka bands, and the kind of parade led by a brass band aimed at raising funds for the local hospital. In all these there was an expression of power and numbers. Chapels aimed to show their strength and dominance as much as did the labour movement. Both demonstrated their respectability, usually through their clothing and cleanliness.

Each of these events would have its participants and its onlookers, both of whom would shift positions for different events. In 1935 there was perceived to be a threat to the whole community and the distinction between onlooker and parader (both of whom are participants in a public spectacle, of course) evaporated. It was the whole range of street events placed end to end and mixed up. Brass bands led the way, Sunday schools and chapels marched much as they did on other occasions, as did trade unionists, political activists and members of the British Legion, who made an annual pilgrimage to cenotaphs. Some marchers may have been remembering their military days. They could sense power and volume as they surged through the confined streets towards a central meeting point: 'Mountain Ash the "half-way house" of the eight mile long valley was the people's Mecca on that Sabbath Day, not for prayer or supplication, but for the united purpose of demanding the adjustment of wrongs and restoration of rights.'[82] Release followed as they disgorged into an open space for the meeting which ended the proceedings.

Initially there was a funereal spirit: 'There was no swing and no zest about this march. It was a grim parade ... feet trod heavily and the banners flaunted nothing but tragedy and bitterness ... it was like a funeral cortege.'[83] This was quickly changed because of the support gathered and the sense of fraternity that was engendered. The marches revealed the strength of the overall community – organizations placed end to end stretched much further than anyone had imagined. Individual chapels were absorbed in their debts, trade unions in their lost memberships, brass bands in paying for their expensive instruments. But collectively the whole community showed it had strength. Here it was on public display. Within a week the processions 'had the atmosphere of a gymanfa ganu or a Sunday School rally!...There were smiles, jokes and laughter on every side. Men, women and children wore their "best" clothes.'[84] Some of the later marches even had instances of carnival within them with marchers allegedly being more interested in posing for photographers than in listening to speeches.[85]

It was respectability which was being defended. The means test threatened the little luxuries which made life bearable for many as well as the basic means of survival for others. If the 1904–5 religious revival was in many ways an expression of guilt on the part of migrants from rural areas for their embrace of urban values and pastimes, this generation would march to defend those urban values and protect them from the attacks of the state. In the sense that they were defending consumer rights – not living by bread alone was a quite frequent phrase used in meetings – they were the true heirs of the looters of shops in Tonypandy.[86] Brynmawr UDC felt the regulations reduced 'the standard of living of the families of the unemployed to a level far below that which any self-respecting British citizen would consider reasonably adequate'. Elsewhere there was talk of 'humiliation', 'being down to the dregs' and a degraded standard of living, while the Act was a 'slave act'.[87]

Part of the sense of community was a recognition that these were now well-rooted industrial societies. Inspiration and perspective were drawn from the past. Consciousness of a history of struggle shone through. The inventive 'Pendar' of the *Aberdare Leader* constantly summoned up his mythical 'Dai' to comment on the present through his memories of the past.[88] In 1935 he could point to the parallel of the hauliers' strike of 1893 and contrast the wildness of the past with the order and the greater numbers mobilized of the present.[89] Other examples were sometimes drawn upon, like 1910 and 1926. However, it was mainly Communists who drew on Tonypandy in a positive sense;[90] more common was the warning against this kind of action. The close proximity to the centenary of Tolpuddle and the Poor Law Amendment Act ensured that it was the world of the Chartists that was most commonly invoked.[91] Commemorations do not always serve right-wing ends.[92] D. J. Williams invoked the

Chartists, along with many others: 'not for a hundred years had the national conscience been stirred ... Then the protest was that of the Chartists, who were fighting for wider Parliamentary representation. Now we were protesting against the handiwork of Parliament.'[93] The image of the Chartists marching down valleys stirred many historical imaginations:

> One hundred years ago the mining valleys of South Wales and Monmouthshire echoed to the tramp of the supporters of the People's Charter ... These same hills and valleys, one hundred years later echo and re-echo to the sound of the tramp, tramp of a vast army of workers, again ... determined to win redress for grievances as intolerable as those under which their forefathers laboured and fought against for years.[94]

The general view was that there had been progress.[95] The past was ransacked for examples including accounts of the days when young children had laboured long hours in industrial occupations. George Hall stressed such things in a series of broadcasts around Christmas 1934. Vigilance was required if there was not to be a return to those days. Bevan suggested that if the Act were implemented the last hundred years would have been lived in vain.[96] Douglas Hughes thought that 'a soulless Capitalist Government forces the standard of life down to the basis of medieval days'.[97] The general wealth of the era – the constant references to poverty in the midst of plenty – also provided a historical perspective. Suffering may have been understandable in the past but was clearly intolerable in the present.[98] Further, knowledge of the past conveyed a sense that history was being made in the present. The actions of the early months of 1935 would ultimately find their place in the pantheon of struggles of which history was composed.[99] George Hall was compared to Keir Hardie.[100] Where once the Chartists had drawn inspiration from the nonconformist tradition, from Cromwell, George Washington and Jesus the radical, they in turn had become the stuff of a progressive view of history. An industrial society required heroes from an earlier industrial era rather than from the remoter past.[101]

The protest movement also tells us much about contemporary conceptions of the family. The responsibility of families for their members in hard times was one of the foundations of the poor law.[102] Up to the nineteenth century there had been what has been called a 'family economy'. The welfare of the unit was placed ahead of that of the individual. It was a form of family rooted in the precariousness of pre-industrial society and one which was under challenge long before the 1930s. By then there was a much clearer sense of individual rights – including consumer rights – which the means test challenged.[103] The means test compelled family members to support each other through unemployment with the contribution of the state correspondingly reduced. This produced a widespread sense of injustice and a feeling that in many cases families would break up rather than endure this humiliation. There was a triple challenge: first to parental authority if offspring were obliged to support their parents; second to filial affection given that parents had to support unemployed adult offspring; and thirdly a test to sibling affection if brothers and sisters became responsible for each other. Speaker after speaker defended the sanctity of the home and saw the regulations as smashing it up. It was referred to as a home-wrecking Act.[104] The break-up of the family was seen as posing moral dangers – the 'premature' release of offspring from parental authority and supervision. Individual rights were asserted: women had struggled for economic rights but were paid lower wages on the grounds that they had no responsibilities, but now responsibilities were being thrust upon them. Those in work were seen as having a right to a higher standard of living rather than being reduced to the poverty line by the support of members of their family. How would young people be able to marry if they spent their incomes on supporting their parents?[105] The conception of the family which was involved was, of course, one in which men had the dominant role, the nuclear family based on a family wage paid to men, as W. H Mainwaring revealed: 'They wanted security for their homes, sustenance for their wives. If they were not prepared to strike a blow for these things then they were not fit to be called men.'[106]

Defenders of the measures tended to take a rather literal view of the biblical rhetorical question: 'Am I my brother's keeper?' Opponents implicitly assumed that in a modern society the state was in this fraternal position. They were forced to define the family. Nye Bevan did so in the modern form of nuclear family, rejecting the kind of family economy on which the means test was predicated.

The family should be defined as father, mother, and children under 16 because employers did not pay family wages to any employé [sic] ... The sons and daughters of working class families had never been wanting in supporting their parents, but there was a difference between doing that voluntarily and being made to do it by law.[107]

How effective was the protest movement? It certainly contributed to the government's U-turn in policy in early February, though it was not the only factor. A general election was on the horizon and unemployment was likely to be a major issue in it. The government was clearly trying to limit the damage to itself and was keen to be seen to be doing something for the unemployed. The Special Areas Act followed the Unemployment Act in Parliament. The ground was being prepared for an election and the protests threatened to upset the carefully considered plans.[108] The victory of 1935 was only a suspension of the regulations and the government bided its time until after it had won the election before bringing the new ones in. Massive protest followed in south Wales but with less overall effect.

The demonstrations of 1936 were in some respects a hangover from 1935.[109] The government's policy had been 'masterly inactivity'. Despite thirty-two parliamentary questions it did not introduce the new regulations until well after it had been re-elected. They became operative only on 16 November 1936, a year after the election. Huge marches were mobilized in many parts of south Wales to counter them, and once again widespread support was forthcoming, including from Conservative Clubs (there were over seventy in south Wales), which claimed that they had been instrumental in causing the turnabout of 1935. Yet these marches seem to have been old hat: the only new element were suggestions to boycott the Coronation. They did not dominate the press as they had done eighteen months previously. They seemed sporadic and scattered. Some of this may have been the result of the pouring of organizational energies into the hunger march to London – aimed essentially against these regulations – in the autumn of 1936. The demonstrations of July 1936 were bigger and more determined than in 1935, even though the widely quoted figure of 100,000 in a demonstration in the Rhondda might need to be deflated to 'only' 50,000.

But they had less punch. The cuts were to be less extensive than in 1935 and, crucially, phased in over eighteen months. A government which did not have to face the electorate until November 1940 had little to fear and was signally unmoved by the protests. The general environment was also less receptive. The middle classes – outside south Wales – now felt that the regulations should be given a chance. International affairs may have been more of a distraction, too. In March 1936 Hitler had reoccupied the Rhineland. South Wales was as angry as in 1935 but now its protest was impotent.

The phasing of the reduction made for less graphic examples of cuts than had been provided in January 1935. If there were any lingering prospects of effective political action they were dispelled by the King's visit to south Wales within days of the new regulations coming into force. This was far from being a plot by the government, for it was embarrassed by the visit; this added to the pressures being exerted by the commissioner for Special Areas, Sir Malcolm Stewart, for industrial relocation to south Wales.[110] But it must have had the spin-off effect of derailing whatever remaining prospects the protest movement against the means test had.

Business owners who almost two years before had made common cause with the unemployed were now asked to decorate their premises for the King. People who had once marched in the streets in protest now lined them waving Union Jacks at a young, film-star-like King who exuded a gentle, informal approach, lacking pomp and patronage: 'HOWEVER BITTER THE PEOPLE OF THE ABERDARE VALLEY MAY FEEL ABOUT THE MEANS TEST AND HIS MAJESTY'S MINISTERS' INDIFFERENCE TO THESE DISTRESSED AREAS THEY TOOK OUR KING TO THEIR HEARTS YESTERDAY.'[111]

In the same week the marching miners reached London in the rain. The message that was conveyed by all this was that the problems of south Wales had been recognized and would be dealt with in due course. In many ways that was what the demonstrators wanted, but now the promise was vague and did not relate to the specifics of the Act which was still seen as a matter of life and death for south Wales. Others had seized the political agenda. The King was shown examples of social-service work in south Wales rather than conditions of poverty. A concept of history rather different from that which had been elaborated in south Wales over the last twenty or more years was paraded:

> The visit of King Edward to South Wales last week is now history. That it will produce good is beyond doubt, for His Majesty has given a personal undertaking that, 'something will be done'. South Wales, which to many people was but a name, has suddenly gained prominence in the news, and the story of its misery has been discussed by Peers and Commoners ... the cumulative effect of the hunger marches, the publication of the report by Sir Malcolm Stewart and the King's visit, have all contributed to arousing widespread attention.[112]

After this, national papers carried articles on south Wales and some were even well-informed. A Tory backbench revolt shocked the government and ensured that it had to promise to come up with definite plans for action within two months.[113] By then the 'people's King' had forsaken south Wales for the arms of the woman he loved, but he had left some mark on the Valleys. Protests against the means test continued to some extent in south Wales, including a 'March of History' held at Tonypandy in March 1937, but they were no longer amplified by the megaphone of a receptive general situation.[114]

The nature of the community in industrial south Wales was demonstrated by its politics. It was solid against a distant government and displayed a strong regional consciousness. Yet it was indubitably part of the British state, aspired to control it, and could even respond to its most archaic trappings. All overtures from Plaid Cymru to join in the campaign were firmly rejected. The regulations threatened the south Wales coalfield and it created a united protest movement. It was the protest movement of an *organized* working class. It drew on the strength of trade union and political organization and was not – unlike crowd actions of the eighteenth and nineteenth centuries – an attempt to work without such structures. Demonstrations were organized by trades and labour councils, the Fed, unemployed clubs and a myriad of other organizations. In several communities there were Councils of Action which drew together the whole panoply of labour and community organizations under one umbrella.[115] There were limits to the amount of popular frontism which was achieved, and Labour and the Communist Party did not at all suspend party conflict, even if there were large areas of co-operation between them in many places. The protest movement drew on the experience and attitudes of the Communist Party but fitted them into a wider structure of community organization. As the popular front tactic recognized, the Communist Party alone could not create mass mobilization of the kind which was seen in 1935. Having created such a widespread basis of support, the parties could contest the control of it fiercely. Labour would ultimately win the struggle, which stretched out over the decade which followed. In doing so it laid the foundations for and anticipated its hegemony in Welsh politics achieved after 1945[116] and for the victory in the general election of 1945. In each case Labour would need to lead an alliance of forces which stretched beyond its own ranks. This need had long been recognized by Labour politicians and was embryonically achieved in 1929: but 1935 was a popular alliance in support of welfare, in the interests of the whole community, which prefigured that which created the welfare state.[117]

The events of January–February 1935 mark a shift in the consciousness of industrial south Wales. It was a mass action adjusted to the realities of the loss of industrial power after 1926. It exerted pressure on government by means of the weight of public opinion rather than by industrial muscle. When the planned strike was defeated by its enemies within the labour movement it was perhaps the final interment of syndicalist direct action even in its symbolic form of a token general strike. In place of industrial strength was an appeal to a larger community, an issue with which industrial unionism had always struggled yet never resolved. A deep and well-honed tradition of popular protest was firmly held within the bounds of constitutional action. In many ways it was the alliance which had characterized Lib-Labism, but it now had the labour movement firmly in the driving seat and setting the course. In capsule form 1930s 'middle opinion' was provided with a popular basis, which it still lacked in Britain as a whole.[118] It would take a war to synchronize them in Britain. South Wales in 1935 achieved something like William James's 'moral equivalent of war' and the kind of political configuration which would transform post-war Britain.[119] The parallel of the war was in the consciousness of one Labour councillor: 'Our lads fought in 1914–18 to prevent a German invasion ... but the biggest enemy in the workers' homes last Friday was far worse than any German invasion.'[120] A similar theme was warmed to by the Revd Bedford Roberts in a protest at Pontardawe. The young men affected by the regulations would be expected to fight for the Empire if it were attacked: they therefore had a right to claim justice from the community. Here there were also echoes of the themes of social imperialism and the military participation ratio that have been used by various subsequent writers to connect war and social reform.[121]

The tramping feet of the marchers would have softer echoes a decade later in the corridors of power. It was entirely appropriate that Aneurin Bevan and Jim Griffiths should be amongst those who remade Britain.[122] Their constituents had given the cause of a humane welfare state a huge boost a decade earlier and demonstrated the broadly based political alliance which would be needed to secure it.

Notes

1. Thanks to Elisabeth Bennett, Hywel Francis, Dot Jones, John Graham Jones and Kate Sullivan for their help in the preparation of this essay. Discussions with Paul O'Leary helped formulate my ideas; he and David Howell gave the text the benefit of a close reading.

2. D. J. V. Jones, *Rebecca's Children: A Study of Rural Society, Crime and Protest* (Oxford, 1989), 214–21.

3. H. Francis and D. Smith, *The Fed: The South Wales Miners in the Twentieth Century* (London, 1980), ch.8; H. Francis, *Miners Against Fascism: Wales and the Spanish Civil War* (London, 1984), ch.3; L. Jones, *We Live* (London, 1939), esp. ch.XIX; G. Thomas, *Sorrow for thy Sons* (London, 1986), esp. part 3; K. Roberts, 'Gorymdaith', *Ffair Gaeaf a Storiau Eraill* (Dinbych, 1937), translated as 'Protest March' in Joseph Clancy (ed.), *The World of Kate Roberts: Selected Stories, 1925–1981* (Philadelphia, 1991).

4. J. Stevenson and C. Cook, *The Slump: Society and Politics in the Depression* (London, 1977; paperback edn 1979).

5. J. Keegan, *Warpaths: Travels of a Military Historian in North America* (London, 1995), 25, 26–7.

6. *Voluntary Service in South Wales: Second Annual Report of South Wales and Monmouthshire Council of Social Service, 1935–36* (SW&MCSS), 3.

7. Portal's deliberations and conclusions were widely reported in the south Wales press, e.g. *Merthyr Express* (*ME*), 5 May, 17 October, 3

November 1934; *South Wales Voice* (*SWV*), 16 June, 10 November, 8 December 1934; *Rhondda Gazette* (*RhG*), 1 December 1934. His report 'South Wales and Monmouthshire' is in Parliamentary Papers, 1933–4, XIII, Cmd 4728; P. Massey, *Industrial South Wales* (London, 1940), 60–3 ; J. E. Daniel, *Welsh Nationalism: What it Stands For* (London, n.d., *c*. 1937), 26–9.

8. *RhG*, 13 October 1934.

9. S. Buchan, *The Scent of Water* (London, 1937). Thanks to Chris Harvie for this reference.

10. P. Stead, 'The voluntary response to mass unemployment in south Wales', in W. E. Minchinton (ed.), *Reactions to Social and Economic Change, 1750–1939* (Exeter Papers in Economic History, 1979), 104–7; *Rhondda Leader* (*RhL*), 6 October 1934.

11. *RhG*, 15 December 1934.

12. *Aberdare Leader* (*AL*), 1, 8, 22 September, 13, 20 October, 12 December 1934.

13. *SWV*, 3 November, 29 December 1934; SW&MCSS, 1934, 22; 1935–6, 7; 1936–7, 21. *ME*, 5, 12 May, 25 August, 3 November 1934; *RhL*, 1, 8, 15, 22, 29 September, 6 October 1934.

14. See D. Smith, *Lewis Jones* (Cardiff, 1982).

15. Cox, *Autobiography*, 69–70, 90, 110–11; second version, pp.20–1, 32, 56, 61; University of Wales Swansea, South Wales Coalfield Archive, Glyn Evans (Garnant) Papers. 'Report on South Wales District [of the Communist Party] – March 1935' (henceforward 1935 Report).

16. L. Jones, *From Exchange and Parish to the P.A.C: For Decency Instead of Destitution* (Tonypandy, 1934), 2.

17. I had written this passage before reading the similar terms in which a recent analysis of the rise of Nazism deals with the heady August days of 1914, when the German public turned from being cheering onlookers at Prussian military parades to demonstrators in favour of war. P. Fritzsche, *Germans into Nazis* (Cambridge, Mass., 1998), 22–5. The book suggests the salience of extending crowd analysis of the kind which David Jones helped pioneer into twentieth-century history.

18. L. Jones (ed.), *Monmouthshire Hunger March of August 1933* (Abertillery, 1933).

19. Cox, *Autobiography*, second version p.38; *Daily Worker* (*DW*), 1, 3, 6, 8, 9, 10, 20, 27 October, 21 November, 1 December 1934, p.1; 1935 Report, p.1; *Llanelly and County Guardian* (*LlCG*), 11 October, 8 November 1934, *Llanelly Mercury* (*LlM*), 6 December 1934; *Llanelly Star* (*LlS*), 8 December 1934; *ME*, 14 July 1934; *RhG*, 22 September 1934; *RhL*, 22 September 1934; *AL*, 20 October 1934.

20. *Western Mail* (*WM*), 26 October 1934; N. Evans, 'Cardiff's Labour tradition', *Llafur*, 4, 2 (1985).

21. *DW*, 30 May 1934; W. Paynter, *My Generation* (London, 1972), 98.
22. *ME*, 2 June 1934.
23. 1935 Report, 4–5.
24. E. Stonelake, *Aberdare Trades and Labour Council, 1900–1950: Jubilee Souvenir* (Aberdare, n.d., c. 1950), 23.
25. A. Deacon and E. Briggs, 'Local democracy and central policy: the issue of pauper votes in the 1920s', *Policy and Politics*, 2, 4 (June 1974); Briggs and Deacon, 'The creation of the National Unemployment Assistance Board', *Policy and Politics*, 2, 1 (September 1973); S. Rh. Williams, 'The Bedwellty Board of Guardians and the Default Act of 1927', *Llafur*, 2, 4 (1979).
26. B. B. Gilbert, *British Social Policy, 1914–1939* (London, 1970), ch.2; Briggs and Deacon 'Creation . . .'.
27. Cited in J. Lewis, 'The relations between central and local government in England and Wales in the period 1923–1933 . . .' (unpublished University of Wales MA thesis, 1936), 149.
28. *Glamorgan County Council Elections 1934: Judge for Yourself: A Record of Labour Rule on the Glamorgan County Council*, 9–11.
29. *WM*, 15, 18 January 1935; *ME*, 19 January 1935. UWS, SWCC, MNA/Pol/2/X Minutes of the Aberdare Trades and Labour Council, 3 January 1935.
30. *LlCG*, 14 February 1935; *SWV*, 19 January, 9 February 1935; NLW, Labour Party Collection, Minutes of the East Glamorgan (Labour) Women's Advisory Council, 23 September 1933; 24 February 1934.
31. R. H. S. Phillpott, *Where Labour Rules: A Tour through Towns and Counties* (London, 1934), 97.
32. *ME*, 1 December 1934; *DW*, 19 January 1935.
33. *WM*, 21, 24 January 1935; *ME*, 1 December, 21 January 1935.
34. SW&MCSS 1935–6, 3.
35. Hansard, vol. 283, 1933–4, 23 November 1933, cols. 1091–2.
36. Lewis, 'Relations between central and local government', 150.
37. Hansard, vol. 289, 1933–4, 15 May 1934, cols. 1471–2.
38. Hansard, vol. 238, 1933–4, cols. 1309–24 for Bevan's major speech.
39. C. Williams, *Democratic Rhondda: Society and Politics, 1885–1951* (Cardiff, 1996).
40. For reasons of space this section is rather schematic and undocumented. It is based on a close examination of *AL*, *ME*, *SWV*, *RhG*, *RhL*, *LlCG*, *LlS*, *LlM*, *WM*, *DW* and the relevant manuscript sources in UWS, SWCC. Much of the relevant narrative is in Francis and Smith, *The Fed*, and Francis, *Miners against Fascism*.
41. F. C. Miller, 'The British unemployment crisis of 1935', *Journal of*

Contemporary History, 14 (1979); J. Stevenson, 'The making of unemployment policy, 1931–1935', in M. Bentley and Stevenson (eds.), *High and Low Politics in Modern Britain* (Oxford, 1983).

42. Neil Evans and Dot Jones, '"To help forward the great work of humanity": women in the Labour Party in Wales, 1900–2000', in Deian Hopkin, Duncan Tanner and C. Williams (eds.), *A Centenary History of the Labour Party in Wales* (Cardiff, forthcoming, 2000); *Labour Woman* (February, March 1935); *DW*, 6, 9, 20, 27 October; 21 November, 1 December 1934; 26 January, 2, 5, 8, 16, 23 February, 4 March 1935.

43. *AL*, 7 July 1935.
44. *Monmouthshire Hunger March*, 5.
45. *SWV*, 17 November 1934.
46. *AL*, 2 March 1935. Similar sentiments were expressed by Cllr A. J. Chick; *RhG*, 23 February 1935.
47. *SWV*, 2, 16 June, 27 July, 20 October, 8 December 1934.
48. *LlCG*, 7, 14 June, 26 July 1934.
49. *LlS*, 27 April 1935.
50. *SWV*, 3 October 1936.
51. NLW, James Griffiths Papers, A 4/40.
52. D. Smith, 'Tonypandy 1910: definitions of community', *Past and Present*, 87 (1980); G. A. Williams, *The Merthyr Rising* (London, 1978).
53. S. Pollard, 'Trade unions reactions to the economic crisis', *Journal of Contemporary History*, 4 (1969), 102–11.
54. The Bridgeman Award was seen as increasing the spending power of the coalfield (*SWV*, 10 November 1934).
55. *SWV*, 19 January 1935.
56. D. Johnston (ed.), *The Complete Poems of Idris Davies* (Cardiff, 1994), 24.
57. *WM*, 7 January 1935.
58. *RhL*, 19 January 1935.
59. *AL*, 26 January 1935; *SWV*, 9 February 1935.
60. *RhG*, 26 January 1935; *SWV*, 26 January 1935; *ME*, 12 January 1935; *WM*, 7 January 1935.
61. *AL*, 29 September, 13 October, 15 December 1934; *RhG*, 23 February 1935.
62. *ME*, 29 December 1934, 12 January 1935.
63. *AL*, 29 September, 6 October 1934; *RhG*, 16 February 1935.
64. P. Stead, 'Vernon Hartshorn: miners' agent and Cabinet minister', in Stewart Williams (ed.), *Glamorgan Historian*, VI (Barry, 1969); Williams, *Democratic Rhondda*.
65. R. Pope, *Building Jerusalem: Nonconformity, Labour and the Social Question in Wales, 1906–1939* (Cardiff, 1998).
66. *AL*, 7 July 1934.

67. *ME*, 9 June 1934.
68. I am indebted to my father's reminiscences. *ME*, 23 February, 2 March 1935.
69. *AL*, 26 January, 9 February 1935.
70. *SWV*, *ME*, 23 February 1935.
71. *RhG*, 9 February 1935.
72. *RhG*, 23 February 1935.
73. *ME*, 9 February 1935.
74. *RhG*, 2 February 1935.
75. *LCG*, 14 February 1935.
76. *RhG*, 9 February 1935.
77. *AL*, 26 January 1935.
78. *WM*, 30, 31 January, 1, 5, 12 (quotation) February 1935.
79. *ME*, 2, 9 March 1935.
80. H. Jennings, *Brynmawr* (London 1934); *A Town on the Dole* (Communist Party pamphlet, *c.* 1937).
81. Pilgrim Trust, *Men without Work* (London, 1938).
82. *AL*, 9 February 1935.
83. *AL*, 2 February 1935.
84. *AL*, 9 February 1935.
85. *RhG*, 2 March 1935.
86. *SWV*, 9 February 1935; Smith, 'Tonypandy 1910'.
87. *WM*, 1 February 1935; *AL*, 5, 12, 26 January, 9 February 1935.
88. J. F. Mear, 'John Davies (Pendar): a selection of his writings', *Old Aberdare*, V (1988).
89. *AL*, 9, 23 February 1935.
90. *DW*, 8 January 1935, reporting a meeting at the Royal Cinema, Tonypandy.
91. *SWV*, 9, 16 February 1935.
92. C. Williams, 'History, heritage and commemoration: Newport, 1839–1939', *Llafur*, 6 (1992).
93. *SWV*, 9 February 1935; *DW*, 2 February 1935.
94. *DW*, 2 February 1935.
95. *AL*, 29 December 1935.
96. *WM*, 4 February 1935.
97. Letter to *LlCG*, 7 February 1935.
98. *AL*, 2 March 1935.
99. *AL*, 9 February 1935.
100. *AL*, 16 February 1935.
101. D. J. V. Jones, 'Chartism in Welsh communities', *Welsh History Review*, 6 (1973), 253.
102. M. A Crowther, 'Family responsibility and state responsibility in Britain before the welfare state', *Historical Journal*, 25 (1982).

103. Louise A. Tilly and Joan W. Scott, *Women, Work and Family* (2nd edn., London, 1987).
104. E.g. *LlCG*, 7 February 1935; *RG*, 2 February 1935.
105. *RhL*, 2 February, *WM*, 11 February 1935.
106. *RhG*, 9 February 1935.
107. *WM*, 4, 11 February 1935.
108. F. C. Miller, 'The unemployment policy of the National Government, 1931–1936', *Historical Journal*, 19 (1976).
109. This account is derived from *RhL*, *AL* and *SWV* for June–November 1936 unless otherwise noted.
110. BBC 2 Wales, *Something Must Be Done*, 1997, based on research by Ted Rowlands, MP.
111. *AL*, 21 November 1936; identical phrasing in *RhL*, 21 November 1936.
112. *SWV*, 28 November 1936.
113. According to Rowlands's research, the crucial decision was taken on the eve of the King's visit and conveyed to him at the station as he left for south Wales.
114. NLW, Cox Papers, Autobiography, 2nd version, p.67.; *South Wales in the March of History . . . Programme for the Communist Party March through Mid Rhondda*, 21 March 1937.
115. UWS, SWCA, 1935 Report, p.2.
116. I. McAllister, 'The Labour Party in Wales: the dynamics of one-partyism', *Llafur*, 3 (1981).
117. J. G. Jones, 'Wales and the "New Socialism", 1926–29', *Welsh History Review*, 11 (1982).
118. Arthur Marwick, 'Middle opinion in the thirties: planning, progress and "political agreement"', *English Historical Review*, 79 (1964).
119. A. Marwick, *Britain in the Century of Total War: War, Peace and Social Change, 1900–1967* (London, 1968; Pelican edn, 1970), 462.
120. *AL*, 26 January 1935.
121. *SWV*, 9 February 1935.
122. K. O. Morgan, *Labour in Power, 1945–1951* (Oxford, 1984), ch.4.

'It's Not All about Nicking Folks': Dramatizing the Police

PETER STEAD

As the twentieth century moved to a close the police were looming large in the national culture of the United Kingdom. For a number of different reasons and in a wide variety of forms the police were always in the public eye with both television and the press displaying an almost unprecedented interest in the whole system of policing. This media concern amounted to a preoccupation. Traditionally, and indeed since the formation of modern policing in 1829, the British had keenly debated the nature of their police, but it would be difficult to argue that either the defenders or the critics of what was always taken to be a uniquely British institution had fully caught the public's attention.[1] Certainly the *Saturday Review*'s 1864 warning that 'we are police-ridden somewhat in the same way that the Italian is priest-ridden' had never become the basis of a general soul-searching.[2] Even in the police-fascinated 1990s the debate was never truly focused, but indubitably one could identify a culture that seemed very inclined to investigate, albeit in a number of uncoordinated political, documentary and fictional modes, the precise meaning of an institution whose good order and ethics were now, more than ever before, seen as being fundamental not only to the nation's identity but also to its well-being.

In the 1990s the police were rarely out of the news, and very little of the police news was good news. The latest headlines concerning the scandals involving individual chief constables and the massive cost of police malingering probably came as no surprise to a public that had almost become accustomed to such revelations. In 1992 Robert Reiner had adjudged that the police were standing at a lower ebb in public trust and esteem than at any other time since they were established in the nineteenth century.[3] He identified a period, a quarter of a century, in which things had seemed to go disastrously wrong for a British police which had hitherto seemed well content with the low-key and non-controversial image of reliability and respectability which it had consolidated as part of the general post-1945 social consensus. Between 1969 and 1972 however there occurred what has been described as 'the fall of Scotland Yard' as a result of which 'a score of London detectives went to gaol'.[4] This was just the beginning of a depressing story in which the whole image of British policing was changed. At the very time when the public perceived that they were not being given effective protection against new classes of criminals, the police themselves seemed riddled with corruption and prone to conspire in 'gross miscarriages of justice'. Valiant attempts were made to re-establish respect, but these efforts tended to be negated by new grounds of complaint in what one historian referred to as a 'dizzily-changing society'.[5]

Much was made of the fact that Robert Mark had been brought in to clean up Scotland Yard and the Metropolitan Police but suddenly attention switched away from the issue of corruption to the wider one of whether the police were behaving responsibly in their handling of what were being freshly identified as all the complexities of a new urban culture. Following the inner-city riots of 1981, the Scarman Report called for new policing methods but, even as suggested reforms were being implemented, there were further scandals and increasingly political controversies. Radical groups who were traditionally critical of the police were given a new credibility by two developments in particular. The industrial disputes of the 1980s gave rise to television footage which prompted many members of the public to wonder for the first time whether the police were being excessively politicized and militarized, whilst the whole debate on the police powers of 'stop and search' triggered off by the Police and Criminal Evidence Act (PACE) of 1981 suggested that racial prejudice might be a permanent feature of urban policing. By the 1990s there were politicians, academics and journalists as well as ordinary citizens with serious reservations about almost every aspect of police work, but perhaps most concern centred on the national system of criminal justice itself. In 1996 the journalist David Rose published *In the Name of the Law*, a book which gave rise to a television series called *The Verdict*. Rose's subtitle was *The Collapse of Criminal Justice*, his argument being that the whole

British system was in crisis, 'for it locks up the innocent while the guilty go free'.[6]

The time was ripe for fundamental reforms, and it was this process that made the police newsworthy in the late 1990s. Not for the first time the key figure was to be the commissioner of the Metropolitan Police, a person who is not only directly in control of 27,000 officers but one who has the potential to set the tone for the nation's police forces as a whole. Each commissioner in turn sets his own agenda and to a degree determines the extent and nature of his media exposure. When first appointed in 1993, Sir Paul Condon, the secondary-modern-educated son of a paint sprayer, had seemed a purely managerial figure, remarkable only for his having started out as an ordinary copper on the beat in the East End.[7] However Condon immediately set up a secret investigation unit which was to report to him directly on matters of corruption. In addition he was adamant that he wanted a force that would be more accountable and one capable of tackling crime and other problems 'in partnership with the community'. As a reforming commissioner Condon needed encouragement, and that he was only to receive following Labour's victory in the general election of 1997. The notion that Labour could steal the Conservatives' thunder on the emotive question of law and order had occurred to Tony Blair during his period as shadow Home Affairs spokesman, and it was he who popularized the slogan that 'Labour would be tough on crime and on the causes of crime'.[8] When Blair became party leader in 1994 his portfolio passed to Jack Straw, who seemed even more resolutely to embody a new Labour attitude. By the time of the general election Blair and Straw had seen the Tory Home Secretary Michael Howard become one of the least respected politicians in the land and had effectively neutralized 'Law and Order' as an electoral issue. In the year following Labour's victory Straw not only emerged as a strong Home Secretary but proved to have the safest pair of hands in the government. In 1998 Straw and Condon together were promising a new era in policing. As the minister prepared his legislation the commissioner estimated that there were possibly 250 corrupt officers in his force, the trouble being that many of them were senior officers whom it was proving difficult to dislodge.[9] Following discussions with Condon and a report of the Commons Home Affairs Select Committee, Straw promised new power to enable chief constables to sack lazy or corrupt officers without delay. Henceforth 'the balance of possibilities' would be sufficient grounds for action, and steps were to be taken to end the infamous dispensation whereby suspected officers took early retirement on health grounds to avoid disciplinary charges.[10] Meanwhile in the Crime and Disorder Bill the Home Secretary introduced a whole range of measures specifically aimed at ending the culture of persistent offending that threatened the quality of life in many communities: Labour was promising increased protection to ordinary everyday victims of crime throughout the land.[11]

The press warmly welcomed the Straw–Condon initiatives. In *The Times* Libby Purves particularly welcomed the government's assurance that working with and reassuring communities was every bit as important as catching criminals. Her argument was that 'aloof, abrupt, macho threatening figures in squad cars ... do not inspire either affection or trust' and that 'the snarling, snapping, sneering, tough-guy culture of TV cop shows is an unhelpful fiction'. Her point was that 'a civilian police force should never forget that its core, its very heart, should be civil in all senses of the word'.[12] In *The Sunday Times* the historian Andrew Roberts explained why the 1997 elections had been such a watershed. The Tories, he argued, had been so dependent on 'the thin blue line at Brixton, Orgreave, Wapping and in 1990 at Trafalgar Square that they had never been in any position to reform the police themselves': consequently the police and the prison officers had remained 'the last two great unreformed trade unions in the land'. Roberts welcomed the way Straw, prompted by Condon and brushing aside the objections of the Police Federation, was introducing the fast-track disciplinary procedures. These reforms were helping to break down what Roberts termed 'the culture of the NCOs' mess which dominates today's police force', a culture which had been useful in its time but which had 'been allowed to take over the system itself' and which was characterized by 'rough justice, corner-cutting, back-scratching, chippiness, grumbling, jobsworthiness and occasional kickbacks'.[13] Perhaps, to an extent they could never have envisaged, the reformers were encouraging a wide-ranging and fundamental analysis of police culture.

All the while the politicians and press commentators were addressing a public who were more fully conversant with the system of policing than any previous body of citizens. Thirty years of complaints by radicals and of investigative journalism particularly on television had disabused a public of their traditional notions. More crucially, there had been an increased awareness of how growing crime rates had either coincided with or been occasioned by new fashions in police methods. Many citizens had developed their own notions about policing and were prepared to debate them, albeit in catchphrases. The way in which the 1960s had seen the officer on the beat replaced by panda and patrol cars was universally adjudged to be a disaster, the usual comment being that 'you never see the police around here'.[14] In particular it was generally agreed that the twin issues of drugs and race had set challenges which the police had been incapable of meeting. Following Scarman, a good deal of faith had been invested in the concept of 'community policing', which had been championed by chief constables such as John Alderson. The police, it was hoped, would come out of their bunkers and proceed to work with a whole range of local community organizations.[15] By the time Labour came to power the new buzz phrase was 'zero tolerance', a system of policing devised in America by Professor James Wilson and implemented with great success in cities such as New York and Baltimore. Jack Straw was greatly enamoured of this method's emphasis on grass-roots action to prevent the exposure of young people to the temptations of crime from the very outset.[16]

The public's increasing familiarity with methods of policing was rounded off by the new emphasis chief constables were placing on public relations. Undoubtedly this was a new strategy devised to counter the notion that individual forces had become less accountable at the local level. Both the conduct and the deployment of the police during the industrial disputes of the 1980s had raised fears that the United Kingdom was moving towards a centrally controlled national police force. In 1985 Roger Geary argued that 'what has disappeared without much notice ever being paid to its existence is the informal control exercised by the community over the police'.[17] This was borne out a decade later, for when the Conservatives set up new police authorities in which the role of elected councillors was severely diminished, there was no national rumpus.[18] In any case the transition was presented in a new wave of publicity which stressed the approachability of the police and their general availability as a service. In October 1997 the Welsh press carried a bilingual twelve-page tabloid supplement explaining every detail of how the South Wales Constabulary operated. A full-colour front page showed PC Debbie Powell of Swansea helping to carry an elderly lady's shopping up one of the city's steepest hills. On inside pages there were lists of objectives and performance indicators, numerous photographs of both officers and authority members, an explanation of the divisional structure, and throughout lots of advice with full use being made of key phrases such as, 'Always on call, always listening', 'The public want a visible street presence' and 'Volunteers have a special role to play in our society.'[19] In subsequent months it was very noticeable that the South Wales force maintained a high profile by releasing stories in which favourable assessments from the Audit Commission and other sources, as well as statistics indicating falling crime rates, were accompanied by individual photographs of young male and female officers and by headlines such as 'Officers will spend more time out on the beat' and 'Constables will target town centre rowdies.'[20]

The icing on the publicity cake came with the *Police Review*'s Community Officer of the Year Award. The first prize, presented of course by the Home Secretary, went to a Liverpool officer, but there was a place on the short list for Inspector Paul Cannon, the South Wales force's sector inspector at Ton Pentre in the Rhondda Valley. In what had until recently been seen 'as an area of high crime' this officer had turned things around by securing a 400-per cent increase in drug-related arrests, by working with community leaders, organizing drink-and-drug-free raves and operating drop-in centres. It was reported that local media were now proclaiming Ton Pentre as 'an area of hope and regeneration'.[21] Upbeat journalism of this kind was doing a great deal to eclipse the more negative image that had emerged from studies such as Nick Danziger's report on Britain's most desolate neighbourhoods. In 1996 he had encountered a police sense of hopelessness. In the Rhondda he had been told of how the community policeman on the Penrhys estate high above Ton Pentre had been awarded the OBE: 'They should have given him the VC', was the comment of one local.[22]

By 1998, then, the citizens of Britain had been encouraged by politicians, the press and the police themselves to take a keen interest in the whole business of policing. The message was that corruption was being rooted out, community relations improved and methods made more effective, as indicated conclusively in falling crime rates. It would be difficult to agree, though, that good news was carrying the day, for in other reports a darker picture was emerging. General crime rates were down but the opposite was true of violent crimes, and increasingly the police were having to deal with what seemed to be a wave of sex crimes, most noticeably paedophilia.[23] Relatively discreetly the press reported on the setting-up of two new national police bodies to spearhead the fight against serious crime, but the need for such bodies was highlighted by a gathering of senior detectives at Bramshill in April 1998 for a briefing relating to 207 unsolved murders.[24] Perhaps more than anything else, it was the failure of the police to secure convictions for highly publicized and brutal murders such as that of Rachel Nickell on Wimbledon Common in 1992 that undermined their authority with the public at large. And all the time there were reports that confirmed that there were still many inadequate and undesirable police officers. There was concern over the number of deaths in custody, reports that the Met. was paying out large sums of money in compensation in assault cases involving serving officers, and hair-raising accounts of Scotland Yard detectives moonlighting as private eyes and selling police secrets to known criminals.[25] In Cleveland, home of 'zero tolerance' policing, the crime figures were encouraging, but the key senior officer was suspended from duty.[26] Several chief constables, nearly all of whom had been regarded as exemplary new-style managers when appointed, had been forced to relinquish office through shortcomings in their own lives or in the conduct of their officers. British policing remained Janus-faced.

At the same time as the public were being encouraged to take an unprecedented interest in the real world of day-to-day policing, they were giving every indication of a huge appetite for fictional policing. On a Saturday evening in April 1998 BBC1, with much attendant hype, launched *City Central*, a ten-part series which it was explained was their first 'major prime-time police station drama since the flashing blue lights of *Z Cars* faded from our screens in 1978'. As envisaged by Michael Jackson, a former channel controller, the new series would be 'a *Z Cars* for the nineties, a fast-moving ensemble drama that lured the Saturday-night audience back out on the beat in style'.[27] The national press willingly fed off the BBC's enthusiasm and gave *City Central* plenty of advance publicity. In so doing they took the opportunity to reflect, in what had become very familiar terms, both on the changing history of police drama since the early days of *Dixon of Dock Green* and on why such shows were popular. Glyn George thought that there would be no shortage of viewers for the new series, for 'cop shows are perennially the most popular on the box'.[28] Nevertheless BBC bravery had to be admired for, as Steve Clark pointed out, they were venturing into territory where there were already several popular and critically acclaimed series. In fact he could reveal that Tony Jordan, *City Central*'s chief progenitor, had been initially reluctant to develop the idea, given that 'the schedules are awash with police drama'.[29] Clearly, though, the BBC were confident that they had a winner and most previews picked up on that. In the *Radio Times* itself there was a special feature on three new crime programmes, with *City Central* highlighted alongside a documentary on a forensic psychologist specializing in criminal profiling and a new adaptation of a crime novel. No wonder an upbeat editor could joke, 'Who says crime doesn't pay?'[30] Just a few weeks after the launch of *City Central* an independent production company announced that, following the great success of Channel 5's repeats of the 1970s detective series *The Sweeney,* filming was to begin of a remake with Dennis Waterman returning in a more senior position in the Flying Squad. Action would again be the hallmark of the armed response team, but some storylines, it was promised, would deal with corruption.[31]

Clearly police shows, either newly minted or recast, were going to run and run on British television. In the mid-1990s Richard Osborne had pointed out the extent to which popular culture was 'undoubtedly obsessed with crime' whilst David Rose identified Britain 'as a society for which crime has become an obsession'.[32] All of this must have been evident to even the casual television viewer, but what was interesting about remarks made by both critics and producers later in the decade was the obvious awareness of a tradition. Police programmes in particular were now being produced and subsequently reviewed by people very aware of cultural patterns, standards and expectations. Both production and debate were informed by a knowledge of how both popular historians and academics had attempted to trace the changing role of police shows in national life.[33] Their combined analyses formed part of a national mythology which is especially resonant for the middle-aged who lived through all the changes from *Dixon of Dock Green*, through *No Hiding Place*, *Z Cars*, *The Sweeney*, *The Bill* and *Taggart* to *City Central*. There has always been a popular appreciation of how this strand of entertainment has developed, and in casual conversations references will be made to the influence of American models – Hollywood initially, and then in the era of television first *Dragnet* and more recently *Hill Street Blues*. There was a ready appreciation, too, of how successive police series had sustained a notion of realism by reflecting their times in terms of the nature of crimes committed, language and in particular bad language used, the role of violence and sex, the relative integrity of police officers, and more recently racial and gender considerations. The place of PC (later Sergeant) George Dixon, as played by Jack Warner between 1955 and (quite incredibly) 1976, is absolutely secure as an icon of post-war consensus, and references to him are as likely to occur in general histories and journalism as much as in specialist articles.[34] Cultural change in post-war Britain can be explained in terms of the extent to which Dixon is either abandoned or clung to as an ideal.

Police series are produced in a cultural context in which the popular mythology interacts with scholarly debate. Simon Frith, Ian Ang and others have explained the ways in which the BBC of the post-war period set out to create, first for radio and then for television, a distinctly British pattern of entertainment, a whole new mass or popular culture that would be middlebrow, non-American, and an embodiment of desirable values. Frith emphasizes how fully broadcasters appreciated the power and significance of 'the home' and in particular 'the hearth'. Programmes were targeted with precision, and in effect 'to become a BBC listener was to join a club'.[35] Ang explained how in the early days the television audience was objectified 'as a set of citizens ready to be unified and disciplined under the central cultural leadership'.[36] Earlier writings on popular television had already discussed the necessary dependence of producers on conventions and genre in developing patterns of entertainment. Neil Postman had referred to the basic rhythms of television and of the knack American networks had developed of getting those rhythms accepted both within individual programmes and across a whole evening. Subsequently John Corner analysed the role of scheduling and generic style in determining the British concept of what was 'televisual'.[37] Police shows emerged out of these general strategies and were shaped by them. Thus, as Geoffrey Hurd has shown, they eschewed all interest in courts and prisons and largely concentrated on how either a hero or a team secured a conviction: selected aspects of police reality were brought together in what had to be above all a coherent pattern.[38] Inevitably, though, explanations of rhythm, convention and even genre were not entirely sufficient, for there was also the dimension of value, of meaning. In this respect the best starting-point was provided by Julian Symons when he attempted to explain the huge popularity of detective fiction. Basically, Symons argues, a puzzle is neatly resolved, but in all the best books and in the work of all the truly memorable sleuths there is the added satisfaction of a social order, and with it a moral order, being saved. In tracing this crucial dimension in the best crime writing from Conan Doyle through Raymond Chandler and into the contemporary era Symons helped establish a pantheon for the literary genre and also neatly defined the litmus test that has in effect always been applied to police films and series.[39] Writing on television, Brooks Robards suggested that 'police shows are obsessed with coming out on top in the eternal struggle between right and wrong' and that they constitute 'a way of reducing conflict to its simplest form and of making the statement that conflict can always be resolved, usually on the side of the righteous'. Inevitably, he argues, such shows 'comprise a deeply conservative genre that works to re-establish over and over again the importance of social order'.[40]

The ideological implications of genre were investigated to some effect in Britain, where inevitably the Reithian notions of 'citizenship' and 'public service' promulgated by the BBC prompted a Marxist-inspired tradition of film and television theory. To the general public the motors of change appeared to be the appetite for social and sexual realism, but students of genre were able to argue that style is most often a matter of surfaces and tends to disguise continuity. Dixon could give way to Regan without there being a meaningful shift in terms of attitude towards the authority of the police. 'The good guys have borrowed from the tough guys' wardrobe', Alan Clarke explained, 'but have left the bad guys' clothes on the peg.' There had been 'an inflection of the moral domain of the hero' but no 'shift in the moral basis of the series and the genre'.[41] For Michael O'Shaughnessy, writing from the perspective of the 1980s, 'much if not most, popular culture ultimately contrives to serve the interests of the dominant groups' and the conventions of narrative and generic form ensured a 'focus on policemen as familiar characters, automatically putting us on their side'.[42] Millions of viewers were seduced by realistic police shows and willingly became fans, but scholars were asking them to reflect on why it was that crime was invariably seen from the police point of view, on why cases were always solved and yet never followed beyond the point of arrest, on why there had to be such a strong identification with a hero or a team, and on why issues of corruption, injustice and of racial and gender prejudice, if shown at all, were treated as occasional aberrations rather than as tolerated norms.

The cultural critics argued convincingly, and their point was substantiated by programmes which were either one-off exceptions or which dealt with themes that were never fully developed or repeated. Jack Gold's 1971 television film *Stockers Copper* told the story of how a detachment of Glamorgan police were sent to Cornwall in 1917 to deal with a strike of tin miners, and of how a friendship developed between a policeman and a striker. Disappointingly television never returned to that theme, and the dramatic possibilities of industrial policing have largely been ignored. In 1978 the BBC ran into enormous difficulty with a four-part series *Law and Order* in which the writer G. F. Newman directly tackled the issue of police corruption. In the first episode, *A Detective's Tale*, the actor Derek Martin presented the most brilliantly convincing portrait of a London cop ever seen on British television, but that and the series as a whole were too much for the authorities. The Prison Officers' Association banned BBC filming in prisons and the Metropolitan Police not only complained bitterly but demanded certain assurances ahead of any further co-operation in the making of police programmes.[43] Villains meanwhile were there 'to be nicked' and only in occasional series did they star in their own right. It was always the cops who hogged the schedules, and in all the long-running series fundamentally honest cops working largely within the system achieved results. Troy Kennedy Martin had originally developed the idea of *Z Cars* because he wanted to get away from the unreal world of George Dixon, but he left the series after only three months because his stories were thought to be breaking the code. He had attempted to show that crime could sometimes pay, and that police officers occasionally had to express frustration. But the series 'pulled back' from that challenging viewpoint and in so doing, he suggested, it lost its 'critical edge'.[44] Stuart Laing has explained how the very successful series earned plaudits because of the realistic way in which it depicted the lives of individual policemen, but for Martin the storylines in which police officers plotted against each other told viewers in the know more about the politics of television than about the police and said little about the society which the programme's creator had wanted to analyse. In 1993 Troy Kennedy Martin developed this point further by dismissing police series generally for giving viewers easy answers, for 'they superimposed', he argued, 'a superficial order . . . over the anarchy of life'.[45]

In this respect police series classically illustrate the central dilemma of popular television. Audiences want all the guarantees and reassurances offered by the familiar, and yet within the predominant formats there has to be some variation and freshness both in the writing and the acting. Within 'the triumph of genre' there has to be a reliance on gimmicks, a search for selling-points. With detective shows this has been easily done as Geoff Tibballs explains: 'We've seen them all. Fat detectives, scruffy detectives, a lollipop-sucking detective, an orchid-loving detective, a Confucius-spouting detective, a snuff-taking detective' and so on *ad infinitum*.[46] It all seems a little too obvious and cynical, but perhaps even producers have been surprised by the extent to which the slightest character quirk is enough to gain both a following and affection. With police-station and police-procedural shows the approach has to be a little different for a whole range of characters need to be developed and then brought together within a tight format and a narrative rhythm. It is precisely here that routine becomes more obvious and freshness rather elusive. In the judgement of scriptwriter Peter Ansorge, 'the police series that now dominate are plot-led and curiously characterless', with the result that 'on prime-time TV it often seems as though we are watching the same characters following the same killers followed by the same lighting cameramen reading the same stage directions'.[47] For all enthusiasts of police procedurals the classic model had been set by the *87th Precinct* novels of Ed McBain, in which a taut plot nevertheless allowed us to develop some interest in the lives of a few detectives. On television, perhaps nothing has ever been so good as the original *Dragnet*, which in the 1950s began to convince many young people especially that perhaps television could be as exciting as the movies. But the danger with police series is always that writers will be drawn away from the society that spawned crime and towards the lives of police officers, will become in other words soap opera. This in effect was what happened to *Z Cars*; and today, under the influence of the hugely influential American show *Hill Street Blues*, it is happening to *The Bill*. Over thirteen years ITV's police-station series had built up a faithful audience of enthusiasts who were intrigued by the mix of officers, the range of crimes, and above all by the intensity and pace of episodes in which more happened within twenty-five minutes than in any two-hour *Morse* story. By 1997, however, it was apparent that on Friday evenings, for example, *The Bill* was losing about half the audience that had previously been watching *Coronation Street*. Stephen Armstrong explained that the trouble was that 'officers have become automata on the beat, they never have problems with the job, fall in love with each other, have kids with problems, or any of the things normal coppers deal with!' Clearly it was felt that *The Bill* was not enough like *Coronation Street*, and that was the direction in which it was now to move. The emphasis would not now be on the 'relentlessly unfolding story but rather on the personal drama and character development of individual police officers'.[48] At this moment of redefinition nothing was said about the rather bland and anonymous London suburban setting of the stories and whether the series could be improved by making Sun Hill itself more dramatic. These changes to *The Bill* were a reminder of the ratings battle and of the ways in which police shows are shaped. In a sense the BBC's *City Central* was a response to the news that there were to be more one-hour episodes of *The Bill*. Significantly *City Central* was to star Paul Nicholls, who had made his name as a heart-throb in *EastEnders*. The decision to put this unlikely star into a blue uniform confirmed that the line between soap opera and police drama had disappeared. Tony Jordan, writer of both *Eastenders* and *City Central*, explained that in the latter the police would 'come across as human beings', there would be 'little solving of crime' but rather crime would be used to 'illustrate our characters' personal lives'.[49] 'It's not all about nicking folks, you know', a veteran cop explains to a rookie in the first episode. Later the critic Alison Graham expressed her enthusiasm for 'TV's first-ever rock 'n' roll police series' in which Paul Nicholls was just one player in 'a tapestry of flawed people'. The police had been reinvented for a new generation of viewers.[50]

The police had proved to be so successful as dramatic entertainment that it was inevitable that documentary programme-makers would feel the need to look at the real thing. Television's greatest contribution to British policing over the years have been the various *Panorama* and *World in Action* programmes that have investigated corruption, but there have also been excellent documentary series which have explained how police forces work, and which have caught moments of real drama. In 1982 Roger Graef's eleven-part series *Police* held its audience's attention every bit as much as the best fictional shows, and was chiefly memorable for the police bullying of a girl who claimed to have been raped, which led in turn to new Home Office instructions. A five-part sequel brought fame to DCI Brian Ward who in the eyes of Kingsley and Tibballs 'looked like John Thaw' in the part of *The Sweeney*'s Regan. The lesson that 'fly-on-the-wall' programmes could be as exciting as they were instructive was quickly learnt. ITV's *Flying Squad*, transmitted in 1989, presented the drama of the police shooting an armed robber whose body was seen lying in a pool of blood. That series was made by Robert Fleming who went on to make two more equally popular series, *Murder Squad* and *Scotland Yard*. Filming the latter in 1993 Fleming found himself working with the Met. at a time when they were being widely criticized and yet were undergoing greater changes than 'at any time since the foundation of the service in 1829'. He found in Commissioner Condon an officer acutely aware of how the police had 'lost a lot of ground with the media' and who felt under 'an obligation ... to try and make a difference, to be accessible, to talk through policing issues'.[51] A new police publicity offensive was beginning, and television was to introduce us to a new type of PR-minded police officer who was managerial, well groomed, well dressed and well spoken. *Crimewatch*, which had first gone out in 1984, now came into its own, with the police spokespersons looking magnificent in their white shirts and matching the professional presenter in confidence and style. Clearly the police find this show useful, given the traditional reluctance of the public to volunteer information and evidence, and given too that they have some control over 'the film material screened'. Whatever the police enthusiasm, there remains something unsatisfactory and disturbing about this programme. 'It has to be a piece of television in its own right which will engage the viewers', explained producer Peter Grimdale, which is presumably why two academics found the programme 'close to popular journalism in terms of its selection of types of crime ... particularly murder, serial crime and robbers'.[52] Surely this is not only 'tabloid journalism' but also basically a relatively cheap substitute for a drama series. And all the while there were yet more documentary series, and one began to suspect that it had become compulsory for all police patrol cars and back-up vehicles to carry film crews. Clearly there are too many series of this kind, and as Ansorge said of the drama series, one chase and one police-enforced entry begin to merge into the next. Extensive voice-over narration lessens the tension and leaves audiences yearning for scripted dialogue. Yet occasionally one's attention is caught either by a good story or more frequently by a police officer with some charisma. In *Murder Squad*'s 1997 episode, *The Murder of Raymond Folks*, unique insight was provided into London's gay culture as the case being investigated became more complex by the minute. There was a remarkable scene in which Detective Sergeant Williams had to reveal the victim's gayness to the bereaved family, explaining that the defence would make much of it in court. This was drama of the highest order and one was left thinking that the articulate, bespectacled and intellectual Sergeant Williams deserved his own series.[53]

What is beyond dispute is that policing demands our attention because, whatever the routine, the paperwork and the sheer plod, the job remains more interesting and more socially relevant than most others. The police are now led by managers with targets, but they are doing something a little more challenging than manufacturing spare parts, spoonfeeding undergraduates or collecting tax. Real police work is demanding because routine, bureaucracy and the unexpected come in a complex mix: the trouble with all police shows, whether fictional or documentary, is that they are seduced by the drama of the streets and by violence. In 1997 the BBC's four-part series *The Force* deliberately set out to convey the range of challenges facing a modern force, and some of the frustrations too. 'We want to get under the surface of the police', said producer Sam Collyns as he explained why they had chosen the Thames Valley force whose detectives, it so happened, had been at the centre of the rape complaint row in Roger Graef's 1982 film. It transpired that Thames Valley were regarded as 'a flagship force ... at the very cutting edge of policing', and in truth, for all the emphasis on frustration, there was a distinct element of PR in the whole project. There was plenty of exposure for the chief constable, Charles Pollard, who thought that 'the overriding consideration' was 'that the public should see what we are doing' for 'most of what people see about the police in the media is either obvious entertainment which bears no resemblance at all to the truth, or documentaries that are skewed towards what will get viewers'.[54] One episode was based on the splendid idea of looking at DCI Evan Read of Oxford, who, like the fictional Morse, loved opera and drove a red sports car, but who, unlike the nation's favourite detective, had no time for leisurely lunchtime pints as he was too caught up in a heroin-fuelled crime wave. 'It's time-driven, it's high-volume crime, significant crime constrained by budgets', the real-life DCI explained.[55]

The transmission of *The Force* provided a wonderful opportunity for Charles Pollard to have his photographs in all the papers, and this was another indication of how, in a new age, chief constables were becoming high-profile figures. There have always been senior police officers who sought publicity, several of whom subsequently fell from grace. At the same time there was clearly a case to be made for looking at the complexity of police work from the perspective of individual officers. It has surely been something of a nonsense to have neglected so much effective police work and so many successful careers in the interests of developing fictional alternatives. The nation deserved to have a police pantheon. In the 1950s we all knew that Robert Fabian had been London's top detective. He had written a couple of volumes of memoirs, but what really made 'Fabian of the Yard' a catch phrase was the TV series of that name in which an immaculately turned-out and incredibly well-spoken actor, Bruce Seton, gave us our first glimpses into the realities of metropolitan life.[56] In those days we would read of a local crime and then realize that things were serious when the announcement came that 'Scotland Yard had been called in'. What that meant was that a dapper man in a suit, Burberry and trilby would arrive in town and proceed to solve the mystery that had baffled local officers. There was a whole procession of these detective inspectors and superintendents whose names were whispered in hushed tones: Fabian, Capstick, Hannam, Crawford, Lewis, with the last of the line being Jack Slipper, who also penned a memoir inevitably entitled *Slipper of the Yard*.[57] These were the men who provided the raw material for the police shows, especially those depicting the work of the specialized Murder and Flying Squads. Their efforts are also celebrated in a whole literature that tells the story of the fight against crime, but that literature belongs to a subculture of market stalls and backstreet bookshops, whilst in the meantime the scriptwriter and actors who feed off it strike it rich. Surely there should have been more mileage in the *Fabian of the Yard* format. Meanwhile, while it is obvious that scriptwriters have read the memoirs of senior detectives, there is less evidence that they have read volumes written by more senior uniformed police officers. They have shown little interest in fraud, white-collar crime, industrial disputes, crowd control and court work, but perhaps their most surprising and disappointing failure has been their reluctance to look at the top-level decisions that determine the whole nature and tone of strategic policing.

Our best-known and most respected police officers have written memoirs, but in a revealing way those generally neglected volumes serve as proof of how little interest not only television producers but society as a whole have in the politics of policing. Quite rightly *The Times* described Gilbert Kelland as 'truly one of the most remarkable policemen of his generation', for this officer, who had started out as PC 458 at Cannon Row in 1946 before eventually becoming Scotland Yard's senior detective, spent nearly forty years fighting organized vice and crime in London, retaining all the while 'a transparent honesty and integrity'.[58] Yet in his memoirs, the assistant commissioner who had led the Flying Squad so effectively could speak of the way in which 'few politicians from any of the political parties have shown until recently any real interest in the long-term measures and strategies necessary to identify, frustrate and control international organized crime'.[59] In the past, of course, the men responsible for strategy preferred anonymity and were happy to take decisions at the Athenaeum. The suspicion of outsiders, and especially journalists, was nicely conveyed in C. H. Rolph's account of his meeting in the 1960s with the Met. commissioner, Sir Joseph Simpson. Rolph, a former policeman who had become a columnist on legal and criminal matters for the left-wing *New Statesman*, noticed a pile of recent copies of this journal on Simpson's desk, and the Commissioner admitted that passages were marked up for him. It was an amicable interview, but Rolph left reflecting on the old adage that 'denunciation of the police is a necessary part of the hygiene of dissenting and greatly assists the circulation of the blood'.[60] Suspicion of the police comes naturally to journalists and broadcasters, and a distancing from the politics of policing would seem to come naturally to the culture in general. What television tends to do is to extract the excitement of police action and to exploit it as entertainment whilst reserving any critique of policing for minority-interest current-affairs programmes. The challenge would be to dramatize the politics, to look again at the careers of commissioners like Sir Robert Mark and Sir David McNee, both of whom published memoirs.[61] Sir Robert's greatest difficulties, it has been suggested, were with his men, Sir David's were perhaps more with the media: 'to my mind', McNee commented, 'there is an excessive interest in conflict and contention with an inclination towards criticism'.[62] Both careers cry out for dramatization.

In 1990 ITV ran a series, *The Chief*, with Tim Piggott-Smith playing a chief constable fighting battles with both the Home Office and his own officers, but it did not strike any real chords and did not change the general nature of police shows. Far more memorable from that year was *Shoot to Kill*, Peter Kosminsky's film dramatizing the remarkable and worrying story that John Stalker, former deputy chief constable of Greater Manchester, had told in his 1988 memoirs.[63] If the British had traditionally ignored the politics of policing on the mainland then that has been far more the case as far as Northern Ireland is concerned. But the demise of John Stalker had implications far beyond the jurisdiction of the Royal Ulster Constabulary which he had been sent to investigate.[64] In the film Stalker was brilliantly played by Jack Shepherd, and his number two, Thorburn, by David Calder, and the deployment of two excellent actors as senior police officers contributed substantially to making this one of the most important films ever made on the subject of how Britain is governed. The news in 1998 that a commission was looking at how Northern Ireland should be policed, as well as continuing reports that Manchester had not yet released all its secrets about the fall of Stalker, will surely prompt film-makers to return to this subject and to this kind of challenge. The United Kingdom is a country crying out for political drama, but as the century ends, Peter Flannery's nine-part series *Our Friends in the North* stands out as the only attempt to examine high-level corruption in the Met. and to relate it to a wider pattern of social and political change. This pioneering series, first shown in 1995 and repeated in 1998, traced the careers of four Geordie friends over four decades. As one strand in the story, a Geordie detective played by Tony Haygarth travels south to Scotland Yard, where he comes face to face with corruption, vacillation and complacency. The sight of a squirming deputy commissioner played by Peter Jeffrey was one of the most memorable television images of the decade. Earlier in the decade the BBC series *Between the Lines* had initially very effectively captured the politics of high-level police complaints procedures before somewhat losing its focus. This was a format that could be profitably revived.

At every point we are forced to conclude that television's interest in the police is very largely a matter of mere entertainment. Television companies obviously realize the great social relevance and topicality of police themes, but with show after show one senses that it is the relative convenience of the format which has recommended it rather than any attempt to come to terms with fundamental political or cultural issues. In the 1990s this general argument would seem to have applied to the depiction of the police on both British and American television. But in earlier decades things had been a little different in the United States. The nature of American society and an understanding of the significance of popular culture had led novelists, film-makers and cultural critics to come to terms with both popular taste and the role of genre in raising fundamentally important issues. By the mid-century novelists like Raymond Chandler, Hollywood directors like John Ford and Howard Hawks, and critics like Robert Warshow understood precisely why the masses could identify with cowboys, cops and robbers, and why it was necessary and important for them to be either written or acted into the culture.[65] Richard Sparks quotes Martin Williams's assertion that 'if the U.S.A. could be said to have a national literature it is crime melodrama', a remark that nicely challenges us into considering the centrality of genre in North America. Alongside it we need to consider David Rose's argument that in Britain 'there is almost no T.V. drama except drama about crime'.[66] The suggestion that emerges is that in America crime writing and crime films have a clear national role, whilst in Britain they are not only less significant but quite possibly serve as a substitute for a national literature and national cinema.

In Britain the enormous popularity of individual television series and the sheer professionalism of the output in general have tended to disguise the limitations of genre and the timidity of the culture as a whole. The preference for series and formats has led to the demise of the single play and the consequent diminution in the status of the television dramatist. Meanwhile the dominance of television has had an effect on London's much vaunted theatre world where, the Irish apart, there has been a noticeable lack of new writing and a heavy dependence on musicals and classic revivals, notably of American plays. There is little contemporary social drama and nothing at all dealing with criminal justice and policing. In 1998 the two most prominent detective inspectors in the West End were both in revivals. J. B. Priestley's *An Inspector Calls*, first produced in 1947, had been brought back as a stunningly staged psychological melodrama in which a mysterious inspector exposes the guilt of a whole family. Also on offer was a new production of Joe Orton's *Loot*, which had first been performed in 1966. In the play Orton had given the English stage its most notorious policeman in the character of Inspector Truscott, a part played most memorably on the stage by Leonard Rossiter and in the film version by Richard Attenborough. Clearly the play had dated in some respects, but not as 'a parody of the conventions of the detective thriller' as Philip Barnes had described it. Once more Truscott (played by Fred Ridgeway) was wonderful, and as he intimidates the other characters he presents a range of police methods that seemed all too familiar: 'Reading isn't an occupation we encourage among police officers', for 'we try to keep paper work down to a minimum'.[67] Orton, of course, had personally experienced police stations and their cells, but few other writers had followed in his path. David Hare was to think of himself very much as the dramatist of British public life in the 1990s and in his book *Asking Around*, based on his research for his acclaimed trilogy which was presented at the National Theatre, he provides one of the best essays written on contemporary policing. 'Throughout the writing of *Murmuring Judges*', explained Hare, 'I liked to return to Clapham Police Station whenever I could, just to hang out.'[68] The essay is full of insights, although the play, which is largely concerned with the courts, is the weakest part of the trilogy. One is left regretting that Hare did not write a police drama.

In the meantime British novelists were much concerned with the police. By the late 1990s it would seem as if the passion for novels of detection was more pronounced than ever. In bookstores the crime sections were always expanding, there were new stores dealing exclusively in crime fiction, and all the while, as if in cahoots, press reviewers gave more and more space to reviews in which increasingly extravagant claims were made on behalf of crime writers. It almost seemed as if the nation were being asked to rethink its literary values and no longer to be ashamed of its passion. Phrases like 'a thoroughly good read' and 'I read it in one go' had been replaced by a different kind of language. Marcel Berlins talked of P. D. James's 'preoccupations with guilt, regret, revenge and redemption', Ruth Padel explained how 'every contemporary British issue is eventually fought out in Ruth Rendell's fictional Kingsmarkham', and Donna Leon asked how it was that every Dalziel/Pascoe novel by Reginald Hill managed 'to be more intellectually and emotionally complex than the last'.[69] Clearly there were good crime novels, and obviously some of the country's best writers were using the genre, but could it be said that crime writing amounted to a national literature? Julian Symons has often talked of the changing world and expanding emotional range of crime novels, but whatever the balance between the mystery or puzzle on the one hand and the degree of social realism on the other, one senses that for most readers the basic psychological requirements have not changed. A crime has been committed, order has been disturbed, and that order has to be restored. That order is all the more appreciated if it is one familiar to and appreciated by readers. This is why P. D. James, like many of her predecessors, opts for what is thought to be the bedrock section of English society. For her 'the essence of the thing is the contrast between respectability and planned brutality', and it is plain snobbery to assume that her 'middle-class people are no less real' than the working class.[70] Norman Shrapnel famously called for a blurring of the line between crime and general fiction, but little has happened in that respect.[71] Crime fiction remains a cult, a game for signed-up members, and the conventions and expectations are there to make things easier for both writers and readers. It seems as if the British can only deal with violence, crime, the criminal mind, the courts and the system of policing itself when the pattern, pace, social range and social perspective are constrained by genre, by format. This is most obviously the case with the fictional shire police, all those books so beloved by television adaptors because of their East Anglian, West Country or Cotswold settings, but the same argument applied to urban cop stories too.

All the evidence suggests that the reading public and television audiences alike are drawn to fictions that offer a real sense of society, and which deal with common fears and anxieties. At one level the police fictions are a neat, convenient, fairly non-controversial and apparently legitimate way of setting up and containing an investigation into the possibilities of illegality and violence. Police shows gain their edge and their prestige from their realism, and yet they are always presented in an essentially controlled and predictable form. The puzzles at their core are rarely dull, confused, shapeless, unresolved and ongoing. Richard Sparks has written perceptively on the ways in which the conventions and psychology of police narratives allow the private viewer 'access to some of the places' where real crime is both found and discussed and yet 'the world's dangers' are contained even as they are evoked, 'anxieties are both invoked and assuaged'.[72] Sparks's superbly sustained analysis explains the process whereby favourite police shows become part of the rhythm and meaning of many viewers' lives, giving structure to their evenings, colour to their conversation, and confirming aspects of their general social identity. But this cultural role needs to be earned by any particular show, and success depends on some vital ingredients.

Dramatizing the Police 229

Acting is all too often taken for granted in Britain, and yet it is one of the greatest strengths of the culture. For writers, the genre can be an easy way out, but for actors the challenge can be formidable. Actors have it in their power to explain and complicate a culture quite as much as writers, and of course the more complex and nuanced a culture, the greater the demands on the nation's repertory company of actors. A sophisticated culture needs brave actors as much as innovative writers. The British have good police shows because there are actors who can play male and female police officers convincingly.

PC Plod 'proceeding along the High Street' saying 'Hello, hello, hello', was easy enough for music-hall comedians to parody, first on the stage and then in film comedies, but more serious dramas were to call for a transcendence of stereotypes. The way forward was indicated by Stanley Baker who created totally convincing policemen in three films from 1958 to 1960. Baker and his directors were certainly inspired by contemporary Hollywood acting, and for the first time British audiences were presented with characters who conveyed all the anger, frustration, energy and professionalism of real police officers.[73] Strangely, British cinema chose not to build on that foundation, but Baker's roles were to form a reference point for later television detectives. It was the swagger of Stratford Johns as Barlow and the ruthless zest of John Thaw as Regan which encouraged the public to believe that *Softly Softly* and *The Sweeney* were keeping them in touch with real life. In every show the uniformed officers had to be well cast and had to be able to suggest personality even as they displayed disciplined restraint, but it was the detectives who were really vital and who had to cope with a far greater range of emotions and with many different aspects of human nature. Our fascination with the more realistic series and shows that go beyond the caricature offered in *Morse* is that of seeing talented actors who are nevertheless recognizably British types convincingly playing professionals doing a job which is more difficult, multifaceted and socially important than any other. In fact, nowhere else are we allowed to see people at work in this detailed way: in a sense police shows are entirely about the role of professionalism in our society generally. There will be nothing bland about this if a group of good actors can develop tension and play off each other. In *The Bill* there were lots of 'uniforms', many of them charming and amusing, doing their job at the double, but the chief interest in the show always was provided by the plain-clothes officers. What gave the programme its authority was the fact that Christopher Ellison's DI Burnside, Kevin Lloyd's DC 'Tosh' Lines, Mark Wingett's DC Carver, Tony Scannel's DS Roach, and above all Simon Rouse's DCI Meadows were so well defined and sustained.[74]

It was the emergence of the modern city that occasioned the formation of the police, and it has always been the changing nature of city life that has determined the evolution of policing methods. It was those novelists who had consciously taken the city as their subject who first spotted that detectives, both in fact and in fiction, had a decisive role to play in saving the city from itself. Dickens, Conan Doyle, Chesterton and Chandler instinctively understood that, given the potential of the city to promote evil, detectives would have to be remarkable people. Policing generally would inevitably be a matter of routine and common sense, and to it would be drawn steady and unremarkable types, but detection would require imagination and flair, as well as courage and integrity. But could such geniuses, as detectives would clearly need to be, emerge from the uniformed rank and file? This dilemma or paradox has always been one of the taking-off points of detective fiction. Conan Doyle and Chandler set up their supermen as private investigators, whilst Chesterton and Philip Kerr allowed the police to recruit officers who were poets, philosophers or qualified psychologists.[75] Kerstin Ekman neatly allowed an intellectual to work in tandem with an ordinary policeman, the former saying to the latter, 'I'll make you human old copper.'[76] But whether a serving officer or no, the detective has to confront a society out of which, at any moment, a threat can emerge. Crime fiction has always been most fully satisfying when there is a sense of the isolated detective staring into the abyss. The writers of Victorian and Edwardian Britain devised that scenario, and then it was the American hard-boiled writers and directors of *film noir* that recast it for modern audiences. As Sparks has argued, it is down Chandler's 'mean streets' and into Warshow's 'strange sad city of imagination' that enthusiasts want to be taken.[77] In a famous essay the American critic Manny Farber wrote of how 'at heart the best action films are journeys into the lower depths of American life' and 'the average gun film travels like a shamus who knows his city and likes his private knowledge'.[78] It was Victorian London and then the Los Angeles and New York of the mid-twentieth century that determined the nature of the challenge facing detectives and that established standards of response against which all subsequent fictions need to be measured.

In 1998 it seemed as if police shows would run and run, and almost every change in the schedules took us to a new city and introduced us to a new squad of officers. Clearly there would always be procedural and police-station shows in which attractive young officers constituting an acceptable racial and gender mix loved and hated each other as they muddled through. At the same time there would be shows set in the shires in which individual officers, with almost the uncluttered freedom of old-style private eyes, would solve murders in picturesque locations after having interviewed a variety of suspects played by actors on loan from the National Theatre. In the midst of all this fictional policing there will be occasional shows which are more ambitious and which sustain a real tension very largely because their detectives are right on the edge. *Taggart*, *Prime Suspect* and *Cracker* were all outstanding because of their excellent scripts, their real sense of the city and memorable acting. The point about the stars of these shows, Mick McManus, Helen Mirren and Robbie Coltrane, was that the sheer professionalism that they were able to convey allowed their characters to come to terms with their self-loathing and anger, whilst at the same time it protected that integrity which gave them the right to judge both offenders and weak-willed colleagues. The characters of Taggart, Tennison and Fitz were as sophisticated and intriguing as anything on television, and the process of their creation and depiction was at the heart of contemporary British drama.[79]

A glimpse at the crime shelves would suggest that there is more to come. The novels of John Harvey and Ian Rankin would seem to cry out for television adaptation. Both writers have cunningly created detectives well able to satisfy readers nostalgic for the Chandler mode, but who yet operate convincingly first in the routines of British provincial policing and then in the utterly realistic cauldron of the contemporary city. In particular it is Rankin's appropriately named Inspector Rebus who enables us to appreciate the extent to which the city, in this case Edinburgh, exploits all forms of human weakness. Rebus, of course, is a divorced, melancholy loner who drinks heavily as he reflects on a

Christian upbringing and a breakdown experienced whilst training with the SAS; he is quite naturally alienated from a city that has passed into the hands of junkies, yuppies, speculators and plutocrats.[80] As one longs for the Rebus stories to be filmed there comes the realization that ultimately one's preference for one detective over another is merely a reflection of one's own cultural style and preferences.[81] Novelists and television producers have become fully aware of that and are adept at catering to all subcultures. They know that for every member of the public who wants to look at the city lights whilst sipping bourbon and playing Coleman Hawkins, there is somebody who wants to walk a dog in leafy lanes which have been made safe by the local bobbies. By the late 1990s it appeared that there was an even larger following for shows which just wanted to confirm that police forces recruit ordinary but attractive young men and women who more or less have the same anxieties and enthusiasms as the rest of their age group. In the Britain of the 1990s there was a culture which enabled many different kinds of people to confirm their own specific social identity by turning to varieties of fictional police that had been devised with them in mind.

Inevitably there have been rebels who have worked to do something more with the police. Andrew Lavender has very effectively highlighted the way in which a Troy Kennedy Martin, all too aware of the constraints on police shows, went on to write *Edge of Darkness*, a much acclaimed series in which a conventional policeman is drawn into a mysterious nightmare that reflected many of the anxieties of the Thatcher era.[82] There have also been subversive novelists. Rather like Joe Orton, Colin MacInnes was well aware of how London had developed a constabulary that reflected many of the characteristics it was there to constrain. 'I think it impossible for police officers to do the work society has set them', he argued, 'without dire temptations to the spirit.'[83] In *Mr Love and Justice* he based a whole novel on the paradox that 'if the copper is a worshipper of the conventional he is also in his inner person something of an anarch: a lover of stress and strain and conflict'.[84] Our police-show-dominated nation needs to rekindle the spirit of Orton and MacInnes. The most recent writer to do that is Scotland's Irvine Welsh for, perhaps as a reaction to the Calvinist despair of Taggart and Rebus, he has created Detective Sergeant Bruce Robertson and invited us to enter the head of a police officer who just happens to be a racist, sexist, perverted, drug-addicted Mason. *Filth* is a timely reminder that if we are determined to retain the police at the centre of our culture then it is certainly the case that we need to know everything about them.[85]

Meanwhile television was doing its best to ensure that police shows reflected as much as possible of the reality of contemporary policing as revealed in the press. In the autumn of 1998 the dramatization of the police reached a crescendo. *The Bill* had been expanded and boosted, but it now had to compete with *Liverpool One*, a series which began with a detective throwing a villain out of the window of a high-rise flat, and with *The Cops*, a much hyped BBC show which promised unprecedented reality, and which clearly intended to win audiences through a storyline involving a policewoman on cocaine. But all this entertainment had a hard time competing with the news headlines, as even the viewing figures suggested.[86] The real police remained the real story. With Commissioner Condon apologizing for how his force had handled the investigation of Stephen Lawrence's death, with the chief constable of Greater Manchester conceding that 'institutional racism' was a feature of his force, and with new evidence of police corruption throughout the United Kingdom, it was the police themselves who seemed to be inviting our attention and possibly requesting our help.

Notes

1. See Clive Emsley, *The English Police: A Political and Social History* (London, 1991); J. M. Hart, *The British Police* (London, 1951); Bernard Porter, *The Origins of the Vigilant State* (London, 1982) and D. J. V. Jones, *Crime in Nineteenth-Century Wales* (Cardiff, 1992).
2. 'The Metropolitan Police', *Saturday Review*, 20 April 1867, quoted in R. F. Stewart, *And Always a Detective* (Newton Abbot, 1980), 136.
3. Robert Reiner, *The Politics of the Police* (2nd edn, London, 1992), 5.
4. Barry Cox, John Shirley and Martin Short, *The Fall of Scotland Yard* (Oxford, 1977).
5. William Purcell, *British Police in a Changing Society* (London, 1974), xviii.
6. David Rose, *In the Name of the Law* (London, 1996), vii.

7. Mary Riddell, Interview with Paul Condon, *New Statesman*, 27 June 1997, 22.

8. John Sopel, *Tony Blair: The Moderniser* (London, 1995), 164.

9. Alasdair Palmer, 'Above the law', *Sunday Telegraph*, 12 October 1997; 'Mr Straw must straighten the bent arm of the law', ibid., 25 January 1998, and 'What makes a policeman bent', ibid., 1 February 1998; Stewart Tendler, 'Condon fights to last against corrupt police', *Times*, 25 July 1998.

10. Stewart Tendler in *Times*, 21 March 1998.

11. Jack Straw, 'Crime and Old Labour's punishment', *Times*, 8 April 1998.

12. Libby Purves, 'A fair cop, Mr Straw', *Times*, 10 February 1998.

13. Andrew Roberts, 'Something rotten in the ranks', *Sunday Times*, 29 March 1998.

14. See D. J. V. Jones, *Crime and Policing in the Twentieth Century* (Cardiff, 1996), 254.

15. John Alderson, *Law and Disorder* (London, 1984).

16. James Lardner, 'Can you believe the New York miracle?', *New York Review of Books*, 14 August 1997, 54, and William Langley, 'The hero of zero tolerance', *Sunday Telegraph*, 31 August 1997.

17. Roger Geary, *Policing Industrial Disputes* (Cambridge, 1985), 151.

18. See Reiner, *Politics of the Police*, 1ff.

19. The South Wales Police, Indicator Special published by *The Western Mail* and *The South Wales Echo*, October 1977. See also the brochure *Policing in South Wales* (Bridgend, 1998).

20. See in particular, 'Healthy era for village policing', *South Wales Evening Post*, 17 October 1997; 'Crime rate falls as the police improve', *South Wales Echo*, 25 January 1998, and 'Officers will spend more time on the beat', *Western Mail*, 23 February 1998.

21. *Police Review*, 106, no. 5456 (30 January 1998), 23.

22. Nick Danziger, *Danziger's Britain: A Journey to the Edge* (London, 1996), 311.

23. See 'Violent crime figures soar to new heights', *Western Mail*, 14 October 1997, and 'Highest drop in general crimes as violent offences show a rise', ibid., 15 October 1997.

24. 'Assaults cost the Met. £80,000', *Guardian*, 21 August 1997.

25. 'Yard officers sold secrets to criminals', *Sunday Times*, 1 January 1998; 'Cautious police blamed as more killers go free', *Times*, 13 January 1998.

26. *Times*, 13 May 1988. The story of Supt Ray Mallon and his suspension from the Middlesbrough CID was examined in ITV's *World in Action*, broadcast on 1 June 1998.

27. 'Z Cars for the nineties', *Radio Times*, 4–10 April 1998, 21.

28. Glyn George, 'A partial TV history of the Boys in Blue', *Express*, 4 April 1998.
29. Steve Clarke, 'Force feeding', *Sunday Times*, 29 March 1998.
30. 'Z Cars for the nineties' (*Radio Times*).
31. *Sunday Times*, 19 April 1998.
32. Richard Osborne, 'Crime and the media', in David Kidd Hewitt and Richard Osborne, *Crime and the Media: The Post-Modern Spectacle* (London, 1995), 29. David Rose, *In the Name of the Law*, ix.
33. See, in particular, T. Vahimegl, *British Television: An Illustrated Guide*, (Oxford, 1994); Geoff Tibballs, *The Boxtree Encyclopedia of TV Detectives* (London 1992); Tony Bennett, Colin Mercer and Janet Woollacott (eds.), *Popular Culture and Social Relations* (Oxford 1986); Richard Sparks, *Television and the Drama of Crime* (Buckingham, 1992); Alan Clarke, '"You're Nicked!" Television police service and the fictional representation of law and order', in Dominic Strinati and Stephen Wagg (eds.), *Come on Down: Popular Media Culture in Post-War Britain* (London, 1992); and Paul Cornell, Martin Day and Keith Topping, *Classic British Television* (London 1996), 209ff.
34. Daniel Jeffreys, 'Dixon of Dock Green can't solve all our problems', *Daily Mail*, 9 February 1992.
35. Simon Frith, 'The pleasure of the hearth: the making of BBC light entertainment', in *Formation of Pleasure* (London 1983), 122.
36. Ian Ang, *Desperately Seeking the Audience* (London, 1991), 13.
37. Neil Postman, *Amusing Ourselves to Death* (London, 1986); John Corner (ed.), *Popular Television in Britain* (London, 1991), 13.
38. Geoffrey Hurd, 'The television presentation of the police', in Tony Bennett et al., *Popular Television and the Film* (London, 1981), 57.
39. Julian Symons, *Bloody Murder* (London, 1972), 13ff.
40. Brooks Robards, 'The Police Show', in Brian C. Rose (ed.), *TV Genres* (Westport and London, 1985), 11ff.
41. Clarke, '"You're nicked!"', 240, and '"This is not the Boy Scouts": television police series and definitions of law and order', in Bennett et al., *Popular Culture*.
42. Michael O'Shaughnessy, 'Box Pop: popular television and hegemony', in Andrew Goodwin and Gary Whennel, *Understanding Television* (London, 1990), 88.
43. Tibballs, *Boxtree Encyclopedia*, 231. For a police corruption novel see G. F. Newman, *Set a Thief* (London 1986).
44. Francis Wheen, *Television* (London, 1985), 135.
45. Stuart Laing, 'Banging in some reality: the original *Z Cars*', in Corner, *Popular Television*, and Cornell et al., *Classic British Television*, 209.
46. Tibballs, *Boxtree Encylopedia*, 3.

47. Peter Ansorge, *From Liverpool to Los Angeles: On Writing for Theatre, Film and Television* (London, 1997), 93.
48. Stephen Armstrong, 'Police rescue', *Sunday Times* 7 September 1997. See also Alison Graham, 'A new beat for the Bill', *Radio Times*, 22-8 August 1998, 20.
49. John Mornish, 'Goodies and baddies in Z Cars for the nineties', *Daily Telegraph*, 3 April 1998.
50. Alison Graham, 'From Britcops to the Old Guard', *Radio Times*, 9-15 May 1998, 130.
51. Robert Fleming with Hugh Millar, *Scotland Yard* (London, 1994), xxiii.
52. See Philip Schlesinger and Howard Tumber, 'Television police and audience', in John Corner and Sylvia Harvey, *Television Times: A Reader* (London 1996), 71.
53. *Murder Squad* was shown on ITV on 8 July 1997. See John Preston, 'Stunned by their detective powers', *Sunday Telegraph*, 13 July 1997.
54. 'Laying down the law', *Radio Times*, 17-23 January 1998.
55. *The Real Inspector Morse* shown on BBC, 28 January 1998. See Joe Joseph, 'Watching the detectives', *Times*, 29 January 1998.
56. Robert Fabian, *Fabian of the Yard* (London, 1950), and *London After Dark* (London, 1954).
57. Jack Slipper, *Slipper of the Yard* (London, 1981).
58. Obituary of Gilbert Kelland, *Times*, 5 September 1997.
59. Gilbert Kelland, *Crime in London* (London, 1986), 8.
60. C. H. Rolph, *Further Particulars* (London, 1987), 171-3.
61. Sir Robert Mark, *In the Office of Constable* (London, 1978) and Sir David McNee, *McNee's Law* (London, 1983).
62. Ibid., 235ff.
63. John Stalker, *Stalker* (London, 1988).
64. Peter Taylor, *Stalker: The Search For the Truth* (London, 1987).
65. See Robert Warshow, *The Immediate Experience* (New York, 1962).
66. Sparks, *Television and the Drama of Crime*, 37, and David Rose, *In the Name of the Law*, ix.
67. Joe Orton, *Loot* (London, 1967).
68. David Hare, *Asking Around* (London, 1993), 63.
69. *Times*, 1 December 1997; *Sunday Telegraph*, 25 August 1997; *Sunday Times*, 2 December 1997.
70. Frances Fyfield, 'Inside a criminal mind', *Times*, 4 October 1977.
71. Norman Shrapnel, 'The literature of violence and pursuit', *Times Literary Supplement*, 23 June 1961.
72. Sparks, *Television and the Drama of Crime*, 57ff.

73. Baker had played Sergeant Bannock in *Your Witness* (1950) and was then Sgt Truman in *Violent Playground* (1958), Inspector Morgan in *Blind Date* (1959) and Inspector Martineau in *Hell is a City* (1960). See Anthony Storey, *Stanley Baker* (London, 1977).

74. See Tony Lynch, *The Bill* (London, 1991); Daniel Rosenthal, 'Give us a break, Guv', *Independent on Sunday*, 7 December 1997; Sean Day-Lewis, *One Day in the Life of Television* (London, 1989), 302ff.

75. See G. K. Chesterton, *The Man who was Thursday* (London, 1908; new edn., 1986) and Philip Kerr, *A Philosophical Investigation* (London, 1992).

76. Kerstin Ekman, *Under the Snow* (Stockholm, 1961; English translation 1997), 41.

77. Sparks, *Television and the Drama of Crime*, 35ff. See also Roger Silverstone, *Television and Everyday Life* (London, 1994), 55.

78. Manny Farber, *Negative Space* (London, 1971), 12ff.

79. For Taggart see Tibballs, *Boxtree Encyclopedia*, 414. For Tennison see Anthony Hayward and Amy Rennert, *Prime Suspect* (London, 1996), and for Cracker see John Crace, *Cracker: The Truth behind the Fiction* (London, 1994).

80. By 1998 John Harvey had published ten Inspector Reswick novels. Coincidentally Ian Rankin had published ten Inspector Rebus volumes of which the finest was *Black and Blue* (London, 1997).

81. For a personal statement see Ian A. Bell, '"We do the police in different voices": representations of the police in contemporary British crime fiction', in H. Gustav Klaus and Stephen Knight (eds.), *The Art of Murder* (Tübingen, 1998).

82. Andrew Lavender, 'Edge of darkness', in George W. Brandt, *British Television Drama in the 1980s* (Cambridge, 1993).

83. Colin MacInnes, 'The criminal society', in C. H. Rolph (ed.), *The Police and the Public* (London, 1962).

84. Colin MacInnes, *Mr Love and Justice* (London, 1980 edn.), 70.

85. Irvine Welsh, *Filth* (London, 1998).

86. 'Police lose their appeal, viewers rule', *Times*, 30 October 1998.

David Jones: A Bibliography

DWYRYD W. JONES

(a) Books

Before Rebecca: Popular Protests in Wales, 1793–1815 (London: Allen Lane, 1973), 282pp.

Chartism and the Chartists (London: Allen Lane, 1975), 229pp.

Crime, Protest, Community and Police in Nineteenth-Century Britain (London: Routledge, 1982), 247pp.

The Last Rising: The Newport Insurrection of 1839 (Oxford: Oxford University Press, 1985), xii + 273pp.

Rebecca's Children: A Study of Rural Society, Crime and Protest (Oxford: Oxford University Press, 1989), ix + 423pp.

Crime in Nineteenth-Century Wales (Cardiff: University of Wales Press, 1992), xi + 295pp.

Crime and Policing in the Twentieth Century: The South Wales Experience (Cardiff: University of Wales Press, 1996), 328pp.

(b) Articles and Chapters

'The corn riots in Wales, 1793–1801', *Welsh History Review*, 2, 4 (1964–5), 323–50

'More light on Rhyfel y Sais Bach', *Ceredigion*, V, 1 (1964–7), 84–93

'Distress and discontent in Cardiganshire, 1814–1819', *Ceredigion*, V, 3 (1964–7), 280–9

'The Amlwch riots of 1817', *Transactions Anglesey Antiquarian Society* (1966), 93–102

'The Merthyr riots of 1831', *Welsh History Review*, 3, 2, (1966–7), 173–205

'The South Wales strike of 1816', *Morgannwg*, XI (1967), 27–45

'The Carmarthen riots of 1831', *Welsh History Review*, 4, 2 (1968–9), 129–42

'The Merthyr riots of 1800: a study in attitudes', *Bulletin of the Board of Celtic Studies*, XXIII, 2 (1968–70), 166–79

'Law enforcement and popular disturbances in Wales, 1793–1835', *Journal of Modern History*, 42, 4 (1970), 496–523

'The Scotch cattle and their black domain', *Welsh History Review*, 5, 3 (1970–1), 220–49

'Chartism at Merthyr: a commentary on the meetings of 1842', *Bulletin of the Board of Celtic Studies*, XXIV, 2 (1970–2), 230–45

'Chartism in Welsh communities', *Welsh History Review*, 6, 3 (1972–3), 243–61

'Crime, protest and community in nineteenth-century Wales', *Llafur*, 1, 3 (1972–5), 110–20

'Thomas Campbell Foster and the rural labourer: incendiarism in East Anglia in the 1840s', *Social History*, 1, 1 (1976), 5–43

'"A dead loss to the community": the criminal vagrant in mid-nineteenth-century Wales', *Welsh History Review*, 8, 3 (1976–7), 312–43

'The second Rebecca riots: a study of poaching in the upper Wye', *Llafur*, 2, 1 (1976–9), 32–56

(with Alan Bainbridge), 'The conquering of "China": crime in an industrial community, 1842–1864', *Llafur*, 2, 4 (1976–9), 7–37

(with Alan Bainbridge), 'SSRC project: crime in Welsh communities in the nineteenth century', *Social History*, 2, 4 (1977), 507–14

'The poacher: a study in Victorian crime and protest', *Historical Journal*, 22, 4 (1979), 825–60

'Life and death in eighteenth-century Wales: a note', *Welsh History Review*, 10, 4 (1980–1), 536–48

'Rural crime and protest', in G. E. Mingay (ed.), *The Victorian Countryside* (London: Routledge and Kegan Paul, 1981), 566–79

'The new police, crime and people in England and Wales, 1829–1888', *Transactions of the Royal Historical Society*, Ser. V, 33 (1983), 151–68

'The Rebecca riots, 1839–44', in A. Charlesworth (ed.), *An Atlas of Rural Protest in Britain, 1548–1900* (London: Croom Helm, 1983), 165–71

'Women and Chartism', *History*, 68, 222 (1983), 1–21

'The Welsh and crime, 1801–1891', in Clive Emsley and James Walvin (eds.), *Artisans, Peasants and Proletarians, 1760–1860: Essays presented to Gwyn A. Williams* (London: Croom Helm, 1985), 81–103

'Crime, order and the police', in R. A. Griffiths (ed.), *The City of Swansea: Challenges and Change* (Stroud: Allan Sutton, 1990), 194–205

'"Where did it all go wrong?": crime in Swansea, 1938–68', *Welsh History Review*, 15, 2 (1990–1), 240–74

'Crime in the South Wales Police District, 1969–1989', in Ieuan Gwynedd Jones and Glanmor Williams (eds.), *Social Policy, Crime and Punishment: Essays in Memory of Jane Morgan* (Cardiff: University of Wales Press, 1994), 15–33

Index

Abegg, Dr Wilhelm 109
Aberystwyth 45, 46
Adams, William Edwin
  (1832–1906) 120–41 *passim*
aliens 113
Anglesey 43, 45, 46, 47, 50, 52, 66
arson 2, 14, 24

Baker, Stanley 229
Bala 47
Beaumaris 45, 46, 48, 50
Beccaria, Cesare 6
  argues against death penalty
    79–83
  different from British penal
    reformers 83–9
  impact on Britain 73–9
Bedwellty parish
  manorial dispute in 59–60
  and poor relief 180
Bevan, Aneurin 26, 34, 183, 192,
  195, 196–7, 201
Bohstedt, J. 48, 49, 53, 55
Boer War 25
Bradlaugh, Charles 128–30, 135–7,
  139
Bridgend 179

Caernarfon 45, 46–8, 62
Caernarfonshire 44, 51, 53, 61
Cannon, Inspector Paul 212
capital punishment 79–81, 85–6, 88
Cardigan 64
Cardiganshire 58, 61, 62, 65
Carmarthen 45, 48, 49, 62, 63
Carmarthenshire 55, 63, 188
Chartism 2, 4–6, 9, 10–14, 22, 25,
  120–41 *passim*
  National Charter Association 122
  remembered in 1930s marches
    194–5
Cheltenham Spa 121–7, 140
Chirk 54
Churchill, Winston 28, 107
City Central 7, 213–14, 219
Close, Revd Francis 121–2, 123,
  126
Communist Party 26, 35
  and unemployment 178–9,
    182–7, 199, 200
'community policing' 211
Condon, Sir Paul 209, 210, 220,
  233
consensus and conflict debate 19ff.
  in American history 19–20
  Communist party in consensus 35
  democracy in consensus 32–4
  linguistic conflict 27–8
  political conflict 25–6
  sectarian conflict 26–7
  in Welsh history 21ff.
  Welsh Labour in consensus 34–5
  Welsh nationalists in consensus 35
Conwy 45, 53
Cove, W. G. 183
Cowen, Joseph Jr. 127–31, 135–7
Cracker 231
crime 2, 6, 14, 23; *see also under*
  poaching

D'Arcy, Feargus 135
Davies, S. O. 181
demonstrations in south Wales in
  1930s 185–7

and community 192–5
  effectiveness of 197
  and family 195
Denbigh 45–9, 51–3, 55–6
Denbighshire 43, 46, 51, 54, 65
Desborough Committee 107–8
devolution 16, 27–8, 39
Dilke, Sir Charles 134–7
disestablishment 27
Dixon of Dock Green 7, 97, 214–16, 218
Dodd, A. H. 56
Dolgellau 44, 56–7

East Anglia 2–3, 7
  poaching in 153, 159, 163, 164
Edward VIII, King 198–9
Emergency Powers Act (1920) 107
enclosure 62, 63
Evans, Gwynfor 35

Fabian, Robert 222–3
Finn, Margot 126, 131
Flint 45
Flintshire 46, 51, 52, 55, 63
France 102, 104, 108, 110–11, 113
Francis, Dai 35

game laws 153, 155, 156, 163, 165
  see also game-preserving
game-keepers 153–6, 158–9, 162–3, 167
game-preserving 149, 152–4
Geary, Roger 211
Gee, Thomas 26
George, David Lloyd 24, 26, 28, 29, 31, 33, 36, 37
Germany 104, 109, 111–12
Glamorgan 66, 178, 179, 181, 182
Glyndŵr, Owain 36, 38
Griffiths, James 26, 34, 186, 188–9, 201
Gruffydd, K. Lloyd 49

Hall, George 185, 192, 195
Hardie, Keir 25
Harvey, John 231
Haverfordwest 44, 51, 53, 63–5

Heycock, Llew 35
Hofstadter, Richard 20, 38
Holyhead 45, 48
Horner, Arthur 35, 179
Howard, Michael 209
Howells, Kim 25
Howkins, Alun 164

Inspector Morse 222, 229
Investigator: A Journal of Secularism 128–9

James, P. D. 227, 228
Johns, Stratford 229
Jones, David 1–15, 16–19, 22, 23, 28–30, 37, 38, 39, 42, 43, 45, 49, 53, 55, 67, 69, 121, 149, 155, 176
Jones, Ieuan Gwynedd 16, 19, 21, 33
Jones, R. Merfyn 30
Jones, Thomas 32

Kell, Vernon 106

Labour Party
  and unemployment 178, 179, 181–7, 199, 200
Lancashire 149–71 *passim*
Laugharne 45
Lawrence, Stephen 233
Lewis, Saunders 24, 29, 35
Lindsay, Captain Lionel 30
Linton, W. J. 124, 125, 126, 127, 141
Llafur 2, 17, 24
Llanelli
  strikers killed in 27
  and unemployment 179, 191
Lloyd, Henry Demarest 121

Maigret 97
manorial rights, disputes over 57–63
  rights to dig turf 60
  rights to encroachments and enclosures 60–3
  rights to minerals 57–8
  rights to timber 59–60

Mark, Sir Robert 208, 224
Marxist historians 12, 23–4, 36
Mazzini, Guiseppe 124–6, 130, 140, 141
McNee, Sir David 224
means test
  marching against 6, 23, 29, 176–201 *passim*
media
  and crime 7, 97
  and police 207ff.
Memoirs of a Social Atom (1903) 120, 124, 125, 141
Merioneth 43–4, 55
Merthyr 3, 4, 25
  and 1930s means test 181
  and administration of transitional benefit 182
  corn riots at 51
  Merthyr rising 13, 22, 24, 29
  storming of UAB offices at 185
  town's sisterhoods protesting against unemployment 191
mineral disputes, within lordships 57–8
Monmouthshire
  administration of poor relief in 182
  corn riots in 52
  manorial disputes in 59
  march of unemployed 178
Montgomeryshire 62, 63
Morgan family of Tredegar house (Mon.) 58–60
Morgan, Jane 29

National Charter Association 122
National Reformer 128–9
National Unemployed Workers' Movement (NUWM) 178–80, 183, 184, 187
Newcastle upon Tyne 129–35, 138–40
Newcastle Chartist Republican Brotherhood 127, 130
Newcastle and Gateshead Republican Club 132, 135, 136, 138

Newcastle Weekly Chronicle 120, 129–32, 134, 139
Newport 6
  Chartist rising 13, 28
  demonstration of unemployed (1933) 178
Night Poaching Prevention Act (1862) 156, 170
Northern Star 123
Northern Tribune 127

O'Brien, Bronterre 14
O'Connor, Feargus 123
On Crimes and Punishments 73–89

Paine, Thomas 122
Parry, Glyn 48, 50
Pembroke 45–7, 52, 53
Pembrokeshire 52, 66
Plaid Cymru 16, 24, 29, 35, 184, 199
poachers and poaching 3, 7, 149–71
  poaching gangs 153, 154, 156, 158, 159, 160–2, 165–7, 168, 171
  poachers as possible social criminals 163–4
police
  dramatizing of 213ff.
  establishment of 101
  and late twentieth-century urban culture 208, 211
  and poaching 156, 158, 164–6, 168–70
  and public demonstration 109–10
  and racial prejudice 208, 233
  and strikes 106ff., 217
policing 6, 12, 23, 30, 97
  and the city 230–2
  England and continental Europe compared 98ff.
  public interest in 210–13
popular protest 6, 10, 14, 17, 22, 24; *see also under* demonstrations
Prime Suspect 231
punishment
  of corn rioters 50–1
  in eighteenth-century Britain 85–8

in nineteenth-century Britain 100
On Crimes and Punishments
   77–82, 85–8
of poachers 162
Purves, Libby 210
Pwllheli 45

Radnorshire 60–1
Rankin, Ian 231–2
Rebecca riots 3, 13, 14, 22, 28, 42, 176
Reith, Charles 101, 118, 216
Rendell, Ruth 227
republicanism 121, 124–41 *passim*
Rhondda 179, 187, 190, 197, 212
Rhuddlan 45, 46, 48–54
Richard, Henry 22–3, 25
riots
   anti-tithe 13, 26, 28
   enclosure 22
   food 12, 22, 42–54
   at Llanelli 28
   militia 54–5
   in parliamentary and local elections 63–4
   racial, in Cardiff 36
   at Tonypandy 28, 29, 32, 194
   at Tredegar 36
   see also Merthyr rising *and* Rebecca riots
Roberts, Andrew 210
Rose, David 208–9, 214, 226

Sianel Pedwar Cymru 16
Smith, Dai 25
smuggling, attacks on local officials 65–6
Softly, Softly 229
South Wales Constabulary, and public relations 212
South Wales Miners' Federation (SWMF), and unemployment 180, 184, 186
Stalker, John 224–5
strangers, antipathy to 55–6
Straw, Jack 209–11
Straw-Condon reform initiatives 209–10

strikes
   at Abertillery, 'stay-down' stoppages (1935) 29
   at Ammanford (1925) 29
   miners' strike (1984–5) 29
   Penrhyn quarrymen's (1900–3) 30
   wave of (1910–12) 107
Swansea 45, 53, 62, 178

Taggart 7, 231
Taylor, Antony 133
Thaw, John 229
The Bill 7, 219, 229–30, 233
The Dragon has Two Tongues 21
The Sweeney 7, 214, 229
Thomas, Wynford Vaughan 21
Thompson, Dorothy 5, 8, 22, 137
Thompson, Edward 5, 23–4, 44, 46, 47, 49, 52
Todd, Nigel 131, 136, 138
Tonypandy 28
torture 77
transportation 81
   for poaching 162, 163, 167, 169
Trevelyan, George Macaulay 98, 100

unemployed in south Wales (1920s and 1930s) 176 ff.
   churches and 190–2
   clubs for 177–8
   middle-class support for 189–90
Unemployment Act (1934) 182–3
   opposition to 183ff.
'ungovernable' neighbourhoods 64–5
United States 19–21, 211, 226

violence, Welsh 29–30
   in food riots 48, 49, 50
   in poaching 155, 156, 158, 160–2, 166, 167
   in protest against Unemployment Act (1934) 185
   Welsh compared with Irish 31

Wells, Roger 45
Welsh Assembly 35, 39

Welsh History Review 16–17
Whig interpretation of history 12, 20, 98, 101, 109, 114
white-collar criminals 99
Wigley, Dafydd 35
Williams, Chris 183
Williams, David 5–6, 10, 16, 22
Williams, Gwyn A. 5–6, 16, 19, 21, 22, 24, 35
Willis, Norman 29

women
  as criminals 8
  in Chartism 8, 13
  in corn riots 8, 52–3
  in marches of the unemployed 178, 184–6, 191
  in Rebecca riots 8
Wrexham 45, 46

Z-Cars 213, 218, 219

List of Subscribers

The following have kindly associated themselves with publication of this book through subscription:

John E. Archer, Preston
T. G. Ashplant, John Moores University, Liverpool
Owen R. Ashton, Staffordshire University
Colin Baber, Cardiff
D. L. Baker-Jones, Llandysul
David Barnes, Cardiff
Logie Barrow, Universität Bremen, Germany
Ken Birch, Aberdyfi
D. George Boyce, University of Wales Swansea
E. C. M. Breuning, University of Wales Swansea
Merlyn Brown, Swansea
Richard Brown, Dunstable
Muriel E. Chamberlain, University of Wales Swansea
Stuart Clark, University of Wales Swansea
Max Cole, Godmanchester
Penelope J. Corfield, Royal Holloway, University of London
Matthew Cragoe, University of Hertfordshire
Malcolm Crook, University of Keele
D. E. Davies, Gorseinon
Derek and Jayne Davies, Newtown
John Davies, Caerdydd
Rees Davies, All Souls College, Oxford
Kirstine and Hugh Dunthorne, Swansea
David Eastwood, University of Wales Swansea
David Egan, University of Wales Institute, Cardiff
Bryn Ellis, Holywell
Clive Emsley, Open University
Elizabeth and Neil Evans, Harlech
Glenys and Vivian Evans, Senghenydd

Hywel Francis, University of Wales Swansea
Edmund Fryde, Aberystwyth
Robert Fyson, Newcastle-under-Lyme
Ralph A. Griffiths, University of Wales Swansea
W. P. Griffith, University of Wales, Bangor
R. Geraint Gruffydd, Aberystwyth
P. H. G. Harries, Swansea
David and Angela Howell, Swansea
Alun Howkins, University of Sussex
Joan Hugman, Newcastle upon Tyne
Rob Humphreys, University of Wales Swansea
Brian Ll. James, Cardiff
Geraint H. Jenkins, Canolfan Uwchefrydiau Cymreig a Cheltaidd
Angela V. John, University of Greenwich
Bill Jones, University of Wales, Cardiff
Brinley Jones, Abertawe
Dwyryd Jones, University of York
Gareth Elwyn and Kath Jones, Swansea
Gwynne and Edna Jones, Guilsfield, Welshpool
Ieuan Gwynedd Jones, Aberystwyth
R. Merfyn Jones, University of Wales, Bangor
Rosemary A. N. Jones, Aberaeron
Sandra and Anthony Jones, Shrewsbury
Stephen Knight, University of Wales, Cardiff
Hideo Koga, Kyoto Women's University, Kyoto
Takashi Koseki, Tokyo
John Latham, Swansea
John Law, University of Wales Swansea
G. Lewis, New Milton
Ian Machin, University of Dundee
Rohan McWilliam, London
David E. Martin, University of Sheffield
Richard Moore-Colyer, Aberystwyth
Alun Morgan, Ammanford
E. J. R. Morgan, Swansea
Kenneth O. Morgan, Long Hanborough, Witney
P. T. J. Morgan, University of Wales Swansea
R. M. Morris, London
Ichiro Nagai, Tokyo
Paul O'Leary, University of Wales, Aberystwyth

Huw and Mary Owen, Aberystwyth
Cedric Parry, Madeley, Crewe
Teifion Phillips, Barry
W. C. Philpin, Little Haven, Haverfordwest
David A. Pretty, Tonteg
Professor and Mrs David Pritchard, Swansea
Bryan Rayner, Burry Port
Sir Stephen Richards, London
Brian Roberts, Leeds
R. O. Roberts, Mumbles, Abertawe
Stephen Roberts, Sutton Coldfield
Edward Royle, University of York
Richard Shannon, London
Michael and Sue Simpson, Swansea
Dai Smith, Cardiff
Llinos and Beverley Smith, Aberystwyth
Robert Smith, Centre for Welsh and Celtic Studies, Aberystwyth
Peter and Elizabeth Stead, Swansea
Catrin Stevens, Trinity College, Carmarthen
John Stubbs, Stafford
Richard Taylor, University of Wales Swansea
Dorothy Thompson, Worcester
Noel Thompson, University of Wales Swansea
David and Margaret Walker, Swansea
Chris Williams, University of Wales, Cardiff
Sir Glanmor Williams, Swansea
Huw Williams, Merthyr Tydfil
J. Dewi Williams, Brentwood
Ivor G. Hughes Wilks, Cribyn
Chris Wrigley, Nottingham University

Bridgend Library and Information Service
Department of History, University of Wales Swansea
National Library of Wales, Aberystwyth
National Museums & Galleries of Wales, Library
Librarian, The Queen's College, Oxford
Department of History, Royal Holloway, University of London
The Librarian, Ruskin College, Oxford
School of Humanities and Social Sciences, Staffordshire University
Thompson Library, Staffordshire University